The Book of Zgierz, Volume II
(Zgierz, Poland)

Translation of
Sefer Zgierz, mazkeret netsach le-kehila yehudit be-Polin

Original Book Edited by: David Shtockfish (Sztokfisz), Sh Kanc, Z. Fisher

Originally published in Tel Aviv 1986

JewishGen

מרכז עולמי לגנאלוגיה יהודית

The Global Home for Jewish Genealogy

A Publication of JewishGen, INC
Edmond J. Safra Plaza, 36 Battery Place, New York, NY 10280
646.494.5972 | info@JewishGen.org | www.jewishgen.org

MUSEUM OF
JEWISH HERITAGE
A LIVING MEMORIAL
TO THE HOLOCAUST

The Book of Zgierz, Volume II (Zgierz, Poland)

Translation of *Sefer Zgierz, mazkeret netsach le-kehila yehudit be-Polin*

Copyright © 2023 by JewishGen, INC All rights reserved.
First Printing: September 2023, Tishrei 5784
Editors of Original Yizkor Book: David Shtockfish (Sztokfisz), Sh. Kanc, Z. Fisher
Project Coordinator: Jerrold Jacobs
Translations: Jerrold Landau
Cover Design: Rachel Kolokoff Hopper
Layout: Jonathan Wind
Name Indexing: Stefanie Holzman

Library of Congress Control Number (LCCN): 2007922624

ISBN: 978-1-954176-81-2 (hard cover: 226 pages, alk. paper)

About JewishGen.org

JewishGen, an affiliate of the Museum of Jewish Heritage - A Living Memorial to the Holocaust, serves as the global home for Jewish genealogy.

Featuring unparalleled access to 30+ million records, it offers unique search tools, along with opportunities for researchers to connect with others who share similar interests. Award winning resources such as the Family Finder, Discussion Groups, and ViewMate, are relied upon by thousands each day.

In addition, JewishGen's extensive informational, educational and historical offerings, such as the Jewish Communities Database, Yizkor Book translations, InfoFiles, Family Tree of the Jewish People, and KehilaLinks, provide critical insights, first-hand accounts, and context about Jewish communal and familial life throughout the world.

Offered as a free resource, JewishGen.org has facilitated thousands of family connections and success stories, and is currently engaged in an intensive expansion effort that will bring many more records, tools, and resources to its collections.

Please visit https://www.jewishgen.org/ to learn more.

Executive Director: Avraham Groll

About the JewishGen Yizkor Book Project

Yizkor Books (Memorial Books) were traditionally written to memorialize the names of departed family and martyrs during holiday services in the synagogue (a practice that still exists in many synagogues today).

Over the centuries, as a result of countless persecutions and horrific atrocities committed against the Jews, Yizkor Books (Sefer Zikaron in Hebrew) were expanded to include more historical information, such as biographical sketches of famous personalities and descriptions of daily town life.

Following the Holocaust, the idea of remembrance and learning took on an urgent and crucial importance. Survivors of the Holocaust sought out other surviving residents of their former towns to memorialize and document the names and way of life of those who were ruthlessly murdered by the Nazis. These remembrances were documented in Yizkor Books, hundreds of which were published in the first decades after the Holocaust.

Most of these books were published privately, or through Landsmanshaftn (social organizations comprised of members originating from the same European town or region) that still existed, and were often distributed free of charge. Sadly, the languages used to document these crucial histories and links to our past, Yiddish and Hebrew, are no longer commonly understood by a significant percentage of Jews today. As a result, JewishGen has undertaken the sacred responsibility of translating these books into English so that the culture and way of life of these communities will be preserved and transmitted to future generations.

In 1986, a group of farsighted JewishGenners started a project to pool their efforts together in groups based upon their ancestors from each town and donate money to get the Yizkor books of their ancestral towns translated into English. As the translated material became available, it was made accessible for free at www.JewishGen.org/Yizkor. Hardcover copies can be purchased by visiting https://www.jewishgen.org/Yizkor/ybip.html (see below).

It is our hope that the translation of these books into English (and other languages) will assist the countless Jewish family researchers who are so desperately seeking to forge a connection with their heritage.

Director of JewishGen Yizkor Book Project: Lance Ackerfeld

About JewishGen Press

JewishGen Press (formerly the Yizkor Books-in-Print Project) is the publishing division of JewishGen.org, and provides a venue for the publication of non-fiction books pertaining to Jewish genealogy, history, culture, and heritage.

In addition to the Yizkor Book category, publications in the Other Non-Fiction category include Shoah memoirs and research, genealogical research, collections of genealogical and historical materials, biographies, diaries and letters, studies of Jewish experience and cultural life in the past, academic theses, and other books of interest to the Jewish community.

Please visit https://www.jewishgen.org/Yizkor/ybip.html to learn more.

Director of JewishGen Press: Joel Alpert
Managing Editor - Jessica Feinstein
Publications Manager - Susan Rosin

Photo Credits

Front Cover:

Illustration: My Home" by Rachel Kolokoff Hopper with Midjourney

Back Cover:

Illustration: "A Garden of Eden" by Rachel Kolokoff Hopper with MidJourney

Poem on back cover: *Memorial* by Esther Krol–Jakubowicz, Tel Aviv, Tevet 5745 (1984 or 1985), page 144.

Geopolitical Information

Zgierz, Poland is located at 51°51' N 19°25' E and 73 miles WSW of Warsaw

	Town	District	Province	Country
Before WWI (c. 1900):	Zgierz	Łódź	Piotrków	Russian Empire
Between the wars (c. 1930):	Zgierz	Łódź	Łódź	Poland
After WWII (c. 1950):	Zgierz			Poland
Today (c. 2000):	Zgierz			Poland

Alternate Names for the Town:

Zgierz [Pol], Zgerzh [Yid], Zgezh [Rus], Görnau [Ger, 1943-45], Zgerzsh, Zgiezh, Zgyerz

Nearby Jewish Communities:

Aleksandrów Łódzki 5 miles WSW
Łódź 7 miles SSE
Konstantynów Łódzki 8 miles SSW
Stryków 9 miles ENE
Ozorków 10 miles NW
Parzęczew 11 miles NW
Lutomiersk 11 miles SW
Pabianice 13 miles S
Rzgów 13 miles SSE
Andrzejów 14 miles SE
Brzeziny 15 miles ESE
Piątek 15 miles N
Głowno 16 miles ENE
Łęczyca 17 miles NNW
Bielawy 18 miles NNE
Tuszyn 18 miles SSE
Poddębice 20 miles W

Sobota 22 miles NNE
Szadek 22 miles WSW
Łask 22 miles SSW
Łyszkowice 23 miles ENE
Będków 23 miles SE
Jeżów 24 miles E
Grabów 26 miles NW
Kutno 27 miles N
Zduńska Wola 27 miles SW
Uniejów 27 miles WNW
Ujazd 28 miles SE
Zelów 28 miles SSW
Łowicz 29 miles NE
Żychlin 29 miles NNE
Krośniewice 29 miles NNW
Dąbie 30 miles WNW
Wolbórz 30 miles SE

Jewish Population: 3,543 (in 1897), 4,547 (in 1931)

BALTIC SEA

LITHUANIA

RUSSIA

Vilnius ●

GERMANY

POLAND

BELARUS

Berlin ●

Poznan ●

Warsaw ●

Brest ●

Zgierz ●

Lublin ●

● Wroclaw

● Prague

Krakow ●

CZECH REPUBLIC

UKRAINE

SLOVAKIA

AUSTRIA

HUNGARY

250 miles

250 Km   500 Km

POLAND – CURRENT BORDERS

Map of Poland showing the location of **Zgierz**

Table of Contents

The Book of Zgierz, Volume II (Poland)

51°51' / 19°25'

Translation of
Sefer Zgierz, mazkeret netsach le-kehila yehudit be-Polin

Edited by: David Shtockfish (Sztokfisz), Sh Kanc, Z. Fisher

Published in Tel Aviv, 1986

———

Acknowledgments:

Project Coordinator

Jerrold Jacobs

Translations:

Jerrold Landau

This is a translation from: *Sefer Zgierz, mazkeret netsach le-kehila yehudit be-Polin*,
Memorial book Zgierz, ed David Shtockfish (Sztokfisz), Sh Kanc, Z. Fisher. Tel Aviv, Zgierz Society, 1986

A. INTRODUCTION

Book of Zgierz

Volume II

Organization of Zgierz Natives in Israel
Address: Chaya Halprin, David Hamelech Street 51, Tel Aviv, Telephone 233870
* * *

Dear Friend!

Forty years have passed since the community of Zgierz was destroyed by the armies of Hitler, may his name be blotted out. However, our hearts are still grieved and filled with agony and grief as we remember the vibrant lives that were cut off in their primes, our families who perished, our brothers and sisters, our relatives and friends who were brought to slaughter during the time of the Nazi enemy.

In order to perpetuate and note this tragic historic event, we present to you today:

The Book of Zgierz, Volume II

which is a continuation and completion of the Book of Zgierz that was published eleven years ago. We hope that this book will also be received with appreciation, through feelings of honor and esteem to the martyrs of our city, may G-d avenge their blood.[1]

The Book Committee
Tel Aviv, October 1986

[Page 1]

Book of Zgierz
* * *
Volume II

[Page 2]

Memorial Book
Zgierz

2nd Volume

Organization of Zgierz Natives in Israel
Ch. Halprin, David Hamelech Street 51, Tel. 233870 Tel Aviv 64237

Printed in Israel 5746 – 1986
Arranged in Lino-Tur, Yesod Hamaale Street 39, Tel Aviv
Printed in "Orly" Printing House, Tel Aviv

[Page 3]

Book of Zgierz

Volume II

The deportation
(Drawing by the illustrator Bromberg)

Published by the Organization of Zgierz Natives in Israel
To Mark the 40th years since the destruction of our community

Tel Aviv 5746 1986

[Page 4]

Book Committee:

Chaya Halprin	Pinchas Sirkis
Rafael Katz	Yeshayahu and Dvora Frugel
Zeev-Wolf Fisher	

Editors:

Shmuel Kantz   Zeev Fisher

[Page 5]

Yizkor Book

2nd Volume

ZGIERZ

Published by the Zgierz Landsmanschaft in Israel
40 years after the destruction of our community

[Page 6]

Dirge and Lament

Woe, Zgierz, my native city
To you I will raise a dirge and lament
For your Jews, for they are no more,
For their destruction and loss.

You are empty, Oh Zgierz, empty of your Jews
No more will the voices emanate from your study halls,
No more will the singing of your children be heard,
A Jewish town, your sons-builders were lost…

Only we, the survivors, will raise in lament, out loud
The outcry of our brokenness, the orphan and bereaved.

Translator's footnote:

1. The above, from "Dear Friend!" is repeated in Hebrew and Yiddish

[Page 7]

Preface to the Book

by Zeev Fisher

Forty years, more than a generation, have passed since our holy community was destroyed. However, its memory, the memory of it people, rabbis, rabbinical judges, administrators, communal workers, scholars, study halls, streets, and landscapes remain alive to this day in the hearts and souls of all Zgierz natives. These additional pages, which we are publishing today as volume II of the Zgierz Book that was published ten years ago, is testimony to this. Through this book, we have attempted to build an eternal monument to our city from the first sprouting of the community, through its period of development, until it was overtaken by the terrible, cruel Holocaust.

Indeed, the Book of Zgierz includes rich, variegated material, with memories, stories, and exciting personal testimonies regarding communal life, its glorious past, and the terrible Holocaust that has no equal in the history of the Nation of Israel, overflowing with tragedy. However, already then, with the publishing of the book, we announced that no small amount of material remained unused in our hands. That material not being included in the book for technical and other reasons. We hoped that redemption would be found after the book, and that everything fitting to be published eventually would be.

Despite great efforts in this matter, ten years have passed, and the material was still waiting for its redemption, until we finally succeeded in overcoming the difficulties. We imbued constructive creative efforts and energy into this. A great deal of work went into arranging and editing the material, into organizational activities and the collection of money – efforts which fell into the hands of few, who did this with a full sense of volunteerism.

Like the Book of Zgierz, this addendum is being published in two languages; Hebrew, the Holy Tongue in which the Jews of our town studied and prayed to their Father in Heaven, and through which their dreams, aspirations, and hopes to return to the Land of their Fathers, the city in which David camped, was expressed; and in Yiddish, the language of the martyrs, through which they conducted their day to day affairs, and through which they educated their children to Torah, the wedding canopy and good deeds.

Through the articles in the two languages, the struggle of the Jews of Zgierz for their existence is expressed. Sections describing the striving toward variegated national life are presented; images of people of many deeds, and expert in Torah are painted; and a flowering treasury of a life of culture and creativity is surveyed.

[Page 8]

The common appearance with the life in other communities is great. Nevertheless, our city exhibits something that is typical and special only to itself.

Indeed, through its way of life, the multitude of images, its internal structure, its religious and secular institutions, our city was a part of Polish Jewry. Everything that transpired in the variegated life of the three–million strong Polish Jewry was reflected in the lens of our 5,000 strong community. The variegated activities of Jewish society and culture continued to grow. Young and old sat in the study halls and the Hassidic Shtibels, studying Torah day and night. When the times changed and new tunes arrived, the youths, male and female, were enthused with ideas and ideals that penetrated to us. They were prepared to dedicate their time and money to the goals of their factions. Every faction had its own headquarters; and conducted lectures, presentations, and especially a plethora of debates. From time to time, every faction would bring in an honorable, veteran orator, a member of the national council, a member of parliament – and there would be joy and gladness in the city. Things were especially joyous when the election time came: elections to the communal council, to the district council, and especially to the Sejm. The debates and disputes extended for weeks. Every free wall was covered with placards, praising themselves and denigrating the opponents. Everyone was convinced that their party was blessed with the most wonderful ideas, and that truth can only be found with them.

The town was not quiet between elections. There was a great deal of cultural and social activities. The libraries, both of the "right" and the "left" were a spiritual gathering place. The youth read with thirst our classics in Yiddish and Hebrew. They regularly participated in evening courses in Hebrew, listened to lectures on literature, politics, and society, and searched for various paths for enlightenment and development.

All of these are written about in the Book of Zgierz with a sense of pride mixed with love. Along with this, however, we know that Zgierz was also exceptional. It differed fundamentally from other cities and towns of Poland.

The famous names of *Admors* [Hassidic masters], writers, poets, and leaders are connected to it. There was certainly something in the air of Zgierz that was conducive to the development of splendid talents. A synthesis between Torah and the people was formed therein. The relationship between all circles of the Jewish community – between the scholar and the simple Jew, between the Yeshiva lad and the maskil – created organized familial relationships. A healthy earthliness, the heartiness of simple Jews blended with the sharpness of thought of the scholars, and lead to the spiritual development of the masses, from whichh the talents sprouted.

From here, a sense of awe, honor, and very deep feelings come to the natives of Zgierz, filling their hearts with a connection to their city all the days of their lives. This is only because of the latent strength hidden in this community, which is close to

[Page 9]

Łódź. Therefore, even those who left it in their youth remain with their unforgettable, childhood love – the source from which they draw their desire to know, understand, and to value the beauty of Jewish life.

The Jews of Zgierz did not abandon their education and culture even during the most difficult moments. Their first concern was to impart knowledge to their children. Lads hastening to their schools, to the cheders or elementary schools were seen on the streets early in the morning. At the conclusion of their course of studies, some lads went on to Yeshiva, which was the crowning highlight of traditional education. However, many continued on to high schools, and there were some who continued on in the universities of Warsaw, as well as foreign universities.

There were also those who studied, expounded, and aroused themselves to cultural activities. They arranged lectures, performances, reading evenings, public debates, and literary trials on the books of Peretz and Sholem Asch, Tolstoy and Archebashev – which became the discussions of the day and the songs of day and night. These literary–artistic evenings attracted a crowd of male and female youths and were accompanied by song, pouring forth from edge to edge. It seems that through their songs, more than through their discussions and debates, they expressed with warmth and enthusiasm everything that afflicted their hearts, that stormed and aroused their souls – souls saturated with the fire and joy of youth, full of longing and desire for far–off places, for the Land of Israel, for a life of toil in the homeland.

When we come today to write something on the life of our town, two types of Jews stand before our eyes – those who were immersed in a firm way of life and its customs, with the Jewish way of life from morning to night, from generation to generation; and those who absorbed the revolutionary spirit, the nationalist Jewish winds, which came to expression through all types of communal, political, and educational activities, as well as in private life and interpersonal relationships. The small groups of Zionists saw themselves as the pioneering brigade of a large movement, which took upon itself the aim of rousing the Jewish world from its slumber, and turning their attention to the solution proposed through zionism. In those days, most of the youths of Zgierz were imbued with the sense of importance of the mission placed upon them, and they invested their entire youthful enthusiasm into it, as they waited for change, and they desired to instigate the change through their deeds.

All of them stand before our eyes, and we write about them in the memorial book, in the Book of Zgierz, and in this additional volume. With all these, we realize that our stage is small, and we cannot state that we have finished. All of this is only an introduction and a beginning. We still have the duty to add, to write, to add another line, to enlarge the mark, to include another image and another vision, so that the memories of a single soul on the large canvas of our great past should not descend to oblivion.

It is our hope that this holy task will also be passed to coming generations, who will accept upon themselves the task of perpetuation. They will remember and learn, for there is no memory without learning. They will learn how their parents and ancestors lived in our city, how they organized their lives, and how the Jewish community functioned.

[Page 10]

The generations will learn how to remember all of them, and to bring to life the values and principles for which they were killed; they will learn to understand their way of life, that was wonderful to a significant degree. This should not only be to pay a debt of honor, even though that is a precious thing, but first and foremost it should be for their own sakes, so that they will know from whence they came, who their parents and grandparents were, what they created, what they fought for, and what they brought here.

They will learn about them, speak about them, write compositions about them, and we will thereby reach a situation that our city, which is no longer, will not only continue its spiritual existence through our hands, but will continue to live in the hearts of our children. From learning and knowing these matters, from uncovering the splendor of light hidden in our community, in its personalities and institutions, they will love them, honor them, and thereby bring honor to themselves and bring preciousness to the path that they are taking.

Therefore, we will talk extensively about our community, about its annals throughout the entire time of its existence, from its beginning to its end – its origins, its spouting, its development, its growth until its setting, until the tragic destruction; about everything that encompasses the spiritual image of the community and its cultural values. We will continue to tell about its social structure, its economic life, and the dynamic life therein. They will learn not only about the supernal Zgierz, but also about the earthly Zgierz – about all the factors that forged the community of Zgierz.

Zgierz has written its own page in the martyrology of our nation. During the first decades of the 19th century, its community was a victim of the establishment of a Jewish ghetto, but despite all the persecutions and harsh tribulations of that period, the members of the community succeeded in overcoming the obstacles and developing the life of the community, both spiritually and economically. The Jews established factories and textile plants, and became an important factor in the development of manufacturing in Zgierz. Just as the restrictions did not quiet the energy of the community members in their concern for Torah and education, they also guarded their strength of spirit in the economic sector. Thanks to their business and organizational talents, the Jews knew how to integrate themselves, as individuals or as small groups, into the economic reality and social structure of the city – at first in a modest manner, and later in much larger proportions. They developed the marketing of textile products to far–off cities in the Russian empire. This was an era of the blending of commerce and manufacturing in the economic life of the Jews of Zgierz.

Thanks to the creativity of work conditions, a great change took place in the social structure of the Jews of Zgierz. A manufacturing and bureaucratic proletariat was created. Fifty percent of the Jewish population of the city earned their livelihoods from the work of their hands. There were also modest workshops, through which the family members earned their livelihoods through the sweat of their brow – themselves or with the help of one or two employees. There were also workshops in all the trade sectors of day–to–day life, everyone according to their expertise. Jewish Zgierz was a working city, but its spiritual form was forged through traditional Jewish value that imparted to the vast majority of the Jewish community a set way of life, and imbued in it an atmosphere of historic Judaism.

[Page 11]

The bearers of the idea of Zionism were members of the previous generation, who bore both the old and the new of Jewish culture in their hearts. They were students of the Talmudic school, with broad knowledge of Jewish sources. On the other hand, they amassed knowledge of Jewish wisdom and general erudition. Thus, they unified all these values into a single, complete harmony.

*

Is it indeed so? Has all of this world of yesteryear been destroyed?

The reality that pervades our feelings and memories answers us in a voice of dread: indeed, this world has been destroyed and is no longer. No more will the voices burst forth from the synagogues. No more will the melody of the cheder students be heard in the city. No more will the stories of Abraham our Forefather and his descendants be heard in the melodic Hebrew language. This entire multi–faceted world has gone to destruction and oblivion.

Let this additional book, just like the Book of Zgierz, guard all the beauty that once was and that will never be forgotten from the hearts of future generations. Let it also serve as a sort of bridge between the past and the future, and testify that it, Jewish Zgierz, lives on in the hearts of its children. It is a sign that eternal life is prepared for it in the annals of our nation.

[Page 12]

Introduction

by W. Fisher

The pages of this section are a supplement to the Book of Zgierz that was published ten years ago. Already then, we estimated that there remained a great deal to tell about the life and destruction of our community. There was such a rich society and spiritual life there among all the circles of the five–thousand strong Jewish community – through all its dimensions and spiritual endeavors, Jewish from all perspectives, not only in its festival and cultural manifestations, but also in its day–to–day, economic, societal and family lives.

The Jewish settlement of Zgierz went through various eras. It overcame many struggles, decrees, and persecutions that were difficult for the Jews. It conducted a bitter struggle against the restrictions on areas of settlement during the middle ages, which placed the Jews into a ghetto. However, not looking at this, the Jews of Zgierz did not refrain from building their homes. By so doing, they demonstrated zest, enterprisingness, love and dedication to their community. They built textile factories and became and important factor in the development and growth of the textile industry in the city. This also created a new source of livelihood for the Jewish population.

A new epoch began when the restriction to be ghettoized was abolished in 1862. Jews began to build houses and various textile enterprises in all portions of the city. The business, the industry, and the hand–working sectors all developed on a large scale. Jews played an important role in all administrative agencies of the city.

The textile industry developed further with the passage of years. Factories grew and branched into other sectors of livelihood. More and more Jews

[Page 13]

left their small–scale sources of livelihood, such as shop–keeping, and branched out into all areas of the textile industry.

Great development of the Jewish community in Zgierz took place as a result of the establishment of business connections with the near and far areas of the Russian Empire, where Jewish merchants from Zgierz would go with their merchandise, which had attained a good name. This also led to an increase in the Jewish population of Zgierz. Jews from Lithuania, Latvia, Volhynia, White Russia, and other provinces settled in Zgierz and quickly set themselves up in industry and business.

We find Hassidic Jews among the Zgierz travelers. In their Hassidic garb, with beards and peyos, they set out for the expanses of Russia for long weeks and months. They traveled with bundles full of samples of merchandise produced in the Zgierz factories, and took orders. Those Jews presented themselves as accomplished businessmen with excellent experience. Through their honesty and respectable, proud poise, they earned respect and trust, thereby making the Zgierz factories famous throughout the world.

In the years prior to the Second World War, Zgierz was already a city with a population of about 40,000, of which 5,000 were Jews. The economic base was the textile industry. Almost all the branches were mechanized, and they provided work and employment for the majority of the population. About 80% of the Jewish population were employed in the textile industry. The others were involved with trade and business.

The Jewish factories in Zgierz had their own union. The Jewish workers belonged to various political parties and organizations, and were active in various social institutions. The Jewish tradesmen were also organized into their own union. They were loved by the population, and many Christians were their regular customers. The union was involved with helping and tending to the needs of its members, with giving advice regarding taxes, examinations, and diplomas, and with granting loans so as to prevent the weakened workshops from going under during times of crisis.

[Page 14]

Our Book of Zgierz discusses the wide branched cultural and educational work of the various institutions and youth organizations. The rabbi, known as "The Elder Tzadik" disseminated Torah study, good character, and refined Kocker style Hassidism in a pleasant fashion for fifty years in his Yeshiva. The study of Torah was accompanied by pride, high flight into the upper worlds, in the world of thought and poetry, with a tune of the outpouring of the soul. The hundreds of students who graduated from the Zgierz Yeshiva invested their entire soul, brain, and heart into their learning. Torah stood at the center of life, and learning was an esthetic undertaking. It was learning for its own sake. A life devoid Torah and following the commandments was considered a hollow and wanton life. A person without Torah and good deeds was like a wild beast to them.

Modern Judaism also sprouted up in that fertile soil. The strict Jewish observance, the deep world concept took on a new manifestation with the maskilim. The *Haskalah* movement produced such personalities in Zgierz as the well-known Maskil, erudite in the wisdom of Israel and worldly knowledge, Avraham Yaakov Wiesenfeld, who sowed in Zgierz the ripest kernels of his *Haskalah* concepts, Galician style; Reb Tovia Lipszyc, considered "the lion of the group," a great scholar, and scholar and interpreter of the Bible and Talmudic literature. He explained Torah science and the ideas of Chibat Zion in accordance with the style of Lithuania; Reb Isucher Szwarc, the scholar and expert of the old Polish literature as well as in modern scholarship, who popularized the modern Herzlist Zionism in Zgierz, Polish style; Reb Moshe Ejger, a rare example of a great industrialist who unified glorious financial activity with proficiency in Jewish knowledge. He was a great expert in the old German literature, and wrote poems in Hebrew and Yiddish. He was immersed in the Zionist ideal and promoted "Zionismus" in an erudite German fashion. Strong nationalistic energy laden with wonderful potential accumulated around them.

[Page 16]

Specifically that multi–colored culture circle, which was permeated with true love of one's fellow Jew, forged the specific uniqueness of the Jewish person of culture in Zgierz through the years. In that atmosphere, the Yiddish language grew into an important cultural factor, with love for the Jewish book and press.

That relatively small Jewish community produced over 50 rabbis, students of the elder rabbi's famous Yeshiva. At the same time, 35 Jewish writers, poets and thinkers, as well as authors of religious books, were raised in Zgierz. Their literary creations had a deep and wide resonance in the Jewish intellectual world. The works of the classicists from our Hebrew and Yiddish literature – David Frishman, Yaakov Cohen, Yitzchak Katzenelson – were treated with special reverence. Like them were also Tovia Lipsyc, Isucher Szwarc, and others, who are mentioned in the Book of Zgierz as being full of Jewishness, of the Jewish culture in Zgierz.

That Jewishness was authentic and integral, not merely a stylistic Jewishness, not external, which is called today "traditional." That which appeared so strongly on the surface in Zgierz was a result of that which was etched in the depths of that hundred percent Jewishness and is a synthesis between the Torah and the people. Since the life of the public was infused with Jewishness, with Jewish culture, the branches of all the strata and circles were like one large family. The spiritual legacy is precious to all – to those were committed to renewing and deepening it, and to those who only want to know and understand it; for those for whom Jewish law is a matter to be understood and drawn from, for those for whom the Code of Jewish Law brought joy every day of the week, from the Modeh Ani upon awakening until the reading of the Shema before going to sleep.

Such were our fathers and grandfathers, with their completely spiritual lives, in all the wonderful shades of Jewish fineness. They imparted to us the belief in our historical path, the understanding of our great responsibility that is expressed in all of our tasks, including the perpetuation of our annihilated community and its martyrs.

[Page 17]

Thus did we Begin

by Zev–Wolf Fisher

At the celebration upon the publication of the book in 1975
Yosef Katz, Pinchas Sirkis, Zeev Fisher, Rafael Katz, Chaya Halpern, Y. Sczaranski, Yeshayahu Frogel, Y. Malkieli

(A few words dedicated to the 30 years of activities of the Organization of Zgierz Natives in Israel on the day of the memorial gathering in 1982.)

On the annual day of memory, permit me to make note of a societal event that took place about 30 years ago, and is also connected with our memorial gathering of today, which had already become a holy tradition for us, with all its Jewish and societal influence.

That event was the founding of the official, organized society that encompassed all Zgierz Jews in the country, and bore the name: The Organization of Zgierz Natives in Israel.

This took place on January 5, 1952. It resulted in the founding of that organization about one month later, on 7 Shevat 5712 (February 3, 1952). The first memorial gathering of the Zgierz Jews in Israel took place in Beit Hachalutzot in Tel Aviv. That gathering was the largest and most influential. That first positive achievement was of great importance.

[Page 18]

The Zgierz Jews, saved from the terrible deluge, had just arrived on ships, and met up with the Zgierz Jews who were already settled in the country, having come here years earlier. They reunited, fell into each other's arms, and reestablished old relationships and friendships.

From that day onward, the newly arrived Jews of Zgierz had an address to which to turn, whether it was for the initial assistance, professional advice to help get established, or merely for a friendly word, warm hominess and encouragement to build up their new homes.

"The Organization of Zgierz Natives in Israel" gained importance and recognition, and became a serious societal factor for the Zgierz Jews in Israel.

That is how they took their first steps, and encouraged the further important goals, about which there is so much to speak and write. Like many great accomplishments, they could not be attained with brief efforts.

Thirty years: the years of a complete generation. In general, these were difficult years. Many difficulties and struggles had to be overcome. Objective situations and conditions were often created that made it difficult to continue with the speedy activity. The difficulties resulted in discouragement more than once. It seemed that we were too weak to continue on with our work, but the Zgierz Jews displayed great steadfastness and continued on with the work, year in and year out, with conscientious responsibility and a deep sense of honor and awe. We observed the historical date of the anniversary of the destruction, and we gathered together in order to unite ourselves with the martyrs of our city in quiet reflection. Were our organization to have been created solely for this single holy aim, it would have been sufficient justification, and to bless the day of its founding.

Great and important was the work that was created in the following years – the Book of Zgierz: the impressive memorial to the Jewish Zgierz that was destroyed. The Book of Zgierz is a work of value for the generations, a work that bring honor and importance as a glorious memorial to the entire community of Zgierz Jews.

Indeed, the 30th anniversary of the Organization of Zgierz Natives in Israel is a great historical event for the Zgierz survivors.

[Page 19]

I would not be historically accurate if I do not mention briefly that the foundation of our organization was laid yet on the soil of our former homeland, Poland. This took place in Łódź at the end of 1946, and the first general memorial gathering took place shortly thereafter, in January 1947.

There, on Poland's soil, in the shadows of the death camps, we lit the first memorial candles for our martyrs. There, on the ruins of our destroyed homes, did we, the survivors, pledge the memorial slogan "Remember! Never Forget!"

By the red light of the congealed blood of our martyrs we swore: we will keep the bygone times, saturated with blood and tears, in our memories forever! We will never forget!

We will never cease to demand the accounting for their destroyed lives.

The 30th anniversary celebration of the Organization of Zgierz Natives in Israel

[Page 20]

Just like the Book of Zgierz, this additional book will be a permanent reminder for generations to come, who will find in the straightforward stories a document and a window into the former rich way of life of our city, which is no more.

Let the shout that emanates from the pages of our books not ceased until the furthest generations.

Every gathering of ours, every meeting and party is imbued with the continuity of that holy oath.

Our gratitude is deep toward all those who helped us continue with this holy work. We express special gratitude for the fruitful activity of Mrs. Chava Halpern, through whose work personifies the soul of our committee, all of whose members excel in their societal responsibility and great dedication.

The first memorial event in 1946 in Zgierz – the speaker is Z. Fisher

[Page 21]

B. Chapters of History

[Page 22]

The City and Its Happenings[1]

by The editorial board

… And it will be if the asker askes about the destroyed cities, about whether there is yet a name and memory in the hearts of its children, the teller will tell: On the contrary, open this book and read it. As it passed through the recesses of the heart, it now passes through the pages of this book in which the hearts beat and nestle over the generations of its children, and whose energy is set in their hearts. Since it is alive in their hearts and memories, it is a sign that it is set for eternal life in the annals of our nation.

The editorial board

*

… At times it happens: you leaf through some old picture, or through a bundle of newspapers and manuscripts from bygone eras, and then suddenly: Zgierz, your city… The blood awakens in your heart… Zgierz – the city that was once an integral part of your life… The city for which you feel yourself as a severed limb in its reality… Zgierz – it arises in your memory as a warm echo, even though we are talking about Zgierz from bygone years.

You read and read with great interest and curiosity, as if it happened just yesterday or the day before. As if you hear echoes from our lives… For that which happened to them [would have] happened also to us – the coming generation – if the years had been in order and as usual…

*

Woe to us! Destruction overtook the community of Zgierz as well, as it did with all the Jewish communities of Poland. The chain of the generations has been severed, and it no longer continues. We are the last of the Zgierz natives. Therefore, let us honor these fragments of memories of our parents and ancestors, for they are also for our honor.

Z. F.

*

Translator's footnote:

1.   This brief section is listed as being on page 21 in the Table of Contents

[Page 23]

Echoes from Years Gone By
(About Zgierz in the Hebrew newspapers of those years)

Hamelitz 1888

Warsaw – Monday (January 2, 18 Tevet) – – one of the honorable people of our city, Reb Shmuel Aryeh the son of Yitzchak Margolis of blessed memory has passed away. – – He lived in the city of Ozorków from 1849 to 1866, where he had a large factory for the weaving of wool, from which many poor Jewish families found their livelihoods. He moved to the manufacturing city of Zgierz in 1866[1] and became one of the large–scale factory owners in that city. There too, he did a great deal for individuals, for his hand was open to any poor person who knocked on his doors. He did a great deal for the city in general, for communal activity was close to his heart. He was a faithful lover of that city, and directed the community and its institutions. Even the gentiles in the city honored him for his good spirit and great worth. When he was forced to leave the city in 1882 and come to our city, all the people of Zgierz accompanied him on his way, and the parting was difficult for them. They many families who found work and support through him wept bitterly. – – –

Hamelitz 1899

The city of Zgierz is a one hour walk from the city of Łódź. Its population is about 20,000, and its Jewish population is about 4,000, mainly Hassidim and the minority "householders." There are two factories for weaving and sewing, in which our brethren also have a share. However the number of Hebrew workers is small, approximately 50, and no more. Jews earn their livelihood from various businesses and trades. There are many wagon drivers who travel the route to Łódź, earning their livelihoods from their frequent journeys. – – The spiritual situation of the Jewish community in the city of Zgierz is also not that different from other such cities; it had a charitable fund, a Bikur Cholim (organization for visiting the sick), and other such institutions, whose purpose is to help the poor during their times of tribulation. – –

The city of Zgierz has now become famous for its Business School, which was founded there and accepted Jews without any quota. Hundreds of students from other cities, near and far, would come here.

[Page 24]

Along with them came work for the tradespeople and shopkeepers. Some of the teachers of the Jews rented large houses and set up rooms for housing and tables for eating for the outside students, and prepared them for acceptance to the school. It is said that the supervisor of that school was an honest man who loved Jews and respected their Torah. He did not at all force the Jewish students, even through moral persuasion, to write on the Sabbath. This should be no small matter in our eyes! For he knew that even some of the children of Orthodox Jews violate the Sabbath at the school, for that is the will of the director, who thinks that Sabbath observance is only for fanatics – and believes that fanatics are not fit to gain knowledge and insight and to later influence the people with their "dark spirit." There are also "government rabbis" who support the opinion of the director through their rabbinical seal! However, more guilty than anyone are the fathers themselves, who compromise their faith and Torah to do the will of the supervisor.

A Jew

The new Rynek [town square], where the monthly fairs take place

[Page 25]

Hatzefira 1901

Zgierz (District of Piotrków). An honorable enterprise operates in our midst, the "*Tzedaka Gedola*" [Great Charity] institution that encompasses all benevolent operatives in our midst. The Jewish community here – – has taken a great stride forward: it has now been two years since several of the prominent people of our city interceded with the authorities regarding the founding of a general charitable society. Now, after many obstacles – the society has been set up and certified.

The residents of our city are solicited for every charitable matter, and they give. Amongst us we have various institutions, and why should we not try to bring order to all of them so that the charitable acts shall be whole?

Through the efforts of several people of our city, and through the work of Mr. Eiger, the head of the workers, the group moved from thought to deeds. The institution was set up, and all the parties participate. There are great results to this day.

After the first meeting, all of those who signed up for the society were called to come to elect directors and functionaries for its various divisions.

The following were elected by majority vote:

Mr. Moshe Tzvi Eiger (chairman)
Nota Heinsdorf (vice chairman)
Shimon Ring (secretary)
Mordechai Margolis (general treasurer)

The directors of the various charitable endeavors, each in accordance with their task and work, are:

Mr. Shlomo Sirkis
Tovia Lypszyc
David Konel
Avraham Weiss
Isuchar Szwarc
Dr. Zylbersztram
Binyamin Szeranski
Eliezer Kotszinski (accountant)
And Mr. Aharon Kaltgrad, recording secretary.

All have been summoned by name, are clean of hands and pure of heart[2]. It is expected that they will set up something proper and respectable for them, and for our city.

At the first meeting, the meeting of members, we immediately recognized their goodwill, for all of them participated and donated what they could to purchase the furniture and other necessities for the rooms of the organization. – – They brought many utensils to furnish the rooms, and everything was set up nicely – everything from private donations.

*

[Page 26]

The members expected to dwell in peace and to carry out their work, but the wrath of the tramway overtook them! At the time when the members began to carry out their work, the tramway from Zgierz to Łódź – Pabianicki, opened up, leaving 70 families, who had earned their livelihoods from wagon driving, without sustenance.

Anyone who is knowledgeable and expert in communal affairs knows how difficult it is for a new enterprise to have a heavy burden fall upon it all at once. Seventy families without the staff of bread, the coffers were small, and there was not an amount to sustain them!

The members of the committee have made efforts to obtain support from the action committee of the tramway. We hope that their efforts bear fruit.

Translator's footnotes:

    1.   There is a typo in the text here – it says 1966, which is obviously incorrect. I rectified it in the translation.
    2.   From Psalms 24:4

Zgierz of the Year 5620 (1860)
through the Eyes of A. Y. Weisenfeld
(from his letter to Yitzchak Mizes)[1]

Blessed be G–d, Monday of the Torah Portion of Ki Tisa, 5625 (1865), Zgierz[2]

To my friend the high priest of his brethren in wisdom and knowledge, the great researcher, Rabbi Yitzchak Mizes, may his light shine.

– – – The reason for my delay in responding is that I know that merely a friendly letter will not be sufficient for you, and that you will want to know not only about my status and situation, but also about the situation of the city in which I live, and I realize that it is a difficult task to understand the essence of people in a brief period. I said that after a few months, I will send at length the material that is fitting to put in a book, and you will receive a booklet on the situation of our brethren in this country, and I would tell you main details about the status of the city, that are worthwhile to know.

The city in which I live has 10,000 residents, including 4,000 of our nation. They earn their livelihood from wool and cotton, and a few of them from small–scale manufacturing. The poorer people are mainly middlemen sitting at corners, tradesmen in various trades – from weavers and embroiderers to heavy coal workers – clean work earned by the sweat of the brow, the likes of which I have not seen in our country.

In general, the city is desolate, and its business is sparse. As all Jewish communities, it had a rabbi, cantor, scribe, administrators, rabbinical judges, physicians, and unemployed people. The rabbi receives a stipend from the communal coffers. He travels several times a year, formerly to Kock and presently to Warsaw. He studies with lads or youths the laws of shopkeepers and their ledgers,

[Page 27]

the cow[3], and the tallis [prayer shawl], but not Bible, Mishna, and proper behavior [and I trust that they will be rabbis and teachers in the Jewish community]. He has no contact with people, and he sits in an inside room rejoicing with his Torah didactics. This is not a complaint, and not to show haughtiness, for we can see in him clear signs of a person who occupies himself in Torah for its own sake in our time. Such individuals merit many things, are not interested in monetary gain, do not have interest in writing or language, and do not provide advice and recommendations on matters of the world or on matters of the city.

The livelihood of the rabbinical judges is very difficult, for they do not receive a stipend from the communal coffers. Rather, they earn something when there is a Torah court case – something that takes place here once in a jubilee – they do not engage in work, for they are either unemployed or frequenters of the *Beis Midrash*. The communal administrators are such in name only, for they keep their distance form communal affairs. There are many ignoramuses who are involved in communal affairs, for it is considered a disgrace here to be a leader of the people. The maskilim here are those people who own valuable books, and learn seven subjects on one foot, such as the book of the covenant, the paths of faith. There are also those who know the Bible well, who can read the fine points of Rashi, and are considered the splendor of the city.

There are two Jewish physicians whom I know, with whom I come into contact at times. The first is a donkey of burden[4], with the books of Walter and the encyclopedias spoken from his throat. He thinks about them as one seeks after the truth. He is of the spirits of the 18th century. He has not seen or does not know about the wisdom and sciences that have taken place from that time until now, for he is a fortress of memory of the previous century.

The second one knows and understands a great deal; whose treasury of knowledge is very great. He was one of the excellent students of the halls of wisdom of Berlin. However, the science of medicine is to him the sum total of the wisdoms. He concentrates on it, and restricts himself to that subject. They are different from each other, and what they have in common is that they do not benefit from each other's company.

I have now brought before you something from all sections of the city, and you will see what has happened in my life, and how I have been chased out from dwelling in the heritage of wisdom, which was the desire of my soul and the life of my spirit. I feared that a worm and a thorn might afflict my meager knowledge. Therefore, I ask that, from time to time, I be granted from the fruit of your knowledge in the fields of the wisdom of Israel, and that you tell me about your family, and your dear daughter and granddaughter, and news from the world of research and the wisdom of Reb Pinchas Mendel and Kirchheim. Please accept my deep gratitude, from your friend who honors and holds you in rabbinical esteem, A. Y. W.

Please, my friend, forgive me for my poor writing, for I am writing this at midnight, and am hurrying to finish the letter, so that I can send it in the mail tomorrow. That way, it should arrive to you on Purim, instead of Shalach Manot [Purim gifts].

(From the book "Exchange of Letters", an anthology of P. H. Wetstein, Krakow, 5660 [1900]).

Translator's footnotes:

1. This letter is written in a very convoluted, almost pseudo–intellectual, style. He addresses the recipient in the third person – which I did not preserve in the translation. The next article, a eulogy written by Weisenfeld, is equally convoluted.
2. It is unclear if the date is 5625 or 5620, as the letters of the Hebrew date are mixed up to form a word "*Haketer*" (The crown) – a common literary technique. The "He" – representing the number 5 in the digits (the thousands number is generally not written, as it is assumed), may be a part of the date, or may actually be a definite article.
3. Possibly referring to the Red Heifer, a law that has no current practical ramifications, and is regarded as theoretical in this day and age.
4. Seemingly a reference to Genesis 49:14.

[Page 28]

The Tzadik has been Lost!

The community of Zgierz shall wail, shall raise its voice in lament and weeping, for the wonderful crown of Torah, adorned with bright sapphires, has been lost. Woe! It has fallen to the ground and its splendor has been removed, the light of Torah has been trampled, and darkness has come to the world on the day of Tevet 6, for that day the angels were victorious, and the holy ark has been taken to eternal life – our rabbi, the Gaon and Hasid, Rabbi Shalom Tzvi HaKohen, may the memory of the holy be blessed. Not only the community of Zgierz, but the entire house of Israel shall weep over this great loss, for the late Gaon of blessed memory was one of the uniquely gifted people, one of the few strong pillars upon which the sanctuary of Torah rests in our generation. Anyone who merited to stand and serve before this late Gaon of blessed memory, and to know a bit about his holy ways, is obligated to rise up and declare publicly about the great loss to our holy nation with the death of his holy individual. The Gaon and righteous priest was crowned with three crowns: the crown of Torah, the crown of priesthood, and the crown of a good name:

Regarding the crown of Torah, he disseminated Torah publicly for the 54 years that he served in the rabbinate of our community. Fine youths streamed to his great Yeshiva from all corners of Poland, for he preserved through his learning style the paths of the great early sages of holy blessed memory. With his great toil and wondrous expertise, he forged a path in the sea of Talmud and in the strong waters of the rabbinic decisors, delving deep into Jewish law, understanding the ideas of the early sages of blessed memory. In all his digging into the Talmud, he did not set his aim solely at the effort of building castles flying in the air, which have no spirit, like the babbling pilpulists. Rather, the spirit of our early ones rested upon him to place all his effort in interpreting, clarifying, and polishing the matters like refined silver. He was granted success from Heaven, after all his great, selfless work, to save many pearls from the sea of Talmud, which had not ben seen yet by the eyes of the great latter sages. More than 50 of his great students are scattered throughout our country. Thus was his excellent manner in holiness, in the courtyards of Torah and Talmud.

Regarding the crown of priesthood, he was a Cohen to the L–rd of High, a student of Aaron, loving peace and pursuing peace, loving his fellow, and drawing them close to Torah[1]. Anyone who basked under his shadow did so without fanfare or

[Page 29]

force, but rather with the spirit of G–d dwelling in his midst, with the spirit of grace etched on his lips, and with the quiet voice drawing near even those who were far–off, returning their hearts to their Father in Heaven.

Greater than all, however, is the crown of a good name. His modesty was extreme. The holy Torah with which he occupied himself for its own sake was that which bestowed upon him that crown overlaid with precious stones, fine and good, with praiseworthy traits. Everyone who saw and knew him, and the many people who visited him, were surprised and astonished. They all said unanimously that they had never seen such a modest person as this laudable person. He never conducted his leadership with a high hand, and he never said to people that they must accept his opinion. He would flee from honor as distantly as he could, even though he earned great honor during his lifetime, and the great rabbis gave honor to his name, with every holy word that emanated from his mouth being holy to G–d in their eyes. These signs of honor did not at all affect his pure heart, and did not even make a small impression on his precious soul. To him, honor was a disgraceful thing, an impure matter that should not be brought into the house of G–d. His door was open all day and a large part of the night to anyone who had something to request, to anyone beaten and depressed. He was available to any petitioner, from the great wealthy people, men of renown and leaders of the community, to the least of the least, the hewers of stone and drawers of water. There was no minute issue for the people of our community that was not brought before him. He would answer the many matters with extra patience, and give words of comfort to anyone who came to his tent. Just like the High Priest who entered the inner sanctum of the temple of Torah, his voice was not heard as he entered the sanctuary to speak about leadership and greatness; he only gave forth the dew of his words calmly, so they would be accepted by the hearts of the listeners. He would direct all his words, in any place that he turned, toward the spirit of each individual, and say to them – purify yourselves[2].

Last Friday, we heard the terrible news that the late Gaon passed away at around midnight. All those who heard trembled, it was a G–dly trembling, and all the people gathered to lament and weep for him. Several hundred people came as well from the neighboring cities of Łódź and Ozorków. The rabbi and head of the rabbinical court of Ozorków was among those who came. The aforementioned Gaon raised a voice of lament and dirge to eulogize him in the large *Beis Midrash* here. However, the voice of the eulogizer could no longer be heard, for all the people were weeping loudly and shedding rivers of tears, for a cedar from amongst the cedars of Lebanon, the mighty ones of Torah, the elder of the rabbis in his character, has fallen. He was 84 years old when he died – his eyesight did not dim and his lifeforce had not abated[3]. Our community is left bereft and desolate, isolated and alone, for its splendor, glory and radiance has departed, and who will bring the likes of him to us – a prince in Torah and charity? Woe over those who are gone and who will not be forgotten. May his name be bound in the bonds of eternal life, Selah. Written with tears by Avraham Yaakov Weisenfeld, Zgierz, Tuesday, 10 Tevet, 5637 (1876).

(From the *Hamagid* weekly – *Hatzofeh LeHamagid*, 1877)

Translator's footnotes:

1. *Pirkei Avot* 1:12.
2. A take–off of the service of the High Priest in the Holy of Holies on Yom Kippur.
3. Used to describe Moses upon his death, Deuteronomy 34:7.

[Page 30]

The "Jewish Street" in Zgierz

by Zeev Wolf Fisher

Dedicated to the memory of the "Jewish Street," a symbol of vibrant Jewish life in our city – 40 years after its destruction; in memory of its builders who struggled hard for their rights, to its residents who were deported from their homes and went on their final journey with their hands on their heads; the street in which the Jewishness of old pervaded, without problems and without disturbances; the street of the melodies of Torah and the spirit of prayer; in which the permanent residences of the rabbis of the city, righteous people, and people of good deeds were situated, in a good and honorable neighborhood along with the simple folk who earned their bread with the sweat of their brow, upright and straightforward – who can remember them without a tear in the eye, without an ache in the heart. The Jewish street – the warm, beating heart of Jewish Zgierz that once was – as an eternal memory.

Two main streets extend out from the Old Market, cross the length of the city, and extend from south to north. On the right is the Jewish street (Yiddishe Gasse, formerly Łódź Street, for the road leads directly to Łódź), and on the left is the Long Street (Lange Gasse), later called Piłsudskiego after the Marshal and Polish President Piłsudski. Jewish life specific to our city arose on these two streets in two planes: While business and commercial life centered and stood out on Piłsudskiego Street, as the primary artery of commerce and the textile trade – the Jewish Street (later, Berka Joselewica Street, named after Berek Joselowicz – a Jewish hero in the Polish revolt against the Russians from 1794) became the center of religious life in the city and anything connected with such – already from the beginning of the Jewish settlement in that city.

Therefore, the Jewish Street was counted among the old roads in our city, but only the main part of it was built by Jews for Jews. In the history of the community (famous

[Page 31]

for its battle against the laws of the *Rewir* (ghetto)[1], we have found the names of people who approached the district committee with requests for permission to build residential houses on the street that was then called Łódź Street (next to the road to Łódź). The first building requests connected to that road were from the years 1823–1848. The following were the names of the petitioners: Nachum the son of Michel Feldon from Lutomiersk, a merchant of wool; Rachel Wajnsztajn, Leizer Bornsztajn, Daniel Rywan, Yaakov Jedlicki (the owner of the tax), Yaakov Sadokierski, Hirsch Horowicz, Yaakov Poznansky, Rada Dobrzynska (the mother of the *Admor* Rabbi Abrahamele of Ciechanów, may the memory of the holy be blessed), Shimon Landau, Jozef Wejlandt (later – father–in–law of the *maskil* A. Y. Weisenfeld), Marek Wajnsztajn, Avraham Salomonowicz, David Hendlisz, Herzl Lewkowicz, and several others whose names are not clear. Apparently, most of the people who appear here had status in the community and were important members of the community, for we find names such as theirs in other places. They are from among the fathers who were the first settlers of the Jewish Street in Zgierz. Along with the first rabbi, the Elder Tzadik, they also imparted their personal and spiritual stamp on the way of life of the street, and the specific manner for future generations.

With the building of the new synagogue (1860) and alongside the Great *Beis Midrash* in the center of the street, other religious institutions sprouted up here, and found their set place alongside them. These included the new *mikva* [ritual bath] building, the slaughterhouse for fowl, and the like. When the first rabbi, Rabbi Shalom Tzvi HaKohen, may the memory of the holy be a blessing, moved his special dwelling into the *Beis Midrash* building, he also set aside a place for his famous Yeshiva, in which lads from all over Poland studied. Similarly, with the passage of time, almost all the religious and Torah institutions moved to the Jewish Street, including the Yeshivas, the cheders, the various *shtibels*, and of course the clergy – the cantors, the *shochtim* [ritual slaughterers], the *shamashim* [beadles] as well as the groups that occupied themselves with communal matters, and ordinary Jews who desired the atmosphere of Torah and prayer.

There were years in which it seemed that Jewish life was conducted here in accordance with autonomous Jewish laws, and the local authorities did not get involved with what was taking place on the street – unless a legal or public complaint was lodged. Life was conducted here in an orderly fashion, and nobody was so daring as to disturb it. Every morning before dawn, Fishel the *shamash* would pass through the center of the street and bang his wooden hammer on the gates of the Jewish homes. He would bang three times on each gate. If he would only bang twice, the residents of the street would know that someone passed away in the city that day, may G–d save us, and one must prepare for the funeral. The *shamash* would pass through the streets on the eve of the Sabbath, and use his hammer to inform everyone that the time of the kindling of Sabbath candles was approaching. There were also times when groups of Hassidic young men, generally of the Shomrim Laboker organization, would pass through every morning at sunrise, both during the summer and the winter, and sing with a sweet and enticing voice in chorus, echoing for an extended period through the festive quite of space: "Jews, Jews! Arise to the worship of the Creator!" Thus did they sing:

[Page 32]

> "Jews, Jews!
> Arise, arise
> To the service of the Creator!..."

The Jews would arise and go to the *Beis Midrash*, where they would recite Psalms with the congregation, and worship the morning service early. Some would then stay to recite a chapter of Mishna. Thus did they greet the new day.

After the First World War, the *Admor* Rabbi Menachem Mendel, may the memory of the holy be blessed, of Stryków lived in our city. His Hassidim set up a residence for him on the Jewish Street with a *Beis Midrash* in the courtyard. Yeshiva lads, even those from other cities, studied there. As was customary, they too filled the street with a religious, Torah based, essence. However, the specific character of the Jewish Street was expressed on Sabbaths, festivals, and other evenings of Torah based celebrations. Indeed, the Jewish Street lived up to its name.

However, with the changing times, the human landscape of the street changed. The sounds of Torah, which had been dominant on the street, changed into a pioneering spirit. There was the house of Reb Yosel Rubinsztajn, the first Jewish master and teacher of this profession in our city, whose weaving workshop became a textile school – from where the theory of weaving emanated and spread through the Jewish Zgierz, and even reached the residents of the area (see Book of Zgierz, pp. 422–423). It is therefore no wonder that Jews involved in labor and trades, who earned their livelihoods from everything connected to this sector, began to gather on this street. There were also entire families with energy and diligence, who had begun their work with hand operated machines, and, after several years, transferred to mechanized weaving machines, and joined well into the textile manufacturing industry, which was the prime source of livelihood of the residents of our city. These were families such as Michowicz, Kaszikec, Ber, and many others who had been involved in this sector for a long time and who established a generation of experts in this sector. There was barely a house on the street, especially the one–story wooden houses, in which there was not one loom, the din of which burst forth outside. In the summer, when the windows were open wide, one would hear the voice of the weaver accompanying his work, along with the monotonous tick–tak–tak of the weaving machine – one with a cantorial piece from Beinish the Cantor, who was beloved by the community, and the second with one of the melodramatic couplets of Goldfaden.

Thus did Jewish life stream in its regular path on the Jewish Street, quietly (even though not always calmly), with a unified blend of holy and secular, Torah and work, which always went forward together under the same sky, which was so typical of the community of Zgierz from the ancient days until the current time; Hassidim and Torah observant people would work in the factories together with simple or independent workers, in unity and harmony. They would also struggle together for a raise in salary and for an improvement in working conditions, in accordance with the demands of the community of workers in this business sector.

[Page 33]

At the beginning of the 1920s, the leadership of he city decided to change the name of the Jewish street to Berka Joselowica as a gesture of goodwill toward the Jewish residents of Zgierz. A splendid ceremony took place on the street, in the presence of communal representatives and a delegation from the city hall. The honor of unveiling the new sign was given to the lawyer Mr. Hilary Sztykgold, the son of Reb Yisrael Sztykgold – a family of *maskilim*, city notables, and veteran residents of the Jewish Street. However, despite the official and festive change of name, the old name "Jewish Street" [Yiddishe Gasse], etched in the hearts of the residents for generations with all the life and action connected to it, remained in the mouths of the Jews of our city until the final day, the most tragic day in the annals of the Jewish settlement of Zgierz.

… Much water has flowed since then in the vistas of the Bzura River, which crosses the Jewish Street. Its clear water still flow at its pace, as in former days – in the same direction and with the same quiet, as if nothing had happened… However, Jews no longer go to its banks for *tashlich*[2], for their "sins" have already been wiped out and expunged in the flames of the crematoria. Children no longer play outside, and no longer call "Mamma!"… for there are no mothers and no children… they went up in fire to heaven. There is no more sound of Torah and prayer on the "Jewish" street, and the din of work has been quieted with a deathly silence. Even the dust and ashes of the burnt synagogue has been scattered with tie in all directions. Zgierz, like other Jewish communities in Poland, is no more. The community of Zgierz has been liquidated, destroyed, and erased from the earth.

However, they still live in the depths of our hearts. They will live within us as long as we live. Each of us bears their images in our hearts, and our souls weep in secret, in secret.

Translator's footnotes:

1. *Rewir* means "district" in Polish.
2. A Rosh Hashanah ceremony at a river bank, symbolically casting one's sins into the water.

The Pogrom Year of 1903 and the Jews of Zgierz

by W. Fisher

The pogrom that took place in Kishinev in 1903, and a few months later also in Homel [Gomel], terribly stirred up Eastern European Jewry, and its frightful echo aroused worry and fear in Jewish hearts for many years. The silent fear of tomorrow peered forth from Jewish eyes. In those years ,the known song (seemingly from Sh. Frug) was commonly heard, and which deeply affected everyone's Jewish mood:

[Page 34]

> "Brothers, sisters, have mercy
> Woe, how terrible is the night!
> Send shrouds for the dead
> Give bread to the living!"

It seems that the murderous pogroms left an oppressive impression in Zgierz as well. People spoke with quiet but meaningful glances, afraid to express the terrible events with their mouths, in accordance with the adage, "Do not open your mouth to the Satan." Even the Zionist meetings, illegal at that time, conducted declamations or readings from Bialik's "In the City of Slaughter." From the itinerant book sellers, one would get the books that described the pogroms and the terrors of the pogromchiks – things that the newspapers were forbidden to write about.

We bring here a letter from one of the Zgierz merchant commissars, Y. A. Rusinow, in which he expresses his impression and deep experiences under the stress of the bloody pogroms. It was written to a friend of his who was on vacation outside the country in Wiesbaden – the distinguished person of Zgierz, Reb Moshe Eiger. There is no doubt the he expresses therein the mood and feelings of Zgierz Jews in general during those days.

The Pogrom Year of 1903 ,and Jews of Zgierz

by Y. A. Rusinow

Zgierz, September 8/21 1903

To Mr. M. H. Eiger in Weisbaden

My dear friend!

They still bear the mark of Cain on their foreheads, the black stain is still on their foreheads, the page sullied by blood and brains in still in their annals. The city of Homel flows with blood, the hand of a person is upon his fellow; those created in the image of G–d have turned into beasts of prey; they gouge out eyes, spill out guts, break legs, and wash their hands with blood. And where is the lamb for the sacrifice? It is not a lamb caught with its horns in the thicket[1]. The lamb for sacrifice is Isaac, not a sacrifice to G–d, not a sacrifice to a holy, lofty and sublime ideal; it is a sacrifice to a coarse force, the force of the fist; these sacrifices are fitting to the destructive demon. Evil spirits rule the world. Night spirits pervade, satyrs dance about, wolves of prey assist them, and we are a poor, destitute nation wallowing in blood. My heart is full of terror, my ideas have become perplexed, my lips murmur, and I utter a prayer:

[Page 35]

Oh G–d!	It is full of agony and pain
As the years pass	To the next year
From atop the skies of our nation	Hasten salvation
Scatter the clouds.	Hasten the redemption,
Blood flows from your nation	To the chosen nation
Here and also there	Bring us to Zion,
Our bitter exile	Speedily in our days.[2]

The iron hand has sealed the mouths of our newspapers with force, and does not permit them to express the naked truth in public. But the land does not cover the evil of the cruel ones, and these evildoers will get their recompence, from the grace of G–d. Perhaps the event is published in the newspapers there as is appropriate to write about us, for the official knowledge will displace the guilt onto the heads of the Jews, for they incited it, and their hands were first in murdering the innocent Christians. It is appropriate to know the truth of the matter, and if you are able to inform me, my desire will be for your good. I bless you will a good, quiet year, a year in which the prophecy of the seer will be fulfilled, and not half–way: that shall live together, not necessarily the wolf with the lamb – but even people with people, and man shall not consume the flesh of his fellow. Your friend, who is embarrassed to be called by the name of humanity.

Translator's footnotes:

1. A reference to the Binding of Isaac.
2. A fascinating poem, which makes sense when read down the columns, and also may make sense when read across.

And it Was When the First Movie Theater Arrived in our City…
(sections from my memory)

by Zeev Fisher

I believe this was in 1911 or 1912, when the first movie theater (called in the vernacular *kinmetograph*, and in Polish *zywe obrazy*) opened in Zgierz. It was housed in the home of Shaya the Baker (Shaya Beker), and later moved to the home of his son–in–law Hershel Luftman.

The day of the opening of the movie theater was an unforgettable experience for all residents of the city. The curiosity, especially amongst the youth, was great and understandable, for how can it be: "Living pictures" on a screen? How can this be understood, that the pictures that we see on the wall in front of us, are indeed coming come the wall behind us… as those who already visited the movie theater in the neighboring city of Łódź tell. You sit in a hall with the darkness of Egypt around you, and if it is dark – how can you see at all? There were more such questions. Therefore, it is no wonder that during the hours of operation,

[Page 36]

Błotna Street was full of people, and no small number of them were willing to pay kopecks (one kopeck is two groszy) to purchase an entry ticket.

Even though we, the students of the Yagdil Torah Yeshiva, were no less curious about the matter than the other youths, we knew very well that this was not a matter for Torah students, and that all the "wonders" that are seen there are nothing other than an optical illusion. We have also heard news that anyone who dares go the movie theater will be thrown out of the Yeshiva. Therefore, we even avoided passing through Błotna Street during the day, when the hall was closed, due to fear and the evil eye.

Then, one day, large blue signs appeared on the walls of the houses, in Polish and Yiddish, that the movie "The Land of Israel Being Built Up" will be shown the following week. In it, one would see the new "colonies" that are being set up, the holy city of Jerusalem, the Western Wall, the tomb of Rachel our Matriarch, the Jordan River, and much more. So, what Jew in our place would not want to see our Holy Land – even from afar? The well–known, renowned Reb Nachum Sokolow would be heard at the beginning of the film, certainly to express his words on the redemption of the Land. Therefore, everyone in the city, from old to young, prepared for the following week, and the youth of the city of Zgierz only spoke and discussed about this matter.

In truth, there were also those among the orthodox, and some of the Hasidim, who strongly opposed this movie, with their reasons: first – this is an act of the Zionists, who are trying to hasten the end, and we all know that their intention is to attract the pure and upright to follow them; second – it is told that men and women sit together "there," may G–d protect us, and how can we support sinners… They had other such excuses. However, these reasons and outcries were ineffective and had no influence. In the evening, when the movie theater opened, Jews from all strata streamed there – entire families, grandparents and grandchildren, to see our Land of Israel with their own eyes, the Land about which every Jew dreams, and every religious student pines for…

Now, with the perspective of years, we can testify that many sons and daughters of our city, who left their parents during those days and made *aliya* to the Land of Israel – that these "living pictures" of this first, modest movie, were, to no small measure, a factor that enthused their imagination and whet their desire to make *aliya* and build up the desolate Land.

*

Appropriate to the title of this article, we describe an episode that surveys in a specific way the social reality in our city (and certainly not only in our city) during the years prior to the First World War – which I found written in "Man of Faith," page 81[1], as follows:

[Page 37]

"In those days, the movie theater reached Zgierz as well. All residents of the town went to see the wonders of the movies – except the Hassidim, who regarded this as a gathering of scoffers[2]. Attendance was not forbidden to their wives and daughters. Chayale also joined the stream of attendees, which was a source of dissatisfaction to her husband, even though he did not disrupt this. Once, when she returned from the movie theater to her home, she found her second son ill with a serious disease. Her husband reproved her, and pointed out the results. On the spot she vowed that if her son would recover, her foot would never tread over the threshold of the movie theater again. Her son recovered, and she, Chayale, kept her vow until her last day..."

Translator's footnotes:

1. There is a text footnote here: "Man of Faith" by Pinchas Sirkes.
2. See Psalms 1:1.

Our Former Home

by Tamar (Tala) Cincinatus

Zgierz, my town Zgierz.

It comes to my memory very often, and I look at it with youthful longing in my glance, with disheveled dreams in my soul, and with quiet pain in my heart.

Zgierz, my small, clean town Zgierz, was a beloved part of my childhood, my warmly beloved parental home, the city of my birth, where I spent the best years of my life.

Zgierz, it is odd, as if that single word spins as if from a scroll of the history of my far–off childhood years, a complete world with all the colors of the rainbow, which dazzles the glance and blurs the pain; a world with memories and associations, which blend together in a confusion of angst, macabre visions of the terrible destruction.

Everything that once was beautiful and good in my personal life is bound up with my hometown Zgierz. A bright world went forth from my home, from the warm, heartwarming circle of my boundlessly dedicated parents, dear beloved brothers and sisters, and many beloved relatives and friends, whose lives were so cruelly cut off.

[Page 38]

The former Jewish Zgierz is dead. Remaining is only us, the survivors – those who left the town long before the destruction of Poland and settled in Israel and other countries, as well as those who were miraculously saved from the horrible destruction.

Our fathers and mothers are no longer here. The dear souls who caressed us and worried about every step of ours are no longer here. They, whose eyes brimmed with tears of joy when we were happy and tears of agony and pain when we were suffering are no longer here.

Our brothers and sisters, all our dear friends with who we spent the best years of our childhood and our youth, happy and bittersweet days, with dreams and hopes for a finer and better life, are no longer here.

All of our dearest and nearest, whom we will never forget, have been murdered with unusual deaths.

A view of Pilsudskiego Street

The years of my childhood and youth live in my memory. You and I constantly feel the living breath of all those who were so horribly annihilated.

[Page 39]

In my glance, I carry all that is fine and soulful from that which the terrible realities destroyed in a manner that exceeds every human fantasy in its horror. Those horrors are our unfortunate reality.

*

I wish to participate significantly in the important work that you have undertaken to perpetuate our martyrs, write about this life of Zgierz Jews, about individuals and entire families whose memories must remain for generations. However, first–of–all, permit me to write a few lines about my own home, about my own wide–branched family, of which only two now remain.

The Cincinatus family was well–known in Zgierz. We were two sisters and six brothers. My father, Shlomo Cincinatus, was a tailor by trade. My mother was involved with maintaining the household, and both devoted their entire lives to raising their children. They also found time for societal work.

I recall how my father, after a hard day of work, found the time and energy to sit an entire night with a seriously ill person. This was one of the tasks that he took on as a member of the Bikur Cholim Society.

My parents possessed a great deal of vitality and life energy, as well as a great deal of understanding for the various problems of life. They invested all this in the daily work of educating their children. They did not satisfy themselves with elementary education and with sending us to *gymnaszja*. They also sent us to study in seminaries and universities, and in those long–ago years, this was a very difficult achievement for a working family. It was required a great deal of energy and perseverance to accomplish such.

The days when our entire family was gathered around the table for a holiday meal always remain before my eyes. Joy radiated from everyone's face. Words, stories and episodes that everyone told about their experiences, about their areas of study or workplace were discussed. This always evoked cheerfulness and joyous laughter, and made us forget our day–to–day worries and concerns.

[Page 40]

The radiant faces of Father and Mother gave testimony to their inner experiences, fine and holy.

*

The town of Zgierz, the town of the years of my childhood and youth, lies in a mound of ash, destroyed and ravaged.

It is hard to comprehend that Zgierz is now a town devoid of Jews, without Sabbaths and festivals; that the houses full of weekday toil, and full of Sabbath grace and holiness, are no longer there.

It is hard to believe that this is all no more, that the life of our beloved and dear ones has been so horribly cut off.

This is the sorrowful and cruel remnants of my home, of my deeply beloved family. I see them day and night. They obscure the entire world before me.

They always remain before my eyes, only them I see. Only them…

There are no words that can express our difficult mood and pain after their destruction. My brother Yaakov and I are the only survivors. We remain mute in the face of the memory of our dear ones, of the murdered Jews of Zgierz, the holy martyrs, and will remain mourners forever.

————

Jewish Pioneers in the Zgierz Hand Weaving Business

by Leon Rubinstein

Leon Rubinstein is among the veterans of Labour Zionism, and was the organizer of the first group of *Chalutzim* [Zionist pioneers] who made *aliya* from Poland to the Land of Israel in 1918. As a teacher and cultural–social activist, he was immersed in the variegated web of Socialist Zionist activity. His interest both in the activities and in the theories, as with all other Jewish problems, always increased, and his personality grew with that. Among other factors, his emotional richness was also drawn

[Page 41]

from the environment in Zgierz, to where he came from Łódź already as a Bar Mitzvah lad.

His fervent striving for *aliya*, drawn at the outset both from Zionist and Socialist thought, and, above all, from the great longing for the Land of Israel that pervaded among the youth in Zgierz, was formed in Zgierz.

We bring down here the beginning of his autobiography, which has a connection to Zgierz, the city of his grandfather, great–grandfather, and close relatives – those dear Jews with good heads and warm Jewish hearts. The relative glory of that wide–branched weaving family of Zgierz is also expressed in the latter chapters of his autobiography.

*

I was born in Łódź on February 2, 1901. My father and my entire family, my grandfather and great–grandfather were all textile manufacturers in Zgierz. My father moved to Łódź when he married my mother, Baltsha, also from a family connected with the textile industry. However, fate had it that my father was incidentally on a business trip to America when the First World War broke out, so my mother with my four brothers and my sister moved to Zgierz. At that time, I was already a Bar Mitzvah lad, and I remained in Zgierz until 1918, when I made *aliya* to the Land of Israel.

I write the history that I am going to tell in the form of a diary. This is the history of my *aliya*, beginning with the journey that I made together with a group of friends through Poland, Austria, Yugoslavia, Italy, and Egypt, until we finally arrived at the coast of the Land of Israel.

*

Like the majority of the Jewish towns of Poland, Zgierz had a vibrant Jewish life, and was full of cheders, Yeshivas, and worldly schools. Zgierz had a large number of Jewish cultural organizations, a large library named for

[Page 42]

David Frischmann[1], an old age home, a literary–musical organization called Hazamir, a drama group, a sporting organization called Maccabee, and a full set of political parties of all colors, starting from Aguda, Mizrachi, and Young Zion, until the Bund, and others. Like many other Jewish towns, Zgierz also produced a large number of Jewish personalities, such as David Frischmann, the renowned speculator Marek Szwarc – the son of the well–known *maskil* and writer Isucher Szwarc, the Hebrew poet Yaakov Kohen, Yitzchak Kacelenson, and others. The Jewish writer Yehuda Elberg also comes from Zgierz.

The Jews of Zgierz were involved with various means of livelihood, but the majority were the textile manufacturers, spinners, and weavers. Zgierz had a number of large factories that employed their own workers. There were also smaller textile enterprises that distributed the work to home workers, daily wage earners, cutters, and stuffers. When the mechanized loom was later operated, the Zgierz weavers got accustomed to the new, modern times. A fair number of the population was employed in the textile industry. The factory owners were Jews and Germans. The employees were Jews, Germans, and Poles. There were factories that sent their own traveling salesman to deep Russia. There were manufacturers who collaborated with factories in neighboring Łódź. In brief: Zgierz lived to a large degree on the rhythm of the weaving industry. My family, including my great–grandfather, my grandfather, and my father, lived to a large degree according to that rhythm. My father Eliezer (Lezjor) Rubinsztajn, was a third–generation textile manufacturer.

My great–grandfather already had a textile factory in Zgierz in the middle of the 19th century. Master weavers were employed for the work, for at that time they had a guild which permitted no others. My father's older sister, my aunt Baltsha, used to love to tell us children stories about her father, our grandfather Yosef Rubinsztajn, who died when I was only one–and–a–half years old. She lived with her mother, our grandmother Malkale Rubinsztajn. Our aunt would always tell us stories about Grandfather when we went to visit our grandmother.

On of her stories is deeply etched in my memory. She related

[Page 43]

that on one occasion, when my grandfather came home from the *Beis Midrash*, he met his father, our great–grandfather, pacing around the room, nervous and upset. When he asked him what had happened, our great–grandfather explained that he had a sharp discussion with the German master weaver, who called him an "accursed Jew." Our great–grandfather then opened the door and threw him out. He, the German, turned around and said to him with a malicious smile that he will yet come to him and beg him to return to work.

When my grandfather heard this, he calmed his father and said, "You do not need to do this, for I will direct the factory." For his father, this was an unexpected statement, and he looked at him with astonishment. It did not occur to him that his son, the *Beis Midrash* student, had an interest in the factory. However, my grandfather then told him that for a long time already, when he came home from the *Beis Midrash*, he would go to the factory and ask the ask the master weaver how the machines work. He took interest in every minute detail of the factory. The master weaver, noticing his sincere curiosity, explained everything to him. To his father's great surprise, my grandfather believed that he could direct the factory.

Indeed, that is how it was.

My grandfather, as my aunt explained further, learned the profession the best of the family. He even took on students from near and far towns, and taught them the profession. Of course, his own sons, sons–in–law, and even the daughters were among the students. My grandfather later played a very important role in the textile industry, not only in Zgierz but also in the entire region. After the Second World War, the Book of Zgierz, a memorial book for the destroyed community, was published in Israel. Some of the participants in the book tell about my grandfather's pioneering role... One of the participants, Leon Lipschitz, states in his memoirs, "My Hometown at the End of the 19th Century"... "The first Jewish industrialist in Zgierz was Reb Yossel Rubinstajn, a deeply pious Orthodox Jew. He studied the weaving trade, and set up future generations of weavers

[Page 44]

who founded weaving enterprises in Zgierz or in the surrounding towns."

A second participant in the book, Y. L. Weinstein, writes about the Zgierz clothmakers, "The influence of Yossel Rubinsztajn, along with others, was evident here. He was the educator of a generation of weaving professionals and master weavers. A recognizable number of Zgierz cloth makers came out of his factory."

Dr. Avraham Eiger gives over more details about my grandfather in his article about his own father Moshel Ejger, who was one of the wealthiest and distinguished manufacturers in Zgierz, and also an important cultural activist. He writes: "My father's life and especially his young years were seriously bound with the life of his uncle Reb Yosel Rubinsztajn. After his father died during the cholera epidemic, Moshele's education was directed by his mother Zisele and her brother Yossel Rubinsztajn… Yossel Rubinsztajn was the first in Zgierz to set up two hand workshops. He quickly mastered the German language and thoroughly learned the profession from the trade literature. He forged contacts with Jewish manufacturers in the Sudeten, and was known as a specialist in the branch of industry. People came to him not only from nearby Łódź, Ozorków, and other nearby towns, but also from Lithuania, Podolia, and other areas."

Translator's footnote:

1.   See https://en.wikipedia.org/wiki/David_Frischmann

The "Ordinances" of the "Union of Youths" in Zgierz

The Union of Youths was established in Zgierz at the end of the first decade of the 20th century. Its purpose was Zionist activity in all areas of Jewish life in our city. In essence, this was one of the first chapters of the Young Zion movement in Poland. This organization was called the Union of Youths on account of the ban on Zionist (political…) activity during the time of the Russian Czar, so as to obfuscate its primary aim.

In its time, we received from our friend Mr. Fabian Grynberg, one of the founders of the union, the original set of "ordinances" or aims of the organization, that were defined and written in minute form in the year 5671 – 1911. We bring them down here in their original language (Regarding Young Zion, see the Book of Zgierz, pp. 299–300).

[Page 45]

1.   The aim of our organization, The Union of Youths, is the revival of the Hebrew language through various means and methods.
2.   In order to achieve this goal, the union organization Hebrew classes, celebrations and lectures. It has opened a library, subscribed to newspapers, etc.
3.   Members of the union can be anyone who pays membership dues, is recommended to the committee by two members, and finds the personal energy to fulfil the requirements of the committee.
4.   A member is removed from the organization when: a) they request such themselves; b) when they have not paid membership dues for three months consecutively, without a reason; c) when they do not fulfil the obligations of a member of the union.
5.   Membership dues are non–refundable.
6.   The leadership of the union is in the hands of a) the general meeting; b) the council.
     a.
          1.   The general meetings elect the members of the council and the members of the committee for the oversight of accounting and the library.
          2.   2. The general meetings are convened six times a year, every two months.
          3.   3. The meetings are official when attended by two thirds of the members.
          Note: General meetings present their recommendations, such as: a change of ordinances, future work, closing of the union, etc.
     b.

1.   The council is divided into two groups: a) the regular council; b) the honorary council.

Note: The regular council must only consist of members of the union.

2.   The general meeting elects three members: three members of the council and three members of the committee for the oversight of accounting and the library.

3.   The members of the council are elected for a full year.

4.   Members of the council divide among themselves the roles of chairman, school supervisor, treasurer, and secretary.

5.   The members of the committee for the oversight of accounts are elected for two months. When a complaint is presented from five members of the union, the council will call a general meeting and the meeting will elect a new committee.

6.   The committee for the oversight of accounts and the library inspects the library and the treasury on a weekly basis.

7.   The union is closed: a) on request from the general meeting; b) when the union cannot continue to exist for material or other reasons.

Zgierz, 5671 (1911)

[Page 46]

The Prospectus

by Z. P.

In former times, it was difficult for authors of books to publish the fruits of their spirit and toil, especially when it comes to books of religion, Torah, and morality. Only an author who has good luck as well as a generous patron will find it easier to actualize his aspiration and achieve his goal. Alas, not every writer merits such. Thus, we recall the wandering of "authors" from city to city and town to town, with a sack in the hand containing their tallis, and tefillin, as well as their "manuscripts" (the fruits of their many years of holy labor, work done for the most part through a life of difficulty, and with intentions for the sake of Heaven – that is to disseminate Torah and books of morality to the masses). They would go about searching for benefactors in the city, whose way was to help and support endeavors such as this, whether through a good recommendation a bit of money, or at times even advance subscription fees for the book when it would be finished.

However, not every home greeted the writers in a pleasant manner with a blessing. There were some "householders" who related to them and their request for up–front payment like "beggars" who were requesting donations. Our author, Reb Chanoch Henich Ehrsohn was one of those in luck, who avoided this obstacle.

Reb Henich Ehrsohn (nicknamed: Henich the Yellow) was an honorable man in our community. He was a scholar who was sincere, splendid in his dress, and pleasant in his mannerisms. He was also the most fruitful of the Torah authors in our city, and there was no insignificant number of such. His mother–in–law, the widow Mrs. Elka, was a woman of means. She was also generous and supportive of rabbis. She literally revered her son–in–law (who married her only daughter) and related to him with awe and respect. She regarded it as a great merit to serve him, to be a support for him, and to help him achieve his spiritual goals. Thus did Reb Henich succeed, without any effort, to publish his first three books in short order. Through them, he earned a name for himself and became famous in the Hassidic and Torah world.

The day came when his mother–in–law, Mrs. Elka the owner of the butcher shop, his dedicated patron, went the way of all people. Then, Henich's luck turned bad. The economic situation of the family declined, and they had to skimp and save. When, with all this, he had three more book manuscripts that had to be published, he had the idea of using the post office as his personal emissary, and the prospectus as a mouthpiece. Thus we see how the printed prospectus was disseminated to the masses, resulting in wonderful things, for not only did this help him in publishing his books, but it also crossed seas and oceans, and reached the YIVO institute in New York…

His economic situation and depressed spirit can be seen in this prospectus. I can testify that the last lines of that prospectus – to not plead or flatter a wealthy benefactor, were written as a parable, as was the custom of authors in those days…

[Page 47]

Pränumerant

הנה עורני ה' ליקן לבית הרפּס ספר יקר להדציאי לאיר עולם. ובו שלשה ספרים נפיהים.

בן רוח על התורה כולל באורים יקרים ומאיר פשׁשׁים גפּלאים ובכּלים. מוהדים ושפצים אור

פקח עינים עוברות על הפסוקים שהם הביניהם לאורה. לבארם על פי דרשות חז"ל שהם לנו לינעם

לאורה. ולהסבירם על ידי בונה עמוקה שבהם לושה ושורה. ולהרובח כמה נר לים דברי תכבים

יקרי המבצאות. ומהם סה שנעורעי מפי השמועות. וגם דברים נרטרים אשר חנני ה' לחידש בנעית:

בוצא טים ידד התוםית ומראה שעני נחםאות ובקשות בקיר בים אבדרם. שתם וקבצי ונאספו הםפוחים.

דברי חנך כדס משולעם ובקשרים דברים נחמדים אשר על ידם נתקני הדדבים וגדישעי התניבית לנטה ולידות מפרי עץ החים הנפוע בתוך תן.

במוה הוא לכל החתום בו וקנה זה הספר. וייהנה וזעין באלה אטרי ישֹר. יתענג בר ממזב שעער ושיחר. ובבו צעֹר עם שב נם ישֹישֹ יפנעי בי דברים תפתאטים לפי טעמו ורוחו.

יכבר דכני ה' להוציא לאיר עולם הם חנוכת התורה. קיל איירו. ומנחת חנך.

עמוקית מני חושך ויצא לאיר ממטונט. ה"ל לאורו. הבטים ושבחותו נטוֹנם. ומקה אני שֹנם הספר הע"ל אשר אנ מתענד בו בעל להדציא לאיר עֹיֹב יצֹא תן ולֹא ימאֹפֹתֹי זכנים ובֹל כֹל ספֹק יתרבו עֹדי הדבה קנֹים.

לכן אבקש מאֹת שוחרי תשיה ותומריה. מחוקי התורה ותוטביח. היו נא במיֹבנב בעֹזדי לבֹמֹע אֹת מֹתֹשֹבֹת ההֹוֹצֹאה לֹפֹוֹעֹל. והֹאבֹו נֹא בֹתֹסֹדֹבֹם לֹהֹוֹת בֹי לֹעֹזֹד ולֹהֹועֹיֹל. ואֹל תֹחֹוֹבֹי עֹל בֹשֹאֹבֹם אֹיֹש לֹפֹי נֹרֹבֹת לֹבֹו כֹסֹף מֹאֹתֹם. לֹתֹהֹוֹם אֹת שֹמֹי עֹל הֹסֹפֹר תֹגֹל ולֹשֹלֹח יֹי דֹמֹי קֹרֹיֹשֹה. ובֹגֹבֹת זֹה תֹתֹבֹרֹבֹו מֹאֹת הֹשֹיֹבֹן שֹבֹם וֹהֹזֹלֹה אֹרֹך עֹל בֹלֹיֹמֹה.

איה כאשר יֹנֹמֹר הֹפֹסֹת הֹסֹפֹר וֹצֹא לֹאֹיֹר. אֹשֹלֹחֹהֹו חֹפֹשֹי אֹל הֹמֹנֹיֹם עֹלֹיֹו. עֹל יֹדֹי הֹכֹי דֹואֹר. ובֹראֹש הֹסֹפֹר אֹפֹרֹסֹם אֹת שֹמֹכֹם הֹטֹוֹב לֹכֹבֹוֹד ולֹתֹפֹאֹרֹת.

תֹהֹי לֹכֹם זֹאֹת לֹהֹכֹרֹנֹא ולֹזֹוֹכֹרֹת. ומֹיֹוֹב בֹטֹתֹיֹנֹי בֹבֹם שֹתֹמֹלֹא בֹקֹשֹתֹי וֹאֹנֹי שֹלֹח אֹנֹי לֹכֹם אֹת הֹדֹרֹי לֹנֹמֹדֹיֹק. ולֹפֹנֹי הֹדֹרֹה בֹבֹוֹדֹבֹם הֹנֹי מֹשֹתֹחֹיֹה ובֹורֹע.

חנוך העניך ערהוואהן

Rabb. Ass. H. Ehrsohn,·Zgierz (Russ.·Polen)

Г. Эрзонъ, Згержъ Петрок. губ.

Photocopy of the prospectus, which is printed on the following page

[Page 48]

Prospectus from an Author

PRÄNUMERANT

Behold, G–d has assisted me in bringing a precious book to print to be published to the light of the world, consisting of three opened books.

a.   *Gan Raveh* [A Watered Garden] on the Torah, including precious and enlightening explanations, simple, wonderful, and strong, enlightening and shedding light on many explanations of our sages of blessed memory, proving how they are checkered with an abundance and a shortage of verses. This will open eyes to the verses that are apparently a mystery, to explain them in accordance with the exegesis of our sages of blessed memory, who are as eyes and light to us, to explain them in accordance with the deep intentions with which they are enveloped, to prove several great statements of the sages that are a tradition for us, for there is nothing that does not have an innuendo in the Torah. These have been gleaned from 500 ancient books of great real value, and some from that which I heard, as well as beautiful things that G–d has given me the grace to innovate through my efforts.

b.   *Motza Mayim* [Source of Water] will delve deeply and demonstrate changes in versions and source material from the sea of the mighty ones, from where the scattered material was gathered and collected.

c.   *Divrei Chanoch* [Words of Chanoch] in which lovely ideas are woven and connected together, through which the paths are fixed and the routes are straightened to arrive and benefit from the fruit of the Tree of Life planted in the garden.

G–d has already granted me the merit to publish the books *Chanukat Hatorah*, *Kol Eliahu*, and *Minchat Chanoch* to clarify the depths from the darkness and expose hidden matters to the light. The wise have seen them and the erudite has praised them. I hope that the aforementioned book that I now intend to publish will find favor, will not be rejected by the builders[1], and without doubt will have many purchasers.

Therefore I request from the masters and studiers of resourcefulness, the upholders and supporters of Torah, to find it in their benefit to help me carry out and actualize my thoughts. I request of you, in your goodwill, to be an aid and enabler. Do not spare your money, each in accordance with the generosity of his heart, for money is nothing when it comes to registering your name for the aforementioned book and to send me advance money. In this merit, may you be blessed from the Dweller of Heaven, who Suspends the World in Space.

And, G–d willing when the publishing of the book is finished, I will send it gratis by mail to all who subscribed to it, and I will include your good names for glory and honor, and let this be a souvenir and memento to you. In my great faith that you will fulfil my request, I am sending you my gratitude in advance, and I bow and prostrate myself before the splendor of your honor:

Chanoch Henich Ehrsohn
Rabb. Ass. H. Ehrsohn, Zgierz (Russ. – Polen)

Translator's footnote:

1.   Based on Psalm 118:22.

[Page 49]

A Fundamental Solution to the Problem of Languages...
Solving the Language Question...

by Reb Moshe Eiger

(As the elder, witty, but always humorous Reb Moshe Eiger solved the old, difficult language question in a simple manner; Yiddish–Hebrew, read and be amazed[1].)

To my friend!
Instead of bathing in Iwanowice, here I sit now –
Come here now, to place a patch
A patch on the old, torn clothing...
As they say: Here instead of the medicine for
My pain in my old feet
And if the doctor decrees – I fulfil:
I drink the water, take the baths,
But I request from you, do not bring any reports from the *cheder*,
I continue to remain the old heretic
I will not believe in this much, and I do not deduce or claim,
That I will find the cure here
That in Iwanowice can be found the wellsprings of salvation...
Perhaps baths could help me sometime
If I would bath in the hot springs of Tiberias in the Land of Israel...
I would sit on the balcony, like an old dreamer,
With the trees swaying in the forest opposite
And I would hear the whisper of the trees of the forest;
There sits an old fool...

Here, you see, my dear one, that the daughters of poetry have surrounded me
The Holy Tongue, just like Yiddish, and each one
Says: let the righteous one rest on my head...
So that there should be peace among Jewish children ——
Here I combine Hebrew and Yiddish, and write them together.
To fulfil that which is written: "And there shall be great peace amongst your children."[2]
Let us all dance with each other:
Zionists, Folkists, specifically in Aleksander...[3]

(From the booklet: "To the son – to the daughter")

Iwanowice, Tammuz 5691 (1931)

Translator's footnotes:

1. The lines of this poem alternate between Hebrew and Yiddish, with the Hebrew line rhyming with the following Yiddish line. Of course, all this is lost in the translation. The last eight lines are in Hebrew.
2. Isaiah 54:13.
3. Referring evidently to Aleksandrów Łódzki, which is the seat of Aleksander Hassidism.

[Page 50]

Names, Family Names, and Nicknames

by W. F.

A memorial light to those Jews of our town, mainly the common folk, whose true names have become obfuscated due to common usage, the times, and the place – and did not reach us.

As with Jews in every town, nicknames stuck to almost all Zgierzers, and when the nickname was a good one and was accepted, it often replaced the true family name, which in time was completely forgotten. It is typical that it is rare that well–connected, wealthy or progressive families in the city were "coronated" with nicknames. They were almost always called by their true names and family names.

The various nicknames, which were certainly created by the anonymous city loafers or simple "light headed folk" generally bore a diverse character: an innocent wit, mockery, malevolence, or were incidental. There were also family names that were intentionally twisted, or simply took on a different meaning and significance in the mouths of the folks.

I will bring here only a few of the popular nicknames with which entire families were designated, to the point that one could only known about whom it was referring through the nickname.

> Di Kasztanes[1] (hatmakers – everyone with fiery red beards)
> Di Smotkes (coach drivers, wagon drivers)
> Di Verem [2] (food shops, business people)
> Di Staniks [3] (butchers)
> Di Szoklers [4] (butchers)
> Di Kurniks (wagon drivers)
> Di Platzkes (weavers)
> Di Pondzszers (weavers)
> Di Tzutls
> Di Muches (householders, patrons)
> Di Snopkes [5]

[Page 51]

> Di Klekls (shoemakers)
> Di Katolikes [6] (householders, merchants)
> Di Chaberikes (iron shop keepers)
> Di Sztompers (businessmen, wagon drivers)
> Di Bekls (businessmen, merchants)
> Di Bielases (porters, coachmen)
> Di Bols (tailor trade)
> Di Paplaks (bookbinders)
> Di Parches (a malevolent nickname)[7]
> Di Soltises (fowl businessmen)[8]
> Di Botszankes[9] — and many more

During the years when Zgierz was growing and Jews taking up settlement there was conspicuous, it was easier to identify the newcomers by the place from where they had come. Some were indeed known as such: Leibel Piliwer,

Hershel Ozorkower, Mendel Linszitzer, Henech Lasker, Yanker Strykewer, etc. It was also easy to identify call them by their trade, or simpler, by their color, weight, etc. : The White Leibush, the Yellow Henech, the Lame Yoel, the Black Yuda, the tall Avramcha, etc. One could also end up [with a nickname only] without a name, such as the Warsawer Butcher, the Black Shoemaker, the Bagel Baker, the Bolimower Baker, the Yellow Tailor, the Tobacco Maker, and further and further – and I knew them all very well…

It was under German rule during the years of the First World War, when, for the first time, everyone had to keep a personal document on themselves. However, especially under the renewed Polish independence when children went to school without exception, surnames became used more and more openly, and began to regain their personal and societal significance. Through their own self–awareness, the new, upcoming generation began to throw off and free themselves from their various family nicknames, which decades earlier "adorned" the status of their parents and grandparents. Slowly, these nicknames became forgotten, and disappeared.

Translator's footnotes:

1. Horse chestnut.
2. Worms.
3. Workbench or assembly line.
4. Shakers.
5. Beam of light.
6. Catholics.
7. In the Weinreich dictionary, the word Parch means canker or ulcer, or (vulgar) rat, or stingy person.
8. Soltis in Polish is a village administrator.
9. Storks.

[Page 52]

A Ray of Light on Cold Days
(from the recent past)

by Z. F.

At the end of 1918, Reb Zeev Eliahu Reichert, one of the Zionist leaders in our city, was elected as a delegate to the national convention of Polish Jewry that took place in Warsaw. A decision was taken at that convention to create a supreme national, political organization to guard the interests of Polish Jewry, with the participation of leaders from the various parties, communities, and institutions from all parts of Poland. When he returned, he presented a detailed, interesting report on this convention in the hall of the Zionist Union on January 9, 1919.

After he provided in his speech a detailed report of the obstacles placed in the path of the national Jewish movement by members of the Socialist parties from one side, and the assimilationists (who were sycophantic toward the Polish authorities) on the other hand, and on the difficult struggle that the Zionists must undertake to ensure that the true interests of the masses of Jews in the communities reign supreme, and on the makeup of communal representation, he described with great emotion the moments that were soul–elevating and won over hearts in that convention. We will now bring a section from his words:

"… We reached the pinnacle of emotion and wonderful spirit when with the reading of the telegram of greeting from President Wilson, from the British government via Lord Balfour, from the Zionist leaders who obtained the historical declaration from November 2 – Professor Chaim Weizmann, Nachum Sokolov, and Louis Brandeis. At that moment, each of us sensed the historical significance that pervaded through the meeting hall. The moods were sublime, creating spontaneous friendship and fraternal feelings among all those gathered – the Orthodox, Mizrachists, regular Zionists, ordinary people, and former assimilationists. All forgot their political aspirations, and everyone sought in their hearts to embrace and kiss each other. We were like one large family gathered for a very joyous event. A stream of boundless joy and gladness passed over us all. Grynbaum, a leftist, hugged and kissed Farbsztajn, a rightist, in the presence of all those gathered. The rabbis delivered sermons on national closeness and unity. The rabbi from Radom spoke in Yiddish, and the rabbi from Sempolna in clear Hebrew. Every sentence emanating from his mouth was a stream of love, faith, Israelite pride, Torah greatness, and national greatness. Our rabbis were not used to hearing such words in the Hebrew language, and everyone asked, 'Who did all this for us?'

How encouraging and heartwarming were the words spoken by the Rabbi of Zamość:

'If one of us came to Warsaw with a heart full of doubts, suspicions, and fear of the status of our nation, torn and ripped to pieces, and was immersed in dark thoughts of what might be, as to whether there is hope to mend

[Page 53]

the rips and to make us into one people who knows its way – its path in life; this most recent convention, filled with hope and security, made it clear that there is hope for our future, that the Nation of Israel will yet live, and that we will inherit our land as in days of yore, returning to the former glory, to reestablish the life of the nation of the foundations of its original culture.'"

(from our archives)

It Once Was…
Memoirs, dreams and illusions from my childhood years

by Mordechai Roisman

The human memory casts out, like the ash from an oven that burnt and warmed on a winter night, many relics and memories. But there are those that are etched in the memory and remain there like hot embers of fire and gold. Thus lie the experiences of my childhood years as if under a thick fog. Once they were perhaps organized in my memory, according to the years, events, and experiences. Now they are tossed about in disarray. Who knows whether our memory is capable of guarding all the experiences in order. Here a beam tears through that reminds, shows the beginning, and then the events that follow. However, it is possible that there is a large portion of our hot desires therein, which helps us create the illusion that this, and nothing different, happened during those distant childhood years. If there are events that have become bleached with time, there are also events, just like people, that have become colored with time.

It begins like in any story: Once there was, once there was a king, once there was a queen… Once there were good times and they disappeared… There was a town Zgierz where everything nestled toward some height, and a longing for loveliness does not stop gnawing. Who can describe the loveliness of all the people, the Hassidim, studiers, and simple Jews; their weekdays, their Sabbaths, and their festivals, the hearty prayers and the wonderful tunes of the worshipping and learning?! Those wonderful melodies still resonate in my ears. With the milk

[Page 54]

from my mother's breast, I absorbed the stories and legends. Years later, I listened to them and desired that nobody would disturb the calm or weaken their holiness.

Years ran buy, children grew up, humming along in the house as in a beanstalk; Yankele, Rivkale, Mordchele, Reizele, Pinchasl. There was also a Berele, who went on a far, unknown journey, where the angel of death took him, and my parents lost a *kaddish*[1].

On both sides of Konstantyn Street stood houses and huts, of wood and brick. A long yard leads far off, to the fields, meadows and gardens. A wooden bucket tied to a metal chain goes down a deep well. Around there, Jewish boys and girls play together with *shkotzimles* and *shikseles*[2]. A branch of a tall pear tree hovers near a window. Naughty hands tear off sweet pears, and children's mouths bite into them with enjoyment.

Days go by, turning into years. I drag myself over our bars from the wooden hut in a neighboring hut in the brick tenement. Our new landlady, Mrs. Sobszinska, casts strange feelings on me. She was a widow with an aristocratic face. She takes measured steps, not too slow and not too fast. She responds to a good-morning with a melodic voice and sharp diction, as if on stage at a theater.

The *Cheshvan* days come. The chestnut trees cast off their yellow-brown leaves. From the unwrapped shells pop forth, as if freed from prison, brown colored, round, shiny chestnuts. The children prance around with enjoyment, filling their pockets with the treasure. The next day, the mother removes the remnants of the previous day's game from the stained pant pockets, and derive satisfaction from the children's pleasure.

Cold winds begin to blow, coming from the heavens with a shuddering chill. The winter covers over the alleyways and roofs with a white blanket of snow. Stalls and cellars are filled with black coal and sticks cut from trees. A heap of potatoes pile up in the cellar.

This means that winter is coming.

A white, snowy *Kislev* brings the Chanukah days with it.

[Page 55]

Shiny eyes gaze toward Father in admiration as the first Chanukah light is lit. It seems that stories from bygone times sprout out from every corner. The night is full of strange dreams, but the early morning smiles upon us with Chanukah gelt.

However, the Christian deity is jealous of the Jewish Chanukah candles; and the gentile houses have green Christmas trees, decorated with colored candles, and silver, paper ribbons surround the green branches. Pictures of people with white beards, but strange faces, hang from the walls… The ringing of bells with their menacing clang rips through the silence, and the Jewish homes are enveloped with a strange fear.

Silver forests with tall trees, growing with long, white beards, burn in my dreams during the long nights. They drop white and red chestnuts… The first glow of the upcoming day approaches my bed and awakens me from my nightmare.

It is light in our house. Green, plush blankets cover the two high beds. In the middle of the house sits a heavy table, covered with a flower tablecloth. There are benches around it. A tile oven is embedded in the wall, reaching to the ceiling, dazzling with its whiteness. Frozen shoulders and ice-cold hands nestle against it. Mother, bent over her pursuits in the kitchen, glances at us from time to time, beaming with satisfaction. Father sits and reads a newspaper, sighing over the Jewish tribulations and worrying about the wide world.

It is already Friday. Hot steam rises from a large pot, and blue-white soap bubbles rise from Mother's caressing hand on the faces of the bent-over children's heads, with crying voices, and red noses that are being rinsed and splashed. Mother's hand give merciful, calming caresses, and the comb smooths and straightens the curly locks.

Two covered, flat challos, which Mother kneaded and baked, already lie on the table. Two white candles stick out of the two silver candlesticks, waiting for Mother's blessing. A flask of wine surrounded by cups and shot glasses proudly awaits Father's kiddush. It is quiet in the house, a Sabbath eve quiet.

[Page 56]

Shortly, Jews in their Sabbath garb, with blond, black or grey beards will emerge from the houses. Children putter around Father's coat hem. From both sides of the Jewish street, Jews go to the synagogue, the *Beis Midrash,* or the Hassidic *shtibels*. We are already at the street corner. Liberman's shop is closed. The aromas from Bolimower's bakery, where Jewish mothers prepared their Sabbath cholent, accompanied with prayers, love, and good wishes, waft from the left side.

Father walks leisurely and calmly, having cast off the weekday concerns. We go together to welcome the Sabbath, to hear the cantor's *Lecha Dodi* [a Sabbath eve prayer], and mingle with the tens of other children and adults.

The iron pump stands like a statue at the corner of Blotner [Muddy] Street. Around it, on the cobblestone pavement, a broad collage spreads out. Candlelight flickers from the rabbi's window. The *shamash* [beadle] waits for him to accompany him to the Welcoming of the Sabbath service. Sabbath candles sparkle from the windows throughout the entire way of the Jewish Street, lighting up the way to the synagogue.

*

It seems that we were strangely earnest children, dreaming and attaining heavenly heights, walking with leisurely steps, not jumping brazenly to be the first. Since our early childhood, we were warmed with the feeling of honor and awe for the grownups, who seemed to us like giants. We breathed the atmosphere of the *cheder* during long days and nights, and we knew that they as well, the giants, had once played the same children's games, but today they shine for us like meteors, like eminent, prominent personalities. Let us at least mention a few of them:

David Friszman, Yaakov Kohen, Isucher Szwarc, Yitchak Kacenelson, Moshel Ejger; and, from the younger ones, Pinchas Bizberg, and, may he live, Yehuda Elberg. Our great rabbis, *Admors*, Hassidim, Torah giants and people of good deeds, eminent and modest.

I walk thus in our pantheon of the spirit and see us surrounded by our simple, toiling Jews, loving and heartwarming mothers, children, youth, educated and growing up in small Jewish Zgierz.

I pass by Jewish houses afflicted with poverty, but they

[Page 57]

comport themselves with honor. The word "honor" shines from them like golden letters on the *parochet* [ark cover] of the Holy Ark of the synagogue and *Beis Midrash*.

It may be that the time will come when it will be difficult to believe that so much fineness and greatness lived in this small town, even though this is the historic truth that has been carried away with the disappearing times.

This is not at all a dream or a legend. This is true, fine reality. A small, modest, but spiritually great and creative community – Zgierz.

Evil winds – no impure hands tore through and burnt our crown.

———

Our "Jewish Street" – in Memory

by Z. W. Fiszer

Dedicated to the fine Jewishness of those generations.

Here life was woven with the woof and the warp,
We count "thousand" as the days and years pass by…
Here we never knew of fat years
And the song was often embittered with pain and tribulations…

The synagogue was fine here, higher than all the houses,
The Gemara chant emanated from the door and windows,
Here, Jewishness dripped from all the roofs –
But the Sabbath and holy days were the nicest.

Everyone wove their life's dream separately,
They requested of G-d that nobody would have to perish;
Only to be able to make a festive celebration for children,
Here, Torah and labor danced together…

*

[Page 58]

To present a bit of the variegated colors that were so characteristic of the residents of the oldest Jewish street in our city, and held on to their uniqueness until the final years of their tragic destruction, we must begin many years earlier, at least from the beginning of the 20th century.

I will begin with Jewish smith, Shimon the Blacksmith, as he was called. His smithy was in the first house of the fish market, which began on the right side of the Jewish Street (at first, this was called Lodzer Street), from south to north – that is, from the old market until the Kurak, which was on the way to Łódź.

We *cheder* children often used to stand near the smithy and gaze with wonder upon the tall, thin, but strongly built Jew with a grey beard as he banged with his hammer on a piece of glowing red iron on the anvil, with sparks flying in all directions – such power in a Jewish hand! We did not realize then that we were standing before the symbol of Jewish toiling labor.

In the area of Shimon the Blacksmith on the fish market one could find the well-known bakery of the widow Lea Ickowicz (Leah the cake baker). This was a wide-branched family from which several sons became weavers. They worked hard and became eminent manufacturers. Leah had a good name in the city and was known for her warm heart toward those suffering and in need. The following families lived in the same house: Mendel Ofenbach – in the weaving business, and Yaakov Okno – a fish seller. From among those who sold all sorts of fish, we must also mention the veteran fish businessmen: Nachum Glowinski (Nachum Shimele's), Sender Gelbard, and several others. Nearby to Leah the cake baker lived Shimon Czernikowski (Moime's) who owned a pasture; Mendel Szejwach, a chair maker; and Shilem Tuch, a water carrier.

The "*Budkes*" [cabins] also stood in the fish market. The five or six wooden cabins were painted brows. One served for selling fruits and vegetables, and the other for the meat and fish business. The cabins were later liquidated. The vegetable dealers also sold sweets for children. We must remember that the area had

[Page 59]

the heaviest concentration of *cheders* and teachers of children in the city. A carousel was placed behind the *Budkes* from time to time, and the children were happy and joyous.

Across from the fish market stood two houses that belonged to two local Germans, Dr. Hesner and Mergel. The following people lived in Mergel's house: Shimon Srebnik, a leather merchant (later a manufacturer of wool articles); Meir Fogel, who owned a vegetable hut; Moshe Sofer (the scribe), who wrote Torah scrolls, *tefillin*, and *mezuzos*, and also sold *Gemaras* to the *cheders* and *yeshivos*; Velvel Kaufman, a printer; and others.

We cut through Szeroka Street (once it had been a part of Piaskes), and we go on the left side of the Jewish Street in the direction of "Kurak." In the corner house of Yosef and Tzirel Poznerzon – Yona Ickowicz, a merchant; Shlomo Szajnholc, a tailor; Yosef Gornicki, a weaver; Yaakov Celgow, has a shoemaker's workshop; Shimon Liberman, a leather merchant; and others. In the neighborhood one finds the house of Leib Feldon, a grain merchant with his son-in-law and partner Leizer Ekbia. The following live there as well: Mendel Ickowicz and Yosef Zszeszowski, bakers; Mendel, Shmerl and Yaakov Wroclawski (stitching workshop); Zalman Wajnsztajn, weaver; Shmuel David Kojawski, food shop owner; Aharon Moshe Szwarc, a cotton producer, and others;. In the house of Meirl Kalski the tavern owner: Nachum Feldon, presser; Ezriel Wajnsztajn, businessman; Yaakov Fajnzilber, wagon driver; Shmuel Lipszyc (the blind Shmil); Mrs. Szenker and her son Yisocher-Mendele, a weaver; and others.

In the nearby house: the previous owners, Avrahamke Wolkowicz, his son Eliahu, later his son-in-law Shimin Princ (son of Michel Princ, owner of a lumber warehouse); Chanan Roiznsztrauch (*gabbai* of Malbish Arumim – for the festivals, he purchased trousers and shows for the children of the Talmud Torah), he was the first cereal maker here; later, his son-in-law Abeh Baum (Abele the cereal maker). His wife Keila Hene was a true woman of valor. From early morning until late at night, she was busy with running the household (they had an open house for poor passers-by). David, the son, toiled in the cereal mill from morning until evening. They were Aleksander Hassidim. Also lived there were: Avraham Yaakov Jankelewicz, the monopoly owner, who studied with older youths. His sons were Pesach, Wolf, Shimon, and Yitzchak. They would play chess with their father in the early hours. All later became merchants; Moshe Nadel, a wool merchant; Mindel-Rivka, and old, learned widow. She would read "*Tzena Urena*"[3] out loud on summer Sabbath afternoons, and passersby would stop to listen

[Page 60]

to her lovely, heartwarming melody from the open windows; Shmuel Zelmanowicz (Shilke the tailor, the "Golden Needle"); Aharon Zalman Wiechucki (The Warsawer Butcher), who had a butcher shop. During the summer, he would provide products for the country houses around the city. He was a jolly societal man, often evoking good cheer and laughter from the neighbors with his jokes and words; Shmuel David Rozalski, a butcher; Berl the joker, a shoemaker. On Fridays, he would go around collecting for the "*Tikun Sofrim*" [book repairing] society of the *Beis Midrash*. While doint so, he would tell stories, jokes, and rhymes to the children. The elderly Berl the Cobbler, an exquisite character; Pinche Brzozowski, connected with the weaving branch; Sender Gelbard, a fisherman.

A nearby house, close to the synagogue and the *Beis Midrash,* was owned by Fisel Bunem Holender (Fishel Bunem the shochet). There lived his sons-in-law, sharp Hassidim and great scholars; Reb Mendel Weksler and Chaim Yaakov Ajzenschmidt (The Yellow Shochet). Reb Mendel Weksler later became the *Rosh Yeshiva* of Beit Meir of Krakow; Bunem Cynamon, who did business with material from torn clothing; Hershel Gelkop (Heshel Smotek), a coachman; Zelig Fogel, a master weaver. He used to perform as an artist in the Zgierz theater troupe. Two sharp Gerrer Hassidim also lived there: Eliahu Baumgarten and Hershel Wagman, merchants, as well as the glassmaker Nachman Turczinski, a veteran teacher at the Talmud Torah.

The synagogue, the *Beis Midrash*, and, to differentiate, the *mikva* [ritual bath]. The cantor Herzl Linden later lived in the dwelling of the rabbi. There, in one of the rooms, the community set up an oven for the baking of matzos for the Jews of Zgierz. This was during the years of the First World War. David Gotlib, a tinsmith, also lived there.

The *mikva* keepers lived in the *mikva* house: Binyamin Lasman, later Pinchas Bentkowski, and still later, Avraham Leibush Michowicz.

Next to the synagogue, in the house of Menashe the oil beater, lived: Sender Malinski, a tanner; Lipman Lipmanowicz (teacher); Wolf Sofer, who was the *shamash* [beadle] in the synagogue during his elder years; Shalom Ber, who had a weaving business; Nathan Szaja, a tinsmith; The Yellow Avraham, a weaver, and others.

We cross the bridge over the stream that divides the street into two.

Incidentally, "the bridge" and "the water pond" come to mind, as does the "Synagogue Street" (Jewish Street) and the Sand Street (the *Piaskes*), which are so often mentioned in

[Page 61]

Frishman's fine story "He Has Passed Away." One can envision that the young Dovidl, like all of us *cheder* children, standing by the bridge and looking at the fish in the pond below…

Next to Borst's long building, which occupied a significant part of the street, in the house of Yaakov-Leib Rozencwajg, lived the rabbi, Rabbi Shlomo Yehuda HaKohen, may the memory of the righteous be blessed. The city provided him with a fine, comfortable dwelling. Every Rosh Hashanah eve, following the evening service, the Hassidim would come there to wish the rabbi a Good Year. The rooms were always full of people and the Hassidic cheer on the festivals spread far along the street.

The following also lived in Itzik Praszker's house: Eliahu Asher Librach, a Hassid and merchant; Shalom Zandberg, the primary trustee [*Gabbai Rishon*] of the *Chevra Kadisha* [burial society], a merchant; Nachman Yechiel Jakier, a tailor; Shalom Hersh Borkowski, a shoemaker; Yitzchak Eksztajn (Yitzchak Ek), a teacher and Gerrer Hassid, Shlomo Zelig Gelbard, a teacher; and others.

The corner house, at the intersection of the Jewish Street with Blotene [The Muddy Street], belonged to the Friszman family. A branch of the Friszman family, Roize Rozenblum lived there. (The house was called "Bei Der Friszmante".) The writer and classicist of Hebrew and Yiddish literature, David Frishmann[4] was born and reared in that house. Living there as well were: Yisrael Yitzchak Gad, a Hassid, scholar, and one of the most elder of the *shochtim* [ritual slaughterers] in the city; Yisrael Mordechai Praszker (the lime maker); Bendit Frenkel, a teacher of the older lads, a scholar, and a fervent Gerrer Hassid. The Strykower Shtibel was also located in that house. Also living in that house were: Shmuel Leizer Grunwald, a coachman; the butchers Zelig and Sender Najman; Yokel Borkowski, a shoemaker; Hershel Rozalski, a cattle merchant; Shaya Feldon, a shoemaker; Wolf Feldon; Godel Frenkel, a merchant; Gedalia Rajzman, a merchant; Yosef Szamszowicz (the Small Yossele), working in the weaving sector; and others. In the further houses and huts lived primarily Christians.

We cross to the other side of the street and return in the direction of the old market. This house once belonged to some villager. Living there were: Pesach Landau, from among the prominent householders, a merchant; Emanuel and Henech Beer, from among the first handweaving businesses; Mordechai Krzykacz, in the weaving business; Kadish Kadysz, a tailor; Shaya Jakubowicz, a weaver; Yudel Konski, a weaver, and others.

In the nearby house, in its time was found the first and well-known

[Page 62]

Yiddish school, led by the teacher Avraham Wachtel. Several Jews lived there a well. This house once belonged to the Nombergs. Jews on handweaving stools worked in the back premises.

The neighboring house belonged to the well-known and wide-branched family of Yudel Szapszowicz and his sons Natan David and Shalom Hirsh. They ran a chicory factory that was known throughout the entire country. In the same house lived Yisrael Frogel, an Ostrowczer Hassid and a great scholar; Butshe Grynfarb, a Jew with Haskalah ideas; Hershel Cohen, from the intelligentsia of that time, and others.

The corner house, on the corner of Konstantyner, belonged to Izidor Sztygold, from one of the eminent families of the city. He was a knowledgeable Jew. He also served as the Torah reader in the synagogue. He was from one of the progressive families of the city. He owned a mechanized weaving workshop. Living there also were: Aryeh Kutner, a weaver; Meir Librach, a merchant; Nota Liberman, a colonial store owner; and others.

We continue onward from the corner of Konstantyner in the direction of the old market. The corner house belongs to Avraham Poznanski, a bakery owner (Bolimower baker); Nathan David Kac, a merchant, one of the eminent Strykower Hassidim; Shmuel Benet, from the weaving trade; and others.

The nearby house belonged to Malkale and Yosef Rubinsztajn and the Wagmans. Living there as well were the family of Leizer Sztachelberg, an eminent and well-connected family; Yitzchak Meir Halperin; the well-known Szeps family; Henech Ber, a broker; and others.

Here, in the house of Yosele Rubinsztajn, also stood the cradle of the Zgierz Jewish hand-weaving guild. Located there was the first Jewish textile trade school in our area, under the leadership and supervision of the aforementioned trade teacher, Yosele Rubinsztajn. Our well-known great industrialist, Zionist activist, and poet, Reb Moshe Ejger, was also educated and raised there. Ezriel Cukier, a merchant, a warm Aleksander Hassid, also lived there. Emanuel Ber ran a large weaving enterprise in the yard.

The farther neighboring house also belonged to partners. Living there were: Avraham Berliner, a traveling agent, a scholar and Hassid. He used to take on fast days; Yosef Pinchas Landau, from the elder Gerrer Hassidim; G. Dresler, a tailor and a volunteer teacher of the Ein Yaakov society; the teacher Yitzchak Jakier; Yitzchak Yosef Blosztajn, (the tobacco maker),

[Page 63]

a scholar, who earned his livelihood with the toil of his hands until he became seriously ill; Shaya Beker, who baked cookies and fan pastry for the *cheder* children. The society of the Jewish clothmakers was also located there.

Behind Napieralski's factory there was a house, which was called "Hotel Kabcanski." It was owned by many partners, and was inhabited by many residents who changed frequently. The following once lived there: Nachman-Yechiel Jakier, a tailor; Shifra Gurner with her two sons, a shoemaker; Shlomo-Zalman Herzog, a merchant; Hershel Ickowicz, a baker; and others. The Strykower Hassidim purchased the old house and built a new house for the rabbi, with a *Beis Midrash* and *Yeshiva* in the courtyard. A new house of Torah and Hassidism stood there. Later, the Kinewer rabbi lived there, who was the rabbi following the death of his father, Rabbi Menachem Mendel Landau, may the memory of the righteous be blessed. Nachman Zajonc, a weaver, also lived there.

The following houses: Living in Michel Praszkier (the deaf Mechel) were: Yaakov Gelbard, a trustee [gabbai] of the *Chevra Kadisha* [burial society]; Mechel Beer, a weaver; Leib Rozencwajg, a tavern keeper; Melech Frajsztat, in the junk business; Aharon Zakon, a scholar and fervent Aleksander Hassid, who owned a shop; and others.

Frida and later Yoel Goldberg, a councilor and president of the Maccabee sport organization of Zgierz were employed in the business and dying enterprise of Brodacz.

We pass by the Polish folk school, which was built (1906-8) in old Russian style, and we are once again near the fish market.

*

With the best of intentions and the greatest effort, we have not succeeded in including more names of the residents of the Jewish Street than these which we have mentioned here. We know well that many are missing – names of former residents. With the passing of years, many names have been forgotten, and the memory has also weakened.

We thank our friends Yeshaya Frogiel, Mira Akabi, and Shaul Blanket for their help in the recovery of the names of the residents, which we have brought down here with great effort.

[Page 64]

To You, Zgierz, my Native City

by Esther Krol-Jakubowicz

"Zgierz," this is a magical word for me –
This is the home of my parents, where I was born and grew up
These were the years of the pleasantness and happiness of my childhood
This – the place of the roots of my family.

This is the pond, famous in the entire area
In the summer – azure, and in the winter – white ice
Sailing in boats in its clear water
With song and melodies, with male and female friends;

This is the "Old Square" with the city hall in the center
With the giant clock, declaring and announcing
With a ringing sound every hour, that the time has come;
And the church rises up proudly next to it,

On Sundays and Christian holidays, to the ringing of the bells
Crowds, crowds stream from all directions;

[Page 65]

Zgierz – This is the synagogue on the Jewish Street
Filled with worshippers on Sabbaths and festivals
With Cantor Linden at the head of the choir
Singing the prayers with his sweet voice

And we, the girls so as not to disturb
Play outside with laughter and commotion
Until the end of the services, and we wait with patience
For our parents and elderly grandparents;

And on the Jewish Street, from the open windows
Aromas of strong and sweet savory foods
Shortly father would recite *Kiddush* for the Sabbath
On wine, and we will sing "To the son and the daughter";

Zgierz – this is the Hashomer Hatzair group
With them, we set out to the outside of the city
And we sang out loud, with our usual tempo;
"Raise a banner and a flag toward Zion" – – –

*

Ha, how lovely were those days that once were…
But suddenly everything was destroyed – and this life was as if it never was…
One winter day, a stormy cold morning –
And everything, everything was liquidated by the hateful enemy…

This, the terrible, tragic, and fateful deportation day
When Hitler's troops broke into the houses with shouts:
"Out Jews!!! *Raus*!!!" as they threatened with deadly shots
And thus did I "part" from my city… –

Worried, sad, overcome by confusion
I sat with my family in the wagon

[Page 66]

Pondering in agony what was happening in my city
Without knowing that I was leaving it forever.

Nevertheless, despite all this, my small city
You remain always dear in my heart
Even though you are so far from me – –
You, my native city, I will never forget…

The pond – property of the weavers' union of the city

Translator's footnotes:

1. In this context, a *kaddish* refers to a son who will eventually recite *kaddish* for a parent.
2. Derogatory term for young gentile boys and girls.
3. See https://en.wikipedia.org/wiki/Tseno_Ureno
4. See https://en.wikipedia.org/wiki/David_Frischmann

[Page 67]

C. Orthodox Zgierz

Religious Life

[Page 68]

Holiness and Nobility

… Zgierz was a fortress of the good spirit of man, and its residence were faithful to this spirit. There, during your youth, we absorbed the ideas of the lessons of our tradition, with its precise concepts and its sublime religious pathos. We merited the charge of thought and the unfaltering source of emotion, which had the ability of directing our deeds. We learned about communal life from the Hassidim. The meaning of communal life was closeness of hearts, dedication of one to the other. We also absorbed into our soul the splendor that enveloped the studiers and worshippers, and the holiness and mystery that enveloped the *Beis Midrashes* and *shtibels* – imparting to us the unique purpose of man and the stringent duties of the heart. Therefore, Orthodox Zgierz calls to us, and we are proud that it unites us with the duty toward good. We present its lines for the generation.

The editorial committee

———

[Page 69]

The Hassidic Movement in Zgierz

by Zeev Fisher

One of the wonderful movements that arose in the Jewish nation during the latter generations was Hassidism, which sprouted in Eastern Europe more than two centuries ago. This movement, which was religious in essence, led to far-reaching development in all areas of Jewish life until our day. As we shall see, Hassidism brought a change in the spiritual and social life of the Jews in Zgierz, as in other cities in Poland. It even laid the first foundations of the national movement of the Jewish nation.

The relationship to Hassidism of the people of our city of Zgierz was always not only as to a historical movement belonging to the past, but rather as to set of values, some of which can be identified even in our time. This was the approach among all strata of the Jewish population of Zgierz, even though it was not typical of the known "*shtetl*" – neither from the understanding of the general population, nor from the external character of life. Nevertheless, Hassidim cleaved to it and settled therein, and *Admors* also aspired to live there. The influence of ideas and words of Torah and wisdom brought with them all streams of Hassidism that existed in our city. Someone delving into them will always find ideas close to those expressed in the ancient and modern philosophic literature, or the ancient and new doctrines of moral learning. Therefore, even the young *maskil* found greatness in the Hassidic tradition.

Indeed, Hassidism in Zgierz found many supporters. It conquered the religious community and the religious institutions and influenced in a recognizable way the character of life of the Jews of Zgierz. Even though it was not a Hassidic center in the accepted sense of the term, but rather a place of concentration for Hassidim, it remained the backbone of the courts of the *Admorim* [Hassidic masters]. It is worthwhile to note that one could find in Zgierz the *shtibels* of various streams of Hassidism, at times opponents of each other, far apart in their ideology and customs. Nevertheless, Hassidic Zgierz brought them together without rivalry and disputes. Each Hassid went according to his doctrine, and all doctrines preached love of humanity, love of one's fellow Jews, and that one must judge every Jew favorably.

All the *shtibels* of the various dynasties in Zgierz appeared as a miniature ingathering of exiles. The Hassidim would frequent them, and faithfully preserve their doctrines and ways. They worshipped in the Sephardic style[1] and lived with faith in the Rebbe. They were certain exceptional individuals among them who studied and delved into Torah, both the revealed

[Page 70]

and the hidden[2] day and night. Several of them woke up every night to perform *Tikkun Chatzot*[3]. They donned ashes and lamented over the exile of the Divine Presence, the destruction of the Temple, and the fallen Tabernacle of David.

On the other hand, how great was the collective spirit that pervaded among the Hassidim. Young and old spoke to each other in the second person. Howe great was the sense of brotherhood and friendship in all the *shtibels*. It was considered natural to assist in various ways a Hassid who was having trouble or who had lost his livelihood.

There were many *shtibels* in our city, each with a different face, unique customs, their own tunes. Each imbued its unique imprint and visage upon its Hassidim, to the point that one could easily tell in which *shtibel* each Hassid worshipped, and to which Rebbe he would travel to visit. Each differed in the mystery of its melodies, which was considered a fundamental value in Hassidim, in the essence of the melody with relation to its fundamentals and the ancient Jewish resonance, for not every dynasty knew or was even careful about "small matters" such as these. However, one cannot describe *shtibel* life without the melody. The heart of every Hassid was attracted to the world of melody as a purifying wellspring, raising the day-to day life as well as that of the Sabbaths and festivals. The prayer, the feasts, and the joyous occasions were filled with hymns and melodies. The Hassidim sang with melodies that attract, that were full of longing and beauty for the people of the sanctuary on the Sabbath eves and the third Sabbath meal before the conclusion of the Sabbath.

As I recall them, the Hassidim of all streams in our city, I have thoughts that the world was not worthy for that Torah, for that love, for those tidings of spirituality, for that hymn that accompanies a person on his path that he follows in solitude. The world was not worthy of those Hassidim, and therefore they were the first to be taken by the storm of destruction.

Nevertheless, we will tell the stories of those wonderful people, for whom the world was not fitting. Therefore, we will pass before our eyes the images of the Hassidim of the city, the beauty of Zgierz Jewry, the charm of that spiritual world in which the poor and the beggar were princes, and the mute who did not have the power of speech were the wise men, for Hassidism was all about the realm of possibility. Everything is possible through the auspices of someone who knows how to listen, to love, to dedicate his soul, for that is Hassidism: the humanization of the fate of mankind.

Perhaps after the confusion of the times uncovers all the grace and beauty, wisdom and understanding in these wonderful stories and descriptions, they will serve as guides and lanterns for those stumbling through the paths of life, searching for a rectification for their souls and a resolution to their complexities.

Translator's footnotes:

1. https://en.wikipedia.org/wiki/Nusach_Sefard
2. The Hidden Torah refers to Kabbalah and mysticism.
3. See https://en.wikipedia.org/wiki/Tikkun_Chatzot

[Page 71]

The Reprover in the Gate

by P. Sirkis

(40 years after the death of the rabbi of the city, may G-d avenge his blood.)

Forty years have now passed since the Nazis, may their names be blotted out, murdered the final rabbi of our community, Rabbi Shlomo Leib HaKohen, may the memory of the holy be blessed (may G-d avenge his blood). He was a scribe and a sword – that is, a scribe and an orator. From all the Torah and *halachic* novella that he succeeded in publishing during his lifetime, there is one book, *Neve Shalom*, that contains everything: Torah, Kabbalah, as well as philosophy. We include here some sections of his book, which will outline some of his customs, human ideas, and moral-human weltanschauung.

The Difference Between Man and Beast

… An immoral human being and a beast require physical guarding of their path so that they do not inflict damage with their beastly powers; One must fence in the beastly part of man with a literal fence, supervise it with guards, placing them at his side, as judges and police to guard the humanity with political laws. Without such, people would be like the fish of the sea, one swallowing the other alive. In order to ensure physical security and private ownership, it is necessary to impose authority and government with a cadre of judges and police, in a hierarchical fashion.

However, evil comes of this: "When a person rules over another for his evil"[1], for the guardians of the state, who are not separate from other mortals, also have animalistic, coarse, and boorish traits. In addition, they have the desire for rulership, power, and authority with all the rights associated with such, to differentiate between thee fortunate ones from those beneath them. From them and their crowds arise wickedness with the staff of evil. These strongmen exert authority upon the masses of people using the damaging rode. This is the root of the evil fruit, the reason for the revolutionaries leading to destruction.

As long as a person does not reach a high level of morality and does not rectify the evil and the bad; and as long as a person requires guardians and supervisors, who are also beasts like them – humanity will not reach sublime fullness." (page 56)

Between Israel and the Nations

The essence of the Israelite people differs from that of other nations – the soul of Israel is intertwined with sparks of the Divine light, a miniature version of the traits of G-d, may He be blessed. This soul fills the entire body of the corpus of Israel and turns it into one unit; its power and string are in the unity, and there is a uniting of the traits for moral wholeness, clear of any stain and filth… Indeed, it differs in essence from the gentiles, which is based on the power of the sword, and is the inheritance of Esau "You will live by the sword," and is built and exists through the force of the sword and the fist – to the extent that a person is stronger –

[Page 72]

The sword determines his judgement, to be or not to be. With the aid of the sword – that kills and destroys – he builds his personality and foundation. From the destruction of other nations he builds his existence and glory. If he succeeded in suppressing the weak and faltering, who have no strength to stand up against him, he overcomes nations, forcing them to their knees and displacing them with his harsh sword. Foreign forces arrive, always trying to swallow up the weak and the small. If we place an eye and look at the history of the governments of nations, we will see… that those that conquered nations not of themselves and excelled in their strength, subduing and slaughtering nations and kingdoms, have earned eternal fame. They are the mighty ones of renown, through blood, fire, and pillars of smoke, rivers of tears, the screams of the murdered and slaughtered under the sword, the destruction of complete cities full of plenty and wealth, now turned into mound of rubble – exalted through the strength of the greatness of the victors, for the wickedness, tactics of war, swords and weapons of destruction serve as measuring rods for the situation… For from the blood of the murdered ones, the clods of earth stick together to become the material for the edifice of the victor.

However, the lot of Jacob is not like this. Its edifice is not based on the destruction of others, for the builders of the nation founded its house on the principle of "much peace." For a measuring stick they used mercy, kindness, love of one's fellow and love of G-d. Through this did the clumps of our people stick to their fellow to become one and to build the sanctuary of the temple of the King. (page 172).

Torah and Culture

The fathers of *Haskalah* perfected the wisdom of language, deepened and broadened it… However, instead of directing it to teach morality and love – they turned their tongue into a destructive arrow – with lies and deceit. They use the iron of the tongue to cause humanity to backslide. They used the pen of the scribe for lies, and the language that speaks grandly to purify the impure, to justify evil, and to accuse the righteous. This is the accursed diplomacy that is termed the running of the state. However, this misleading light brings myriads upon myriads of people to slaughter as we have seen in the world wars, and in battles, tribulations, disputes and hatred among nations – all these are a result of diplomacy, as is known. In the Torah of Moses, whose light is the candle for our path has given the path of life to humanity, the prohibition of "thou shalt not murder, thou shalt not steal," and the Ten Commandments is the crown of splendor and completeness. The precious light and sublime morality of the Torah of Moses has penetrated the hearts of all humanity – that a nation shall not rule over a nation and a person shall not rule over a person to their detriment, that they not send their sons out to an internecine war, that the oppressor and oppression shall cease. The absolute command of "thou shalt not murder, thou shalt not steal" has protected humanity and ensured its life, not permitting it to lose the wealth of its possessions. The community and the individual found protection and preservation of its existence under the queen of wisdom and the morality of the Torah, for its light chased away darkness, lies, hypocrisy, and sycophantism. The sparks of its light burnt the snakes and scorpions. The spirit of Torah imparted life. The traits were cleaned, refined, and whitened, and how refined and exalted was the man. (page 176).

[Page 73]

Regarding Baseless Hatred

… The bullies, leaders, and heads during the time of the destruction [of the Temple], the lowliness of the regime and decline of the nation, the removal of the miter and the crown, and the horn of priesthood has descended to the dust. The factions and parties increased and multiplied. There were people who attracted the crowds to themselves, and confusion increased and filled the land with blood. Things reached the point where a person of strong heart and subterfuge, as well as the cattle-herds and those who ambushed the routes – did not find it lowly in their eyes to become the awaited savior or to be the straightener of the route… The masses were left to the obstinacy of their hearts through the guilt of the deceitful chiefs and leaders, disgracefully wanton. In the disputes and arguments among the chiefs and leaders, the battles at home and outside, the riots and revolts, for disputes increased – the victor prevailed, and hearts and opinions of the leaders separated. A nest of baseless hatred and jealousy among the leaders was placed…

*

These words and many more words of value, whose force is proper even today, were written by the rabbi of Zgierz in his aforementioned book during the 1920s, when the State of Israel was still in the realm of a dream.

What would he have been able to add had he lived in our day?

It was not for naught that the writer A. Sh. Litwin, in his article about the final rabbi of our city, nicknamed him "The Prophet Jeremiah of Zgierz" (Book of Zgierz, page 359).

Translator's footnote:

1. Kohelet [Ecclesiastes] 8:9.

[Page 73]

Stories and Legends of the Elderly Tzadik

(From the book *Tiferet Adam* by Pinchas Zelig Glicksman)

His Method in Directives – Toward Leniency

Rabbi Shalom Hirsch haKohen was a pure Tzadik and also a Hassid in the usual understanding of people in the latter generations. – – – His countenance was bright, exuding goodness, sincerity, grace, and nobility. Everyone who knew him loved him and honored him as a holy man. Anyone with a bitter spirit would go to him to pour out his bitterness, and anyone who had a sick person in the house would go to him to get a blessing and to request mercy. Some said he even worked miracles.

I heard a wonderful legend from a man of faith: once one of the wealthy people in the city got sick with urinary retention. The sick person and his relatives had already decided to summon an expert doctor from abroad. The sick man was the only person in the city with a shaved beard. The rabbi sent his assistant to him to inform him that if he accepts upon himself

[Page 74]

to no longer shave his beard, and to do one of: paving the synagogue yard with stones or replacing the broken tin sheets of the roof of the synagogue, he will be cured of his illness. At first the sick person refused to listen to his voice, but when he saw that evil was decreed upon him, he agreed to fulfil the command of the rabbi. Then his insides quickly reopened, he had relief, and he returned to his health.

Rabbi Shalom Hirsch excelled in that he always tended toward the lenient rather than the stringent. When a question about whether something was permitted or forbidden came before him, and he found that the Taz was lenient and the Shach was stringent[1], he would decide in favor of the former, stating how great the Taz was, and how it is fitting to follow him. If the situation was the opposite, he would sing the praises of the Shach, and decide in accordance to him. Thus was his manner in issuing decisions, to decide in accordance with the more lenient view. The *shochets* in the city knew this very well.

… One of his decisions that I knew about from Father is worthy to be written in the book for eternal memory: one Passover eve, our fellow townsman Reb David Hendlisz, who was known as Davidche, a wealthy, erudite householder, came to a certain person's pharmacy. The pharmacist and Rev Davidche began to discuss the essence of the Jewish people, with its weaknesses and good traits. "The Jews are the friends of thieves," said the pharmacist, "Their eyes are only toward monetary gain, and this is their ideal." Reb Davidche said to him, "I will show you that this is not true. For if you give today to the lowliest Jew as much money as he wants in order to drink a cut of liquor, he will not listen to you, for this is forbidden to him by the laws of our religion. Thus, you will see that the aspiration of the Jewish soul is not solely for money." The pharmacist retorted, "I will show you that any Jew I summon will drink liquor in my home." Reb David said, "Let us make a bet for the sum of eight ducats" (A ducat is a golden dinar that has the value of approximately nine marks, and was called *Tkuten* by the Jews of Poland.) The pharmacist sent for the Jewish barber to come to his house to give him a haircut, and Reb David hid in one of the rooms in his house. The barber came and did his job, and the pharmacist paid him generously. Then he placed a glass of liquor before him in a friendly manner, and said, "Drink, it is a good drink." The barber humbly said, "Do you not know, my master, that it is the eve of Passover today, and it is forbidden for us to drink." "Drink," the pharmacist enticed him with words, "do not speak foolishness." "I will not drink." "But I will give you a ducat if you drink," the pharmacist enticed him. "I will not drink; it is forbidden for us." "But I will give you two ducats, or three – you will even get eight whole ducats from me if you drink," said the pharmacist finally when he saw his stubbornness. "I will not drink, even for one hundred," responded the barber with complete decisiveness, as he took his hat and left. Then Rev Davidche came out of his hiding place triumphantly, took the money of the bet, and returned to his home. On his way home, he went to the rabbi's house and told him what happened in the home of the Polish pharmacist. The rabbi told him that, according to the law, it is appropriate to give this money to the barber. He immediately summoned him to come to his house and gave him the money.

Translator's footnote:

1.   Taz: https://en.wikipedia.org/wiki/David_HaLevi_Segal Shach: https://en.wikipedia.org/wiki/Shabbatai_HaKohen

---

[Page 75]

Wonder from Previous Times[1]

(About whom the Elder Tzadik appeared in a dream)

by Pinchas Zelig Glicksman

Here we will tell of the greatness and wonder of the "Elder Tzadik," the first rabbi of Zgierz, Rabbi Shalom Hirsh HaKohen, may the memory of the holy be blessed, as is brought down in the book "*Tiferet Adam*," by the well–known writer and biographer of his time, Reb Pinchas Zelig Gliksman. This was a letter that his father, Reb Avraham Hirsh Gliksman of blessed memory (one of the first Zgierz manufacturers and prominent activists) wrote to his wife, who was in rehabilitation in Carlsbad. We bring down the letter in the form and language in which it was written. It probably portrays the "enlightened" Jewish middle class in Zgierz of that time (the letter is dated: with the help of G–d, Friday of Torah portion of Noach, 5655[2]):

"To my dear wife... Last Sabbath, I witnessed one of the greatest heavenly wonders, of the resurrection of the dead, and I joyously recited the blessings 'He who quickens the dead,' and *Shehecheyanu* [He who kept us alive]. As you certainly know, Reb Moshe Wieland became paralyzed before Passover, and lost consciousness completely shortly thereafter. It appeared that he would soon completely go to oblivion. On the Sabbath, our neighbor Reb Motel Gliksman came to us and told me, 'Reb Moshe Weiland sent to him that he should come to him, and if possible, he wishes to speak to us.' Reb Motel said that it is indeed difficult to speak with him. The situation had already become hopeless on Passover. He visited him for the last time over Shavuot, and was convinced that, unfortunately, soon everything would over and he would never see him again. He did not understand what the invitation meant, that he wished that we should go together and be convinced what is happening. To our great surprise, Reb Moshe Weiland was happy, and well dressed, and extended his hand to us. He looked well, and spoke well, happy and cheerful. Reb Moshe captivated us and told us the following:

[Page 76]

"That which happened to him from Passover until Rosh Hashanah, he knows nothing about. He does not know how he became ill, how they dealt with him at first, how good friends visited him. In one word, he knows nothing and cannot describe that bitter time. Only one night after Rosh Hashanah, the righteous rabbi, the rabbi of blessed memory from Zgierz came to him while sleeping [i.e. in a dream]. He was greatly moved by that happening, and began to tremble violently. The rabbi then said to him: 'Moshe, you must not be afraid. You will be well.' After these words, Moshe began to weep profusely. The rabbi of blessed memory said to him: 'Moshe, I will tell you again, you will be well.' However, Moshe continued to weep very strongly. The rabbi of blessed memory stood by him for a long time with his friendly smile, appearing as if alive. Moshe did nothing other than weep. He felt very weak, as if he had no energy. He could not utter a word. Then the rabbi of blessed memory started to leave. As he noticed that the rabbi of blessed memory was leaving, he gathered all his strength, and shouted loudly: 'Rebbe! Rebbe! Rebbe!' With that shout, his wife came to him. He woke up, and saw his wife there. He could barely speak a word. Hi wife gave him some wine in a spoon. He tasted it and said to his wife, 'Now I can assure you that I will be well. A very honorable man told me this twice.'

"His wife appeared very emotional, and wondered how he was able to speak so clearly after being without the power of speech for such a long time. She gave him a bit more wine. He held himself for a short time, and his wife extended both of her hands to him. Then his wife noticed that he was able to move both legs, and was able to move various other parts of his body. The lameness completely disappeared. He felt stronger. They called the two physicians, Kohn and Janszer, who had treated him earlier. They barely agreed to come to him. They could not believe that he was still alive. Finally, they came, and they saw him speaking

[Page 77]

and moving. When they saw that he could move all parts of his body, they both said simultaneously: '*to jest widocznie cud boski*' [It is a miracle of G–d].

"They prescribed kefir, wine, and soft–boiled eggs. The improvement speeded up. On Yom Kippur, he already was able to worship appropriately, and recited the Yizkor for the holy rabbi of blessed memory with great feeling, such as he had never felt previously. Today, he is well, blessed be G–d. At first, he asked to be able to go out, or at least for his friends to come to him. It is barely possible to comprehend how both blessings came true.

Your husband, who appreciated and honors you."

Translator's footnotes:

1. This article is written in non–standard Yiddish. I was unable to translate it literally, and some of the nuance may be missed. However, the main idea of the blessing given by the Rabbi of Zgierz to a very ill man, which then came true, should be clear.
2. There is a footnote in the text here indicating that this is 1895, but in reality it would be in the autumn of 1894.

The Hassidim and Shtibels in our City

by Z. Fisher and P. Sirkis

For various reasons, few lines were dedicated to the *cheders* in our town in the Book of Zgierz, despite their great influence on day-to-day life. Therefore, in this addendum, we include some of the essence of the *cheder*.

The Hassidic movement, which conquered and enthused the hearts of a significantly large portion of Polish Jewry, did not pass over our city of Zgierz. It penetrated our city at the beginning of the 19th century, that is with the founding of the settlement and the start of the Jewish community there. However, the Hassidic community of our city only grew and expanded during the years of the first rabbi of the city (5587-5637 / 1827-1877), who was the Tzadik and Hassid Rabbi Shalom HirschHaKohen, may the memory of the holy be blessed, a major student and associate of Rabbi Mendele of Kock. The large Yeshiva founded, famous in its time, which was founded by the rabbi and in which he served as Rosh Yeshiva, was a cause of this. It attracted lads and young men from the cream of the crop of the studiers of Torah and Hassidism from all ends of the country of Poland. In this way, Zgierz became a city of Torah and Hassidism through the years, and its fame spread widely.

Indeed, it was not only the students and Torah studiers who were attracted to Zgierz, for scholars and *Admorim* also took up residence there. At the end of the 19th and beginning of the 20th century, the rabbi of Brzeziny

[Page 78]

(nicknamed "The Brzeziner Rebbe") lived in our city. He lived in the home of Moshe Baruch Szwarc on Łęczycka Street. Many Hassidim from Łódź and the area came to his funeral. The community set up an honorable *Ohel* [cemetery canopy] and a wooden fence around his grave, which was always full of *kvitels* [petitionary notes]. His grandchildren were known as "*The Brzeziner Rebbe's Einiklech.*" The Rabbi of Żyrardów, Rabbi Todris, may the memory of the holy be blessed, also settled in Zgierz during the First World War. He lived on Strykówska Street in the home of Reb David Weis. He had Hassidim, mainly local. He is buried in the *Ohel* of the Rebbe of Brzeziny.

The following settled in Zgierz after the First World War: The *Admor* of Sochaczew, Rabbi Shmuel Bornsztajn, may the memory of the holy be blessed; and the *Admor* Rabbi Menachem Mendel Landau, may the memory of the holy be blessed, of Stryków (see Book of Zgierz, page 374-379), one of the veteran *Admorim*, who imprinted his stamp on a splendid community of Hassidim for about a half a century, and played an active role in the arena of observant Judaism. He excelled greatly as a leader. His grandson, the *Admor* Rabbi Avraham Landau, may he live long, continues in his tradition of Torah in Israel.

The Hassidic community was quite recognizable and honorable within the Jewish population of our city. It often had a decisive influence with respect to local and communal programs. Its representatives were active in almost all areas of societal life in the city, and one of them served as the head of the communal council for many years. His humane disposition was attuned with the social and class structure, which came from all classes and segments of the Jewish community. Worshipping together, shoulder to shoulder in the *shtibel* (Hassidic prayer house) were: industrialists and workers, wealthy merchants and poor workers, Torah giants, authors of books, and simple Jews – all united in a feeling of Hassidic unity, the Hassidic essence, and the aspiration to reach the level of holiness, Hassidic trust, and love of one's fellow Jew.

On the right side of the rabbi in the dissemination of the Hassidic doctrine in Zgierz stood also veteran Hassidim of renown such as Reb Nota Heinsdorf of blessed memory, a sublime personality with generous traits, a scholar, one of the fervent Hassidim of Kock and Ger, who spent most of his day occupied in Torah, and also directed the young men of the city in Hassidism and the service of the Creator; his brother-in-law Reb Leibush Pozner of blessed memory, who in his youth would travel to the Rebbe Yitzchalkl of Worka, and who also followed Reb Mendele of Kock after his marriage. He was recognized as one of the fervent Hassidim of the city. These two entered under the wings of Gerrer Hassidism. During the days of the *Admor*, the author of *Sfas Emes*, the philanthropic Hassid, of the finest of the city, Reb Shlomo Sirkis of blessed memory, also joined Gerrer Hassidism. After the death of Reb Nota of blessed memory, he became the standard bearer of Gerrer Hassidism in our city. And finally: the rabbi of the city, Rabbi Shlomo Yehuda Leib HaKohen, may the memory of the holy be blessed, was also one of the veteran Hassidim of Ger – however that holy service did not disturb him one iota from his regular learning regimen and classes.

[Page 79]

There were also family and personal connections between the House of Kock and one of the first Hassidim of Koch in Zgierz, Reb Yaakov Moshe Pozner of blessed memory, one of the pioneers of textile manufacturing in our city. His son-in-law, Reb Yitzchak Zelig Frankiel of blessed memory, was also an enthusiastic Hassid of Kock, married the daughter of the middle Rebbe of Kock, Rabbi David Morgensztern, may the memory of the holy be blessed. Reb Yitzchak Zelig's daughter Yocheved married Rabbi Chaim Yisrael Morgensztern, may the memory of the holy be blessed, who later became known as the Rebbe of Pilow, the author of the book *Shalom Yerushalayim*. Thus, a double bond was formed between Kock and Zgierz (see the Book of Zgierz, page 203). The following were also among the first of the Hassidim of Kock-Aleksander -Ger: Reb Yosef Hirsch Kahana Szapira, an elder and honorable person of the community, and his son Reb Refael Yaakov Kahana Szapira (a student of the Rebbe Henich of Aleksander, may the memory of the holy be blessed) who was known in the city as a generous host of guests, with an abundance of love and blessing; Reb Itzl (Yitzchak) Orbach, from a well-known rabbinical family, a man of kindness and much action; Reb Yosef Zaklikowski, nicknamed Yosef Sokolower, who merited to visit the Chidushei Hari'm[1], may the memory of the holy be blessed. He was afflicted by tribulations throughout his life, and nevertheless always maintained an elevated spirit and happy face. Elder Hassidim took every opportunity to repeat his sharp statements; Reb Leizer Holander, one of the first *shochtim* [ritual slaughterers], who took up residence in Zgierz on the direction of Reb Mendele of Kock; Reb Moshe Bendekower, who had a sharp tongue in his many debates with Hassidim of various *Admorim*; and several other Hassidim, longstanding members of the communities and among the first of the Hassidim of Ger, whose names we have forgotten to our dismay, and about whom we know only from hearsay.

Shtibels

The Shtibel of the Gerrer Hassidim

Ger grew upon two founding pillars of Polish Hassidism – Przysucha and Kock – and forged its own path with the passage of time, that was more fitting to the needs of the new times. In Ger, Hassidim attained, in the common sense of the term, a democratic form and populist character. Its emphasis was on Torah, the fulfillment of the commandments, and good deeds. It was at the pinnacle of Polish Hassidism in numbers of Hassidim and in its broad social character which had a place for anyone who accepted the yoke of its authority.

There were many Hassidic personalities in the Gerrer Shtibel in Zgierz, including exceptional singers and prayer leaders, Torah scholars, an authors of books.

People such as this, who were raised and educated in this sublime environment and atmosphere – as far as our memory reaches – with appreciation and reverence, the names of those Hassidim who worshipped in the Gerrer Hassidic house, almost all of whom were murdered by the Nazis, may their names be blotted out – according to their set place in the *shtibel* in the home of the Hassid Reb David Bendkowski of blessed memory – I recall as follows...

[Page 80]

It is Friday night between *Mincha* and the Welcoming of the Sabbath service. The *shtibel* is full to the brim with Hassidim. The silk and atlas *kapotes* sparkle in the light of the candles and polished chandeliers. The heads are covered with velvet hats and *streimels*. The faces are resplendent for great the Sabbath Queen. In a few moments, Yosele Baluter will approach the podium and begin *Lechu Neranena* with his sweet, pleasant voice. In the meantime, some are reviewing the weekly Torah portion and others are melodiously humming the Song of Songs.

Around the long table, covered with a white tablecloth, sit mainly the old people; the communal elders sit at the head of the table: Reb Lipa Berliner (nicknamed Lipa Zelcer, as he was once a salt merchant), one of the elders of the city and one of the chief *gabbaim* [trustees] of the *Chevra Kadisha*; Reb Chaim Leibish the children's teacher, who, in his time, basked in the shadow of Rabbi Henech of Aleksander; Reb Shmuel Yechezkel Turberg, a prominent Hassid, who occupied himself with Torah for all his days: Reb Moshe Hirsch Porisower, the prayer leader in the shtibel; Reb Shmuel Koren (nicknamed Shmuel Hassid, due to his Hassidic prominence); Reb Laib Parizer, a Hassid of Trisk, one of the honorable householders of the city, and his son Reb Aharon, the son-in-law of Reb Natan Adar; Reb Shabtai Hauszpigel, the prayer leader for *Shacharit* on Rosh Hashanah and Yom Kippur, one of the excellent teachers of children in the city, along with his sons Reb Avraham Aharon, an artist, whose works included the *Kegavna* and *Berich Shemei*[2] in gilt frames decorating the walls of the *shtibel*, and his sons Yosef and Bendet; Reb Leibish Rozenberg (The White Leibish), who always had a book open in front of him even though he was a travelling agent, and his son Reb Michael-Mendel who served as a prayer leader on Sabbaths.

I recall the melancholy that imbued us in the *shtibel* during the Third Sabbath Meal, when Reb Michael-Mendel would sing *Bnei Heichala*. His son Itza was a young scholar. Michael-Mendel's son-in-law was Reb Yechiel Yitzchak Rappaport (the genius), who later became a preacher for Mizrachi and a rabbi in the city of Uniejów.

Among these upright people, who tended only toward the good, I recall: Reb Mendel Baron (Mendel Lencycer), a Gemara teacher; Rebi Leibel Haron, elderly, with fine traits, who gave charity in secret; Reb Yisrael Moshe Rozanowicz, a *gabbai* [trustee] of the Yagdil Torah Yeshiva; Reb Yosef David Garzon; Reb Leibel Buzyn (Leibel Lipa's), a prominent scholar, and his son Feivel; Reb Efraim Bornsztajn, a Hassid and G-d fearing man; Reb Noach Mendelson, a scholar and G-d fearing man, who knew and told stories of *Tzadikim* and *Admors*; Reb David Berliner (David Lipa's), a modest, G-d fearing man, and his sons Yitzchak, Yaakov and Yehoshua, and his son-in-law Yehoshua Reisman.

Reb Shimon Fiszer, a modest, humble man with fine traits, who would greet every person. He had the rights to the honor of taking out and putting back the Torah in the shtibel. Along with his sons Wolf and Yaakov; Reb Mordechai Shmuel Cudkowicz, a scholar, *mohel* [ritual circumciser], who composed the annual calendars for Sabbath candle lighting times for all the cities of Poland; Reb Falik Kohansztam, who was known for his wonderful memory; Rabbi Natan Elberg, the son of Rabbi Yechiel Ichel , the author of books, who, after years, also served as the rabbi in the cities of Błaszki and Sanok, and his sons David, Tovi and Yehuda (later a known author in Israel); Reb Yitzchak Eksztajn (Yitzchk-Ek)

[Page 81]

the teacher and educator of the children of the Hassidim; Reb Chaim Moshe Kohen, one of the elders and notables of the community; Reb Michel Princ, one of the city honorable and his son Reb Daniel.

Standing next to our eyes: Reb Mendel Noach Koren, a prominent scholar, the head of the Yagdil Torah Yeshiva in Zgierz; Reb Fishel Bunim Holander, the elderly *shochet*, one of the veteran Hassidim. His son-in-law was Reb Mendel Wechsler, a sharp scholar, one of the students of the author of Avnei Nezer, who later was accepted as head of the Yeshiva of Krakow. His sons were David, Leizer, Leibel, and his son-in-law was Reb Yaakov Shimon Izbicki; Reb Chaim Eizenszmidt, a *shochet*, the second son-in-law of Reb Fishel Bunim, one of the fervent Hassidim of the shtibel; Reb Avraham Kuperman, a Torah scholar, and his son Moshe, veteran Hassidim; Reb Pesach Gurner, a Hassid and G-d fearing man, and his son Shlomo, one of the fine students of the Yeshiva.

The following were revered by all their acquaintances: Reb Yosef Bialistocki (Yosef Shmuel Chasid's), a fervent Hassid, a teacher of Torah to the public, the author of the book *Mesora Gedola*, and his sons Shmuel and Simcha; Reb Yitzchak Nekriz (Reb Itshka), a great scholar and fearer of Heaven, who had authorization to give halachic decisions, the Torah reader in the *shtibel*, as well as the shofar blower. Anyone who never saw him during the shofar blowing does not know what holy awe is: and his sons Yaakov, Avraham, Nota, and Chuna; Reb Baruch Nekricz, the brother of Reb Yitzchak; Reb David Bendkowski, who dedicated several rooms in the courtyard of his house for the shtibel, and used to receive the *maftir* honor regularly: and his sons Reb Shmuel, Reb Pinchas, Leibel, and Mordechai; Reb

Moshel Aharonson, the son-in-law of Reb Yisraelche Boas, his sons, and his son-on-law Reb Yaakov Aryeh Minc, a philanthropist and charitable man, who employed Hassidic young men in his business.

The list is even greater, and we recall the people in one breath. With this we also express the trait of equality of the Hassidic community.

These included: Reb Shalom Henich Boms and his sons Yosef Izik, Tovia and Nota – he occupied himself with charity and benevolence all his days. He concerned himself with guests in the *shtibel*, and arranged Sabbath meals for them with the worshippers; Reb Yitzchak Meir Cohen and his son Yossel; Reb Avraham Shmuel Weisberg; Reb Itza Meir Sztajer and his sons. He served as prayer reader on Sabbaths and festivals; Reb Yitzchak Praszker, a *gabbai*; Reb Moshe Lipszyc and his sons-in-laws, the young men Reb Avraham Yaakov Kac and Aharon Kac; Reb Avraham Baum and his sons Chaim and David; Reb Henich Banda, a pious Hassid, who lived from the toil of his hands; Reb Elya Tenenbaum (the Tall Elya), a tall man, who was also a *gabbai* in the *shtibel*; Reb Elya Zalman Bornsztajn, a veteran Hassid; Reb Pesachya Praszker; Reb Yeshaya Henich Segal and his son David; Reb Shmuel Yosef Lypszyc, who also sat in his store and studied; Reb Yosef Ber Lewkowicz, a veteran Hassid and his son-in-law, the scholarly Reb Hirsch Leib Zelcer, and his son Yerachmiel (the author of the book *Ner Lameah*); Reb Yaakov Librach and his sons: Reb Shimon, a fine young man, who years later was accepted as a rabbi in place of Reb Ichel, and Zeinwil; Reb Mordechai Natan Kupersztoch, who was authorized to issue *halachic* decisions; Reb Yosef Hirsch Szpira and his sons: Moshe Wolf and Yehuda; his brothers Reb Avraham and Reb Moshe – the sons of the well-known Hassid Reb Refael Yaakov Kahana Szpira, charitable people, honorable people of the city.

[Page 82]

The aforementioned Reb Shlomo Sirkis, from among the fine people of the city, a generous philanthropist and benevolent person, well-known for hosting guests, a man of many deeds and action, one of the heads of the community of Zgierz, close to the *Admor* of Ger and his sons, a representative to the Polish Sejm, a member of the leadership of the city council of Zgierz; his brother Reb Daniel Sirkis and his sons. He was also a communal leader, who did a great deal for religious Zionism; Reb Hershel, Rev Pinchas, and Reb Peretz Sirkis; Reb Binyamin Szaranski and his sons Yitzchak, Meir (later the author of books), and Nota; a modest, G-d fearing man (the son-in-law of the aforementioned Reb Nota Hajnsdorf), who was also in the religious institutions of the city; Reb Berish Bechler, an administrator in the communal council; Reb Kalman Mendel Zajda, a teacher of young children and his son Reb Moshe, who was also a teacher in the Yesodei Hatorah School.

Reb Yosef Mandelman (nicknamed Reb Yosele Baluter) was a fine singer with a sweet, pleasant voice. He served as the prayer leader for *Musaf* on festivals and the High Holy Days. He was always in a sublime spirit. He aroused people to joy and dance. His tasteful and meaningful words made the rounds among the Hassidim and scholars; Reb Meir Mandelman; Reb Hershel (Hershel Ozerkower), a scholar from among the young Hassidim; Reb Eliezer Korcarz, a modest man, a Hassid and scholar, who lived from the toil of his hands, with his sons Yehuda Leib, Meir, Gershon, and Yosef, and his son-in-law Reb Yechiel Meir Mankita, active in the religious educational institutions; Reb Henich Ehrzon, great in Torah, an author of books; Reb Asher Izik Gelbard and his sons Eliahu, Shmuel Zelik, and Leib; Reb Shimon Wronski and his brother Eliahu; Reb Tovia Kopel Boms, a prominent scholar, the son-in-law of Aharon Parizer; Reb Yisrael Zaken, a sharp Hassid.

The following spent all their days immersed in Torah: Reb Yehoshua Kaufman and his brother-in-law Reb Leibish Dimant, also a scholar, formerly a Hassid of Sadagura; Reb Shlomo Rozencwajg, a man with an upright heart, beloved by people, the son-in-law of Reb Yudel Szapszowicz; Reb Bendit Frenkel, a prominent scholar, a teacher of older students; Reb Yona Krakow; Reb Daniel Lencycki, an enlightened Hassid; the two brothers-in-law: Reb Zeev Elya and Reb Zev Michel Rajchert, honorable members of the community, lovers of the Zionist idea. Later they left the *shtibel* and founded a house of prayer for Mizrachi supporters along with other Hassidim of the city.

The following Hassidim moved with them to Mizrachi: Reb Baruch Bizberg and his sons Pinchas (later an author of books) and Yosef; Reb Manis Engel; Reb Bunim David Przytyk and several other Hassidim and enlightened Torah scholars; Reb Shmuel Zelik Gelbard, a teacher of young children; Reb Mendel Frohman, a modest, Torah scholar; Reb Betzalel Gutgold and his son Baruch; Reb Wolf Gliksman, elderly, a veteran, fervent Hassid; Reb Avraham

Chaim Michelson, the son of the chief rabbi, and head of the rabbinical court of Warsaw Rabbi Tzvi Yechezkel Michelson, the author of books on Hassidism and *Admorim*; the rabbi and Gaon Rabbi Yitzchak Mendel HaKohen, the son of the first rabbi of Zgierz,

[Page 83]

expert in Torah and the wisdom of Israel. After the death of the rabbi of Żyrardów (who lived in Zgierz), is Hassidim chose him as the rabbi and spiritual guide; Reb Fishel Gliksman, a well-known teacher of young children in the city, his son Shimshon Wolf, who was also a teacher; Reb Berl Celnik; Reb Leibel Wyszygrodski, active in the religious institutions of the city; Reb Pinchas Celnik, the son-in-law of Reb Binyamin Szcraranski, secretary of the community of Zgierz; Reb Moshe Sofer, a pious Jew stringent in observance of the commandments; Reb Itzel Tuchman; Reb Meirl Librach, a veteran Hassid, the son of Reb Elia Asher Librach, an honorable member of the community; Reb Mendel Tugendreich; Reb Yaakov Luksenberg; a man of a pure path, who owned a strictly kosher restaurant in the city; Reb Ozer Kirsztajn; as well as Reb Manli, a righteous, upright man, needy, with many children. His wife had been sick for many years, and he, in his straits, worked hard to support the household and bore his yoke silently and submissively. Oh, how sad and desperate was his gaze, which was always directed downward.

However, today is the Sabbath, and the splendor of its sanctity also lit up his thin, peaceful face.

Many other Hassidim, students of Torah, modest in their ways, upright of heart, of a pure path, imbued with grace and knowing how to take an accounting of their souls were numbered among them. Many of them influenced the masses of the residents of the city with their exemplary behavior and traits – especially the youth – to maintain and respect the Jewish values, and to continue in the traditions of the nation.

We loved these uniquely wonderful people, but, to our great sorrow, we are unable to present their names here, for, due to the pressures of the times and the passage of times, their names have departed from our memories. All we can do today is to beg the forgiveness of their families and relatives.

From all of Polish Jewry, which was annihilated by the Nazis during the Holocaust years, the Hassidic movement undoubtedly suffered a harsh, terrible blow. In every city and town conquered by the Germans, the Hassidim were the first to be beaten and degraded to the dust even before they were deported to the crematoria. May their memories be forever, and their good deeds remain as an example for all of us for generations.

The Shtibel of the Hassidim of Aleksander

The Hassidim of Aleksander went with the great tune and nobility, along with the heartfelt melody of Worka Hassidim, with religious fervor, internal Hassidism, and external simplicity.

The *Shtibel* of the Hassidim of Aleksander was second to the *Shtibel* of the Hassidim of Ger in size and number of worshippers in our city.

[Page 84]

The following are the names that are still in our memory, or that we have succeeded in gathering from others:

The rabbi of the city Rabbi Yechiel Ichel Elberg and his son Eliezer, Rabb Yisrael Yitzchak Gad, the *shochet*, and his son Berish, the cantor of the synagogue and a shochet; Ezriel Cukier and his sons Feivel-Mendel and Yonatan; Mendel Kuperman and his sons Michel and Moshe-Aharon (alive in Israel); Chaim Mendel Herzog; Shlomo-Zalman Herzog; Shmuel (Shmuelke) Landau, a descendent of Rabbi Yechezkel Landau, the author of *Noda BiYehuda*, a prayer leader on the High Holidays, and his sons Moshe and Yechiel; Hershel Ickowicz; Moshe Ickowicz; Yankel Ickowicz; Leibel Goldberg, a member of the communal council, and his son Moshe; Berish Rozenblat and his sons David, Avigdor, and Moshe; Yankel Liberman and his sons Yechiel and Boaz; Shimon Liberman and his sons; Anshel Waldman, one of the heads of the *Chevra Kadisha*; Kalman Kalmanowicz; the Adler brothers; Meir Lerner; Chaim

Kohen; Abba Kohen and his son Yitzchak; Henich Shaar (Lasker): Shimon Czernikowski and his son Avraham; Fishel Rus and his son Nechemia; Aharon Zakon and his son Menachem; Abba Baum (cereal maker) and his sons Yaakov and David (lives in Israel); Yankel Himel; Mendel Cwajghaft and his sons; Avraham Yaakov Jankielewicz, a teacher (nicknamed Monopolnik) and his sons Pesach, Wolf, Shimon and Yitzchak; Mendel Jakubowicz; Zisha Turcinski (nicknamed Zisha Glezer) and his son Yaakov Meir, who studied *Ein Yaakov* in the evenings with the householders in the *Beis Midrash*. There were many others, many Hassidim and their children, whose names have been forgotten from our memory due to time and the era of tribulations. We hereby beg the pardon of their family members for this.

The Small Gerrer Prayer House (Klein Gerrer Shtibel)

From Mordechai Glazer the son of Reb Yaakov of blessed memory

As I remember the Small Gerrer Prayer House (also called the Parizer Shtibel) on Pilsudski Street in the home of Reb David Szmuklerski of blessed memory, the following names of worshippers, who worshipped together with my father, remain with me: Reb Leib Parizer, the elderly Torah scholar, and originally a Hassid of Trisk. He moved from the Gerrer Shtibel and founded the prayer house (which was called by his name); his son Reb Aharon Parizer; Moshe Meir Bryn, the *gabbai*, and his son Mordechai; Moshel Dawidowicz, the Torah reader, and his sons. There were excellent prayer leaders who knew how to sing among the Hassidim of Ger in the small *Shtibel*; Mendel Morgensztern, who served as the prayer leader for *Musaf* on the High Holy Days, whose pleasant voice attracted worshippers from outside the circles of Gerrer Hassidim as well; Avraham Leib Kohen, the shofar blower; Eliahu Yaakov Glazer, who lead the *Shacharit* service on Sabbaths, and his sons; Mendel Warszawski, who lead *Shacharit*. They were all musically inclined in their prayers; Shalom Hirsch Grynberg, the deputy *gabbai*. These had a constant role in the *shtibel*.

I still recall the following worshippers: Aharon Yosef Berger, who was a member of the city council

[Page 85]

and chairman of the community council in our city, and his son David; Natan Adar and his son Yaakov (lives in Israel); Gedalia Grynberg, a veteran of the community; Wolf Lipszyc; Mendel Librach; Leizer Landau Itche Meir Zylberberg; Eliezer Shlumiel; Feivish Praszkier; Kastiel Ginzberg; the Braun brothers; Shmuel Dawidowicz and his sons; Zalman Yeshayahu Kohen; Mordechai Jakubowicz and his sons; Avraham Morgensztern, a communal activist and member of the town council; Mordechai Dawidowicz and his sons; Yisrael Jakubowicz and his son Mendel; Yisrael Yudofsky; Baruch Lipowicz; Yudel Kohen; Yisrael Lenczyski; Chaim Meir Frenkel; Asher Weinbaum; David Libow; Yosef Meir Haron; Michel Morgensztern; Issucher Lerner; Aharon Kaltgrad; Mendel Kaufman; Binyanim Krisztal; and other worshippers whose names I no longer remember, but their images are always before my eyes.

After the *Mincha* service on weekdays, some of the worshippers would study a page of *Gemara* or *Mishna*. This house of worship also served as a meeting place for the youth who came with their parents for services. Most of the youths in Zgierz belonged to Hashomer Hatzair during the years after the First World War and onward.

On the Fast of Esther and the eve of Yom Kippur, there was a plate for the Jewish National Fund alongside the plates for charity and the Half Shekel. Emissaries and speakers from the World Zionist Organization would also often appear there.

The House of Prayer of the Hassidim of Sochaczew

From the time that the *Admor* of Sochaczew, the rabbi and Tzadik Rabbi Shmuel Bornsztajn may the memory of the holy be blessed, moved to the city of Zgierz, this branch of Hassidim spread out in a significant fashion through the city and its area.

The connection between the Hassidim of Sochaczew in Zgierz and the *Admor* strengthened, and the fame of the Rebbe spread as a disseminator of Torah to the flocks of students, whom he educated toward refined Hassidism.

Important people were among the Sochaczew Hassidim, and thanks to this, the influence of the Sochaczew Hassidim in the life of the community and communal institutions was significant.

All of the Sochaczew Hassidim in our city worshipped in the house of prayer, which was built specially and served also as a *Beis Midrash* for *Yeshiva* students. Many people studied there, and some were quite prominent. This was through the influence of the *Admor*, the author of *Avnei Neizer*, who placed his mark on the Torah studies.

We express our sorrow that, due to the passage of time and the years of tribulation, we have been unable to recall very many of the numerous Sochaczew Hassidim of Zgierz – and we apologize to their relatives! The following are those whose names still live in our memories: Rabbi Yisraelche Boas, an honorable member of the community, one of the elders of the city and a leader of the Sochaczew Hassidim, and his sons:

[Page 86]

Chaim Boaz and his sons Yitzchak and Mendel; Shalom Boaz and his sons Avraham and Meir; Avraham Boaz, a member of the city council; David Boaz, Noach Boaz; Leizer Poznerzon and his sons Yaakov and Zecharia; Chaim Poznerzon; Mendel Bornsztajn (Siedlicer); Wolf Kwiabski and his sons; Feivish Szerman, a teacher; Yitzchak Meir Halpern and his sons; Yitzchak Yakir Lisak, a teacher; Aharon Bornsztajn and his sons; Shimon Sribnik and his sons Moshe Yaakov and Leibush; Yaakov Szerakowiak and his sons Yechezkel and Fishel; Reb David Kozlowski; Reb Yisrael Paltiel Frogel and his sons; Reb Shlomo Dawidowicz; and other Hassidism whose names, to our sorrow we no longer recall.

The House of Prayer of the Stryków Hassidim

When the *Admor* of Stryków, the rabbi and Tzadik Rabbi Menachem Mendel Landau, may the memory of the holy be blessed, moved to Zgierz, his Hassidim set up a special home for him, with an adjacent *Beis Midrash* for *Yeshiva* lads and a House of Prayer. The *Beis Midrash* was filled to the brim on festivals, and especially on the High Holy Days.

The names of several of the regular worshippers of that place still remain in our memory:

Rabbi Avraham Berliner, elderly, and one of the honorable members of the community; Leizer Sztachelberg; Yudel Szapszowicz and his sons; Natan David Szapszowicz and his sons; Shlomo Szapszowicz and his sons; Avraham Szapszowicz and his sons; Shalom Hirsch Szapszowicz and his sons, Shmuel Benet; Yitzchak Berliner; Natan David Kac and his sons; Yisrael Mordechai Praszker; Godel Frenkel; Melech Frajsztat; Mendel Laskier; Leibush Szrerakowiak and his son Fishel; and many other good Jews, followers of Torah, whose names, to our sorrow, have been lost from our memories. We apologize to those who are still alive.

The House of Prayer of the Stryków Hassidim served as a center for Torah and Hassidism. Tens of lads and young men studied there. There was no battle there with various opponents, but rather living Torah and Hassidism, lighting up the path of life and deeds for people, and actualizing the traits of Hassidic piety: modesty, love of one's fellow Jew, fervent prayer, devotion, brotherhood, charity, chastity, etc. In the center stood education toward diligence in Torah as a primary rather than subordinate value. The entire routine and curriculum of the *Yeshiva* was under the constant supervision of the *Admor*, From time to time, he would test the students and present some of his novel ideas to them. The Rebbe's dedication to the *Yeshiva* was his daily bread. No effort was too hard when it came to the existence of the *Yeshiva*. The students returned the love to him as well.

His Torah discussions at his table on Sabbaths and festivals lasted for many hours, and attracted studious, knowledgeable Hassidim, wo cleaved to him with boundless faith and reverence. After his death, his place was filled by his son,

[Page 87]

the *Admor* Reb Yaakov Yitzchak Dan Landau, may G-d avenge his blood, who perished in the Holocaust (The rabbi of Kinow). His son, the *Admor* Rabbi Tovia Landau, may he live, serves as the Stryków Admor in Tel Aviv.

There were other houses of worship and regular *minyanim* [prayer quorums] in private house in the city, such as the House of Prayer of the brothers Pinchas and David Wand. From among the worshippers in that prayer house, we remember Itza Meir Bialystocki and his sons; David Honiksztok; Michel Radogowski.

The worshippers of the Hassidim of Żyrardów included: Avraham Mandel, the *gabbai* [trustee]; Shlomo Cyncynatus; Yosef (Yoshke) Lewin and his sons, and others.

Translator's footnotes:

1. See https://en.wikipedia.org/wiki/Yitzchak_Meir_Alter
2. Certain portions of the prayer service, evidently drawn in calligraphy.

In the Old Gerrer Shtibel

by Natan Nota Nekritz

In Zgierz, the Gerrer Hassidim were the majority of all Hassidim. The large *shtibel* at the home of Reb David Bendkowski encompassed over 200 Gerrer Hassidim as worshippers.

The regular prayer leaders on the High Holy Days were: the teacher Reb Yitzchak Eksztajn – *Shacharit* and *Kol Nidre*; Reb Shabtai the teacher (Hauszzpigel) – *Musaf*. It is interesting that despite the fact that Reb Yitzchak was known for his lovely voice, the prayers of Reb Shabtai, tasteful and from the heart, moved the worshippers more deeply. His voice was infused with soul and feeling, and emanated from a veritable Jewish broken heart.

My father, Reb Yitzchak of blessed memory, was the shofar blower on Rosh Hashanah, and the regular Torah reader. Mourners or people who were observing yahrzeit would lead the services on weekdays. On regular Sabbaths, Itche Meir Sztajer or Michael-Mendel Rozenberg lead the *Shacharit* service. Yisrael Moshe Razanowicz would lead *Musaf*.

There would be a break between *Shacharit* and *Musaf* on Sabbaths and festivals, during which the youths and lads would sit at long tables and study. On festivals, after the break, Yosele Baluter (Yosef Mandelman) would always lead the services.

After Reb Shabtai the teacher passed away, Yosele Baluter became the

[Page 88]

regular prayer leader for *Musaf* on the High Holy Days. We children literally idolized him. His appearance in the *shtibel* would evoke a cheerful feeling. A happy smile of Hassidic sublimity always shone from his full face and thin beard. He was a young man with a hearty, lyrical voice, who enchanted everyone with his singing. His joyous Hassidic marches and enthusiastic dances carried away the old and young. Where Yosele was, there was no sadness. He would especially lead the youth and make things joyous in the *shtibel*.

He and his close family would always dress up in costumes on Purim. He would sit at the table and conduct himself in accordance with the Aleksander style, as those gathered would enjoy with contentment. "A Heavenly blessed artist," people would murmur in amazement.

Yosele Baluter was also a great scholar with an excellent knowledge of Bible. His sweet, melodic recital of Hebrew penetrated everyone's hearts. When he led services on regular Sabbaths, he was assisted by a few musically inclined youths, of whom there was no shortage in the *shtibel*. On the High Holy Days, however, he sung with a special choir of youths and older lads. One of these youths was my close friend Wolf Fiszer.

Almost every Hassid had his Sabbath when he travelled to the Rebbe. Thus, every Sabbath, several Hassidim were absent from the *shtibel*, as they had gone to Ger [Góra Kalwaria]. Naturally, this was also the primary source for Yosele's new tunes. He had a fine, musical ear, and an exquisite, quick grasp for new "things." Yosele would rehearse in the *shtibel* the new tunes and marches several times a week with the musically inclined Hassidic youth. We children had already finished our school day. We returned from *cheder* at noon and went to the *shtibel*, where were sat around the table and listened with wonder as Yosel Baluter taught the new Gerrer melodies to the youth.

When Yosele sang, who thought about livelihood or food?! One did not feel hunger at all. The teaching of the melodies lasted until late afternoon. Only when the wives and mothers arrived in the *shtibel* with a commotion did people remember that they also had a house and home. They returned home, as if carried by the wings of the Divine Presence. The taste of Yosele's singing with his singers accompanied us the entire way.

[Page 89]

In Memory of the Worshippers of the Synagogue and the Beis Midrash

We are sorry that we have not succeeded, despite our strong desire, in bringing down more names of the synagogue and *Beis Midrash* attendees, the vast majority of whom were householders of the intelligentsia and regular Jews of the city. The vast majority of them do not have even one survivor to recall their names and perpetuate their memories. Indeed, the following names of people that are memorialized here were brought to memory with great difficulty, as the memory weakens with time.

May their memories be a blessing, and may G-d avenge their blood.

Aharon Hirsch Kompel (the last head of the community)
Shalom Zelmanowicz
Hirsch Gelkop
Hirshel Luftman
Shimon Ring
Noach Trocki, from the former communal council
Yosef Miechowski
Yaakov Gelbard, lawyer
Barak Cohen
Elia Szwarcbard
Moshe Cygler
Moshe Librach
Chaim Itche Segal
Avraham Morgensztern, journalist and activist

Moshe Skosowski, *gabbai* of the *Beis Midrash*
Avraham Skosowski, political activist
Avraham Leib Sloma
Moshe Gelbard, *shamash* of the *Beis Midrash*
Fishel Feldon, *shamash* of the synagogue
Baruch Gilbralter
Mendel Gibralter
Moszek Dziak
Yisroel Yudofsky
… Yudofsky
Moshe Szydlowski
Michel Szydlowski
Avigdor Rozalski
Henich Grand
Avraham David Grand
Yitzchak Trojanowski
Shaul Trojanowski
Zanwil Sochaczewski
Moshe Hirsch Grand
Yisrael Grand
Ziskind Grand
A. Y. Szperling
Wolf Szmietanski
Yoel Speiwak
Meir Szwarc
Yaakov Meir Kuper
Nachum Glowinski
Izidor Strykówski, former secretary of the community
Michel Radogowski
Getzel Szwarcbard
Gershon Petrowicz
Moshe Glowinski
Leon Krikus
Shmuel Kuperman
Yisrael Yitzchak Finkelsztajn
Wolf Lipszyc
Moshe Praszker
Moshe Reznik

[Page 90]

Avraham Meir Rochenzon
Yaakov Rozensztrauch
Avraham Szlumiel
Henech Frajsztat
Eliezer Mendlowicz
Avraham Wald
Shia Rotenberg
Fishel Lipszyc
Asher Horn
Motel Margulis
Pesach Landau
Hirsch Leib Landau
Shimon Srebnik, *gabbai* of the *Beis Midrash*
Shimon Henich Srebnik

David Gothajner
Zalman Grundwald (*feldscher*)
Yaakov Gliksman
Isucher Szwarc
Moshe Gross
Chaim Wolkowicz
Daniel Sirkis
Shmuel David Lefkowicz
Ch. N. Szrubka
Ber Cukier (Bezhe), active in the *Chevra Kadisha*
Shalom Zandberg, *gabbai* of the *Chevra Kadisha*
Meir Kolski
Berl Wajsbaum, *gabbai* of the *Chevra Kadisha*
Izik Sieradzki
Aharon Grychendler
Yisrael Mondszajn
Moshe Baruch Szwarc
Zalman Wiechucki
Mendel Warszawski
Avraham Pantl
Mendel Jakubowicz
Hirsch Gedalia Godlfarb
Henich Pantl
Aharon Jedlicki
Shlomo Szajnholtz
Shimon Princ
Henich Princ
Zisha Turczynski
Yosef (?) Turczynski (his son)
Nachman Turczynski
Meir Temerzon
Nachum Glowinski
Baruch Gibralter
Mendel Gibralter
Mendel Krisztal
Aharon Horn
Yosef Celgow
Hirsch Gelkop
Leib Feldon
Yaakof Gelbard
Yaakov Leib Rozencwajg, lawyer
Itzik Praszker
Gedalia Rozman
Yisrael Sztykgold
Shlomo Goldberg
Yeshaya Goldberg
Avraham Temerzon
Meir Fogel
Yerachmiel Bornsztajn
Nota Broner
Avraham Himelfarb
Nachman Baruch (Nachman Bisk)
Naftali Hirsch Rozenes, prayer leader in the *Beis Midrash*
Tzemach Rozenfeld, *shamash* of the *Beis Midrash*
Postowelski, *shamash* of the synagogue
And many other worshippers

[Page 91]

The Beis Midrash and its "Guard"…

by W. Fisher

Since the time of creation, the small stream, the Bzura, has flowed behind the massive eastern wall of the communal *Beis Midrash*. Its source is in the Łagiewniki Forests behind Zgierz. This stream separates the *Beis Midrash* from two large factories that stand opposite, so close that their din often disturbed the fervent silence during the festival services.

For generations, a tall, wide-branched, poplar tree stood between the stream and the *Beis Midrash*. It spread its long, heavy branches over the roof of the *Beis Midrash* such that it seemed that it was some sort of High Priest raising his hands in blessing over the sanctuary in the Priestly Benediction, with the leaves uttering prayerfully: May G-d bless you… and protect you…

Elderly Jews used to relate that, since the *Beis Midrash* was standing there, the tree protected it from all types of disasters. More than one storm wind tore off the roofs of the houses, but the *Beis Midrash* remained intact to this day, for the tree covered it with a paternal hand. More than once did the calm stream overflow its banks and flood the houses and yards with its waters, but the waters never reached the threshold of the *Beis Midrash*. The swollen roots of the tree always held back the gush of the water. Also, no fire every affected it. Indeed, the factories were affected by fire several times, and the flames burst forth to here, heaven forbid… but, literally miracles! Several times, the tree received a zinc scorch from the other side, but the *Beis Midrash* was always protected.

Reb Wolf Sofer and Reb Fishel Bunim Shochet, from among the long-time neighbors, remember that they had received a tradition from the old Tzadik that, as long as the tree would stand there, it would protect and guard the *Beis Midrash* like a trusted guard…

The years flowed by like the calm waters of the stream, and they, the old, holy *Beis Midrash* and the old, majestic poplar, held an idyllic calm, as if they were spinning their heavenly thoughts and dreams for the Messianic times. Who knows how many stories and legends would have still been interwoven in their fine, interconnected lives, where it not…

[Page 92]

Then, just the other day, indeed one year before the war broke out, we heard that the tree near the *Beis Midrash* was no more. Only the broadly rooted, smoothly sawed down stump remained in the ground. There were various reasons as to why the heads of the community did so, but the reasons, whatever they may be, no longer have any relevance to our story.

The elder householders of the Jewish street wandered around unhappily with their heads crossed. One cannot permit this, under any circumstances… an unheard-of brazenness… the world is not wanton… one must ask the community, one must… others will yet feel the pain, some sort of a hint of something not good, G-d should protect us! And indeed, it became clear how an evil hand will cut down the powerful, green canopy of leaves that always graced the top of the *Beis Midrash*….

However, what is there to talk about now? That which happened cannot be avoided. The coming days and weeks would bring worry and uncertainty. There was talk of a war; the Germans were threatening to attack Poland. Dark clouds covered over the Jewish skies… The Jews felt that they were being left to wantonness…

It began specifically on a lovely, blue-skied Friday: the first bombs… And from then the subsequent events unfolded like a film reel. The Germans took over the city… The deathly frightened Jews were bullied… Every day brought new deathly decrees… The synagogue was burnt, and the *Beis Midrash*was set afire as well… They arrested, they beat, the shot… Now they were holding to only a bit of barren life… No, one does not ask, one does not speak. The tongue has been removed; Only the silent glances shout out fear and terror of death…

… And on one cold, gloomy winter-day, the Jews were driven out of their homes. Their final journey led to Che³mno and Treblinka.

*

Only sometimes, when mentioning the former Jewish reality, does one now also hold the thought: In essence they were both taken, they were both removed and annihilated by the decree of man, and simultaneously – the *Beis Midrash* and its "protector." But for whom does this have meaning today?

———

[Page 93]

Two from among my Neighbors at the Eastern Wall
(From my youth in the old Aguda Shtibel)

by P. Sirkis

… Their set place in the Ger Shtibel was next to the Holy Ark. One, Reb Falik Konsztam was much older. He was one of the communal notables and of the veteran Hassidim of the Shtibel. He was close to the rabbinical families of Zgierz. The second was Reb Shimon Fiszer, nicknamed Reb Shimon Pabianiczer (he came to Zgierz from there)[1]. He had the regular rights to taking out and putting back the Torah in the *shtibel*, and nobody tried to take that away from him. Even though both of them were bound with bonds of friendship and good neighborliness, and would honor each other greatly, the differences between them were obvious, both in their personal comportment and in their character, to the point that these are etched in my memory.

In contrast to my neighbor, Reb Falik, who was a conversationalist by nature and was involved in every debate and dispute among the Hassidim, so as to make his opinion heard – the voice of Reb Shimon was not heard within the walls of the *shtibel*. The children of the Hassidim scurried around him, some talking about matters between one Admor and the other, others talking about elections to the communal council or other communal institutions – while he, the level-headed Reb Shimon, did not get involved. At such times, his lips were uttering chapters of Psalms or reviewing the weekly Torah portion. He did not stand out, he did not pursue honor, for his way of live was to comport himself modestly with the L-rd your G-d[2] and with one's fellow humans.

Translator's footnotes:

1. Pabianice: see https://en.wikipedia.org/wiki/Pabianice
2. Micha 6:8.

Jewish Education
(Chapters of memory)

by Zeev Fisher

To the extent that we remember it from the distant days of our childhood and youth, the *cheder* was, without doubt, a type of phenomenon in the general arena of education and pedagogy, a product of its times. The researchers will certainly yet weigh in on its various influences, whether directly or indirectly, whether negatively or positively, on the Jewish child, and in a greater sense – also on the spiritual (and perhaps also physical) development of a large and important part of the totality of the Jewish people.

In our book, especially in the autobiographical section, we almost always find the *cheder*, in which the writer, poet or artist absorbed the special atmosphere that accompanied him and his creations, sometimes

[Page 94]

in all aspects of his life and activity. The well-known scholar and philosopher, Shlomo Maimon, who lived in the latter half of the 18th century, already studied the essence of the *cheder* and its influence on the way and thinking and modes of behavior of the child. He dedicated a broad, detailed description of the *cheder*, in which he took his first steps toward his understanding of Judaism and its spiritual world.

We include here two descriptions of the realities of the *cheders* in Zgierz. This first is of a *cheder* at the end of the 18th century, and the second, one generation later, is from the 1920s.

Cheders in the Memories of People of Zgierz

In the Cheder (from the memoires of the man of many deeds, Reb Daniel Sirkis of blessed memory)[1]

I began to attend the *cheder* of Reb Yaakovl, a Jew prone to anger, thin and weak, but strong enough to give his students slaps "of fire." I suffered greatly from his beatings. This teacher did not show us any signs of love, and we did not bond with him at all. I spent a long time in that *cheder*, until I transferred to the *cheder* of Reb Shabtai-Feivish, who was loved and appreciated by his students. We especially liked his wife, who was good to the children and treated them with bread sprinkled with fine sugar. At times, we would even get mushrooms or fried potatoes. I began to study Gemara with Reb Shabtai-Feivish. We studied the chapter of *Hamafkid*, the third chapter of *Bava Metzia*. The teacher's house had two rooms. There was a long table surrounded by benches in the room in which we studied. The teacher was G-d fearing and meticulous in the observance of commandments. He fasted on occasion, and rose early for services. We also studies with him matters of morality and proper behavior. I spent three years in that *cheder*, and remember them lovingly.

At the age of eight and a half I transferred to another teacher – Reb Yosef Pomeranc, who tormented us mercilessly. To this day. I tremble when I recall this teacher; with his whip, his grabbing of our ears, and the blows from his heavy stick. It was through miracles that we were not permanently maimed. We were so afraid that we were wary of complaining to our parents. There would be no point in this, for the teacher was always correct. All his blows were "for the sake of Heaven" and we were lazy. There was no benefit in these studies, for we were full of fear of the future beatings that we would receive. Therefore, all the tests on Sabbath with

[Page 95]

my father turned into a hell on earth. Father used to test me in my studies in the presence of the strict eyes of the teacher. Of course, many of his questions were left unanswered. On Sunday, the teacher took his revenge upon me, and beat me soundly for the embarrassment I caused him.

I continued to bear this yoke for many more years, for this Reb Yosef succeeded in earning the reputation of a successful teacher. My father was busy with his wide-branched businesses, and depended on the teachers to impart knowledge to us. To my good fortune, Reb Yosef got tired of teaching and transferred to commerce. Then I was able to recite "blessed is He who freed me"[2]. When news reached our home that Reb Yosef left his teaching position, I was overcome with deep joy. However, I was wary of displaying it – lest that teacher return and repay me in multiples. So great was my fear of that teacher. When I was ten and a half or eleven years old, I transferred to the teacher Reb Chaim Leibush, an elderly, sickly Jew.

(From the book Zekof Hakoma [Straighten your Posture] by Pinchas Sirkis)

Translator's footnotes:

1.   There is a footnote in the text here as follows: See the Book of Zgierz, pp. 454-455 for the personage of Reb Daniel Sirkis.
2.   A blessing recited by the father of a Bar Mitzvah boy upon being freed from the responsibility of his son's sins.

In the Agudas Yisroel Cheder
(Memoires from childhood days)

by Yaakov Chaimowicz

In memory of the institution in which very many of us had some connection to. Is this not – the *cheder* – and I refer here to the *cheder* of Agudas Yisroel in Zgierz.

I recall my native city of Zgierz only from my childhood, for I left it when I was fourteen years old. Therefore, I will of course tell here primarily of the life of *cheder*-age children.

The two-story building on Blotene Street that housed the *cheder* looked like it would topple over. The ground floor served for studies. It housed seven large rooms and one small room for the teachers. As I recall, the teachers were: Reb Hershele, the teacher of young children. A weak, short Jew, who did his best to impart reading skills to the young children; the second was Reb Simcha-Wolf, also short, who took interest in all matters in the running of the *cheder* and very little in his students. However, when he had to recite Psalms for a sick person, he would do this with his students with his full heart and enthusiasm. He also taught all the students of the *cheder* to write in Yiddish, and he taught his own students how to understand Chumash and Rashi.

To this point they related to us like children – with some understanding, and some patience. However, from that point, the relationship changed... The third teacher was Reb Avraham Woler (from the city of Wola). The students

[Page 96]

nicknamed him *Der Sheleger* (the beater). There was no relationship between the Torah that we absorbed from his mouth and the beatings that we absorbed from his hands. He was a bitter Jew who also embittered our lives. Our studies began at 7:00 a.m. and continued until 8:00 p.m., with small recesses during the day. We had general studies from 3:00 to 5:00. The teachers, primarily Poles, would come daily to teach us secular subjects. Through this, we also fulfilled the obligations of the state, which was particular about compulsory education. Our pious parents would never have considered sending us to a government school, for three reasons: a) it is forbidden to waste most of the hours of the day on the vanities of this world, b) girls and boys study together there, may G-d protect us, c) they study there without a hat, may G-d have mercy. Therefore, they found a solution: the teachers would come to the *cheder* for two hours, which would satisfy all opinions.

I studied for a very brief period with Reb Lipman, and I barely remember him. Someone called Rep Pinchas (nicknamed by the students Der Grober – the fat one) came in his stead. He also beat his students no small amount, but he also taught us, and we knew by heart everything that he taught us. Our fifth teacher was our acquaintance Rabbi Yitzchak Ek. He also managed the financial matters of this enterprise. He was the son of Kalman-Mendel the teacher. His relationship to his students was more refined and personal. His manner of explanation was also more understandable, and everything was in good taste and calm. Therefore, it is no wonder that he was liked by his students.

Nevertheless, any time I think about those days, I remember an event that took place with Yitzchak Ek, the teacher, and is etched in my mind to this day. The story was as follows: as has been noted, we were involved with the *cheder* from morning to night, and he did not even have a little bit of time for enjoyment or a game. Indeed, of what importance are such things to young Jews who were already studying *Gemara* with *Tosafot* [commentary on the Talmud], and who would shortly be 13 years old and could then be counted in a *minyan* [prayer quorum]. The days of Chanukah came, and we were free from studies from 5:00 p.m. When we returned home at night and saw how the young people were sledding with sleds over the frozen ice on the slope of Pilsudski Street, with sounds of joy and laughter filling the street – we were filled with jealousy and a great desire to be among them. Then the Satan stole the hearts of several of our friends, who decided to infiltrate the sledders and enjoy together with other lads in the area. We tried once or twice, and felt that we too were lads who could enjoy like the rest of them, until we forgot about the danger that would await if the matter became known in the *cheder*.

And suddenly – hey! In the darkness of the hour, someone exited the *shtibel* on that street, stumbled upon our sleds, and fell upon us with his full stature. We all fell in the snow and were quite confused, but when we realized that the strange guest was not one of us, but was rather our acquaintance Rabbi Pinchas the teacher, we fled and scattered in every direction.

[Page 97]

The next day, when we came to class, we were afraid and full of worry about what would take place that day. For if the matter would become known to our rebbe, Rabbi Yitzchak Ek, our end would be bitter. Indeed, the rebbe already knew everything that had happened, for he began to interrogate one of our friends with his typical strictness, and the friend immediately admitted to our sin. Then Rabbi Yitzchak rose from his chair, approached the place where his stick stood, took it in his hand, and turned to the rebellious child: "From you, Yechezkel, nothing will come. You will be and remain a street child. But tell me, please, who were your collaborators in this disgraceful act, through which you damaged the good name of the *cheder*?" The lad began to call out names that were made up, and ended by stating that these lads were not from our *cheder*. When Rabbi Yitzchak heard the "explanation", he got very angry and raised his voice, "Such a *shegetz*! It is not enough that you embarrassed me and the *cheder* with your deeds, but you are now so brazen as to lie to me!?" Suddenly he stopped speaking, without words and without beatings. He remained seated in his seat. His face became white as plaster, and nothing came from his mouth. It was as if he fainted. After he recovered a bit, it was as if he forgot the entire matter. He rose from his chair, and let us go home. Even our rebbe, Rabbi Yitzchak, went home. He became ill and bedridden, not to rise again. He passed away. May his memory be a blessing.

The Hidden Light

by the editors

– – – Without any doubt, it was possible and necessary to broaden the story on religious life in our city, but we did not pretend, and it was not possible to provide all the spiritual wealth, and the spirit and soul of the Jewish community of Zgierz in this book.

For generations, our community was always rich in personalities and people of renown. We cannot quantify the powerful contribution that they made to the flourishing of Torah thought in the tents of Torah from generations ago until the destruction of the community. They raised the honor of Torah with the imagination of their ideas and the clarity of their intellect. Geniuses rose up within the walls of the *yeshivot* and *Beis Midrashes*. At times, they became famous as Torah giants, whose names preceded them, geniuses in wisdom, people of the sanctuary, people of logic with ethical values.

The articles and memories in this section are only a small slice of the body of the tree, hinting to the aromatic canopies in all realms of religious life in the city. However, they prove and stress that this was a rooted Judaism, full of strength, with a bustling soul, imbued with faith and dedication to human values, the values of life and the values of tradition, which imparted to the vast majority of the Jewish community.

[Page 98]

a constant way of life, and imbued it with a spirit of historic Judaism. A sort of blend between Torah and the nation was created, and relations were forged between all strata of the community, between the scholars and the simple folk, between the *yeshiva* students and the workers – relations of an organic family.

The cordiality of the simple Jews, a simplicity of the preachers, the healthy earthiness of the tradesmen – all this penetrated the *Beis Midrash*. Toiling Jews, merchants, porters – all were partners in Torah. The greats of Torah and Hassidism did not suffice themselves with words of preaching and guarding the spiritual image of their community. Rather, they aspired to improve and raise the faithful masses to a more developed level. People of stature forged the spiritual image of the community, guarded and developed the values of culture within it, and continued to guard the traditional heritage and image.

Among the tens of houses of worship, there were many Hassidic *shtibels* and groups for the study – of *Talmud* and *Mishnah* on one side, and of *Midrash* and *Chayei Adam* [a book of Jewish law] on the other side. Jews from all strata and ages would sit in them, whether for a communal class or alone, studying Torah, which was the heritage of the many. Each Jew saw himself as a partner in Torah, and all together formed a community of a unified will and a common lot.

In Zgierz, there were Hassidim of various streams, as well as Misnagdim. The unifying force in the community of Zgierz was that the differences of opinion that pervaded among the various streams never led to a chasm of the hearts. Indeed, at times there was tension between the camps, especially before elections, but in general, the Jewish community was typified by internal essence and soulful connection – this also made Zgierz unique among all other holy communities.

[Page 99]

D. Personalities and Characters

[Page 100]

People of Zgierz

by the editorial board

… This section presents to the reader a long series of people of Zgierz, simple folk and precious people worth of praise, families who struck deep roots in the events of the city and Jewish tradition, with the love of their fellow etched very deeply in their hearts and their personalities – simplicity, modesty, and proper behavior between man and his fellow, and between man and his Creator. The personalities and characters that composed this community were people of distinct personalities. Each was an element in the tapestry of the community, from which they drew their spiritual nourishment – both influencing and being influenced. The pulse of life beat in them with strength. Their souls secretly aspired for the sublime and lofty in life.

[Page 101]

David Frischmann
(60 years after his death – 10 of Av, 5682 – 1922)

by Z. F.

In the memorial article for David Frischmann from *Haboker*, September 26, 1952, the well-known writer Baruch Karo writes the following with the title "A Memorial Candle to David Frischmann."

"How have we all passed in silence the 30th anniversary of the death of David Frischmann? For his words still vibrate with life to this day." If those words were accurate for the 30th anniversary of the passing of giant among the classicists of the new Hebrew literature – it is no wonder, therefore, that the name of this writer, poet, translator, and researcher, wo gave so much to its development and renewal of modern Hebrew literature, in form, content, and style – is not recalled, even with a whisper. He was a man who left behind a legacy whose value remains for generations, who "taught the writers how to write in the language of human beings." (Sh. Sh.)

However, it is our desire this time to include here several items from the aforementioned article, regarding the relation of Frischmann to Messianism – an eternal topic for us, actual in this day as well:

… but he (Frischmann) was among those who did not yet sense the footsteps of the Messiah, who felt that the generation was not worthy. He wrote two poems on the topic of the Messiah. Both had the undertone, "Until a new generation will arise, a generation that wants to be redeemed and that will prepare its soul to be redeemed" – (referring to the preparation of the hearts that was demanded by Ahad Ha'am, and regarding which the wise people of our generation of course mock).

The following are sections of the second poem in which he turns his attention to the Messiah redeemer himself – whether he is completely ready at this time for his high, historic task? Let us delve into the essence, the soul of the Messiah, as the poet saw him in his poem "On the Path of the Messiah."

> Next to the Jordan there is the house of a smith
> An iron smith, light as a knight
> He is doing his work there
> With a flaming bellows,
> Pach-pach! Pach-pach! It is flaming
> An eternal flame – burns beneath it.

What are you doing here, oh smith?
"I am doing here, I am now,
Preparing and laying
An iron horseshoe, and this is for,
Hurray! Hurray! This is for
The horse of the Messiah!"

[Page 101]

We can, therefore, surmise that when the sound of the Messiah's shofar is heard – his horse will be waiting for him, prepared for the journey. And a weaver is sitting there, weaving a silk tunic "for the Messiah." He is also knitting with his needle, also stretched over his work, preparing a precious flag "for the King Messiah." Indeed, he is working faithfully and enthusiastically preparing the splendid and glorious accessories of the Messiah, without any doubt waiting for the advent of the great, awaited day. And the Messiah?

There are seven cherubim in the heavens
Silent like dreams, quick as flies
Carrying out the work;
They are before the Throne of Honor –
Hurray! Hurray! With honor they
Are standing in formation.

Everything sublime, everything uplifted,
Everything lovely, everything above,
Everything good and pure
All of these they take,
Hurray! Hurray! They take
An everything that is splendorous and luminous;

Everything that has mercy upon the weak
Who in their pain wallow in blood,
All this they take –
Everything protected, everything tender,
Hurray! Hurray! Everything tender,
Prepared in a mixture.

What, oh Cherubim, are you doing here? –
"Everything we bear,
We prepare, and even leave
And the soul is made such,
Hurray! Hurray! Made such
For the Messiah!"

"However we have a secret, a secret!
All the workers around us
Have already finished the work;
Only we still are falling behind,
Oy! Oy! We are still falling behind,
There is no more sign of success.

This is nothing but this soul,
This pure one, this exalted one,
For it there is not yet sufficient raw material
That we have collected to this day,
Oy! Oy! To this day
From all the passers-by.

It is not sufficiently sublime, it is not sufficiently exalted
It is not sufficiently lovely and raised,
There is not enough splendor and light;
Even groaning is no more,
Oy! Oy! Perhaps it is not
Refined and pure."

And the angels, seven cherubim,
Raise their voice, the voice of abandonment,
The voice of moaning and talk –
To this day they have not completed,
Oy! Oy! They have not completed
The soul of the Messiah!

And with all this, we shall await him; for, when the day comes – he will surely come.

Z. F.

[Page 103]

David Frischmann – the Jewish World Spirit
(60 years from the time of his passing)

by the editors

G-dly blessed talent and great mastery, moral steadfastness and stormy, pugnacious cheerfulness – this is what the readers gleaned from David Frischmann's pen. However, his close friends knew the great extent that his creative work derived from the atmosphere in Zgierz, where he was born and educated, where he studied and began to write his first creations. That atmosphere, which we recognize from the Book of Zgierz and the additional book, also had its effect on later works, on his critical feuilletons, stories and poems.

One is born with a talent, but a writer's talent, mastery and consistency in creativity is not sufficient to ignite the souls of the readers. For that, one's moral qualifications must also drive one's pen: with personality, character, and conscience. This is forged by that which one was shaped during one's youth and childhood. This is what David Frischmann received in Zgierz. There, he also found the characters and personalities for his first fiction creations.

In David Frischmann's writings, from his "formlessness an emptiness" through his poems and stories, until his *Bamidbar* series, the legends of our national-social childhood – everything has an inner persuasion of the craft of a great personality. His sharp criticisms did not come, heaven forbid, from hatred or jealously, but rather from a deep desire to better and beautify Jewish life, Jewish creations in all areas of literature and art.

David Frischmann wrote both about literature and art, and about writers, poets, and politicians. He also wrote about theater and actors, and above all about the problems of life and death, love and hate. He was an artist and raconteur, editor and translator. All of his work excelled with freshness, fruitfulness and timelessness. His creations in all areas demonstrated the will to try all avenues to walk and seek, to not stop, to not allow himself to get caught in the web of complacency. From stormy

[Page 104]

feuilletons, he set out to tomorrow in the inner world of elegant poems, of self-appraisal, and gentle sadness.

From the intimate Jewish world, he sought a way to the world arena, not of gladiators, but only of people of worldly spirituality. His translations of Shakespeare and Byron, of Heinrich Heine and Rabindranath Tagore[1], Oscar Wilde, Anatol France, Pushkin, Ibsen, Elliot, Andersen, Grimm, and others, were great artistic achievements. All were imbued with so much intimate living spirit that they became blessed mutual creations. They burst forth in song as if from the same melody, the same rhythm as if from the source, the same beauty, the same radiating light; and frequently gave the impression that Frischmann provided a rectification of the creation in Hebrew, which, according to his intent, were wallowing in other languages.

He had an eye for all the important cultural events in the world of literature, art and politics. He brought his readers into partnership with all the movements and winds blowing in the civilized world, with all the changes and announcements of the great people of spirit who disrupted the literary world in Europe.

Like an uncomfortable spirit, albeit also harmonious, David Frischmann did not hide from the world in an ivory tower. Rather, he was always wide open to it, and fought incessantly against the chaos – for harmony. The great discomfort always runs against the world. It peers deep in the eyes, burying its deep secrets, laying them deep in the ground of despair, and rising again to the peaks of the spirituality of beauty.

David Frischmann was such a great, turbulent spirit. He had a great deal of pessimism in him, but he never satisfied himself with pessimistic formulas. After every sorrow, he called life toward a new struggle, and expressed a stubborn sense of invincibleness, certain in the victory over the muddle of questions and problems; a victory that is laced with understanding and belief, and came to expression both in his feuilletons and in his works of fiction. Who can forget the impression that his *Shlosha Sheachlu* [Three who Ate Together] or his *Titchadesh* [Let it be Renewed] had upon our childhood years? He was a creative pessimist, but when all the optimists dropped their hands, Frischmann set out to his work. Every one of his sighs was accompanied by hope.

[Page 105]

Like a thunderbird, he destroyed dreams and his heart pulsated with great Jewish hope. He did not believe in any plaited beliefs. He was no picayune pessimist. Above all, he stitched up everything that was flat, an everything that he touched was immersed in holiness.

The editors

Translator's footnote:

1. See https://en.wikipedia.org/wiki/Rabindranath_Tagore

In the Circles of the Maskilim of Zgierz
(Memories)

by Moshe Helman of blessed memory

In his time, the communal activist from Łódź, Mr. Moshe Helman of blessed memory, would frequently visit Reb Isucher Szwarc, and was a friend of the writer David Frischmann. We include here several sections of his memoirs (still in manuscript form) regarding his connections and impressions of these two Zgierz natives.

P. S.

… Rabbi Eliahu Chaim Meizel, may the memory of the holy be blessed, the rabbi of Łódź, greeted every person pleasantly and treated them with honor. It was not only scholarly rabbis who frequented his home, for Maskilim also visited him for communal matters. It was in the home of the rabbi that I first met Reb Isucher Szwarc of Zgierz in 1888. The grandson of the rabbi introduced him to me, adding that Mr. Szwarc had a large library full of valuable books. Mr. Szwarc invited me to visit him in his home in Zgierz, where I could also meet David Frischmann, the poet of Israel. He added in jest: a poet – not a cantor, but a poet in Israel[1]…

This meeting drew me near to both Isucher Szwarc and David Frischmann in the future. At my first opportunity to be in Zgierz with my brother-in-law Reb Shlomo Sirkis, I asked him to show me the way to the home of Reb Isucher Szwarc. My brother-in-law told me that Reb Isucher Szwarc worships in a different synagogue, and is considered to be a scholar, but since he is more progressive than a scholar, the Hassidim are not content with him. He was surprised to hear that the rabbi of Łódź drew him so near.

Nevertheless, he sent one of his officials with me to show me the way. When I entered his home, I saw him setting at the table with a book open before him. Next to the wall, there was a bookcase full of books, among which were many

[Page 106]

whose titles I was not yet familiar with. Reb Isucher was very happy to greet in his home the young brother-in-law of Reb Shlomo Sirkis (as he expressed it), and chatted with me briefly.

His first question was: what am I studying and what do I read? Do I read *Hamelitz* and *Hatzefira*? Have I read his articles signed with the pseudonym "Black Sea"[2]? When he heard that I was mainly studying Talmud, Talmudic commentaries, and the Code of Jewish Law, and read little, he pointed out to me that it would also be good to read a great deal, for a Jew is not only supposed to understand his past, but also to present, looking toward the future. He advised me to read a Hebrew newspaper as well as a Hebrew monthly such as *Hashachar*. He introduced me to his young son Shmuel and said, "My young son also studies, but he also reads."

… I often went to visit my parents in Zgierz. I felt that my brother-in-law Shlomo wished to educate me in the way of Hassidism. However, he did not know that my heart was drawn to Reb Isucher Szwarc and Reb Moshe Ejger of blessed memory, my brother-in-law's partner, one of the first *Maskilim*, a member of Chovevei Zion, and a friend of Isucher Szwarc. I spent most of my time in their company every time I visited Zgierz.

… In the year 5658 (1898) I spent time in Odessa for business. Mr. Shmuel Barbash invited me to the Sabbath eve meal. He asked me about the engineer Shmuel Szwarc, the son of Reb Isucher Szwarc, who was in Spain at the time. I understood that this was a question about a marriage match. I spoke the praises of the youth, stating that he was scholarly, a Torah student, with fine character. I took that opportunity to tell him about the following fine episode. Shmuel Szwarc studied engineering in Paris, and one of his friends was Rothschild's son. Once, Shmuel Szwarc told his friends that he was blessed with a wonderful memory for numbers. He recited hundreds of numbers for them, which they were to write down. He then would repeat them, number by number, in the order that he had given them over. They had made a bet for a charitable institution.

A short time after they wrote down the numbers, he repeated them exactly as he had given them over. This was a surprising thing, and they considered the young Szwarc to be exceptionally talented. When Szwarc once went to visit his friend, the Rothschild father entered, and started a conversation with the youth from Poland. He asked how he had gotten such a wonderful memory. Shmuel Szwarc smiled and responded: "The matter is very simple. I am a Jew, and for us, the numbers are represented by the *aleph beit*[3]. I choose a chapter of Psalms that I know off by heart, let us say *Ashrei Yoshvei Beitecha* [4] and translate it to the numbers: *aleph* – 1, *shin* – 300, *reish* – 200, *yod* – 10, etc. Rothschild liked this "invention" and gave him a recommendation for Spain, where he received a job as an engineer.

Mr. Barbash enjoyed the invention of Shmuel Szwarc very much. After a few years, he became his son-in-law.

.. At that time, I hosted Reb Isucher Szwarc in my home, and a sharp debate broke out between us on the topic of Haskalah [enlightenment]. He admitted to me that the incident I saw with… (who wrote on the Sabbath) was already known to him, and that person was not the only one, but such was the way

[Page 107]

with most Maskilim. Reb Isucher Szwarc was not content with the fact that, for example, the hero of the story *Le'an* by Fierberg, published in *Hashiloach*, extinguished a candle on the Sabbath in front of the entire congregation in the synagogue. Despite all this, the *Haskalah* was separate from the behavior of these *Maskilim*. "Reb Isucher stressed, people such as you and I are obligated to forge a blend of opposition based on the Code of Jewish Law, and of life in the spirit of the *Haskalah*, that is, in the spirit of tolerance.

We decided between us to found a circle of Torah-oriented *Maskilim*, and to gather from time to time for reading and discussion in the spirit of research without appeals, without searching for the truth and accepting the truth from those who state it.

… In those days we were – we, the Maskilim of the old generations – used to gather once a week "over a cup of tea" at the home of Mrs. Batya Turkeltaub. Her house was a meeting place for the writers of Israel, and David Frischmann was a regular there. He once said that Batya Turkeltaub was his friend to whom he writes letters on literary matters. She admired Hebrew literature as the supreme ideal. The famous illustrator Glicenstein would also stay at her home when he visited Łódź. We would sit around in that house over a cup of tea and listen to the creations of Frischmann before they were published.

… In his discussions, Frischmann would always request that we teach Hebrew not only to our sons, but also to our daughters.

We would visit the home of David Frischmann whenever we were in Warsaw. It was spiritual enjoyment not only to read his writing, but also to hear his regular conversations. His jokes reminded us of Boccaccio's Decameron[5]. He only told them to special individuals. He showed me his jokes in writing, but did not want to publish them. He stated in his will that they are only allowed to be published fifty years after his death.

… After his wedding, David Frischmann sent us a thank you note for the gift we sent him

(published after the death of the poet in "Letters of David Frischmann," page 162)

———————

Translator's footnotes:

    1.   Here, Israel refers to the Jewish people and not the land. Also, the word for poet used here could also mean a singer, hence the reference to a cantor.
    2.   Szwarc is black in Yiddish.
    3.   See http://www.jewfaq.org/alephbet.htm#Numbers
    4.   An important part of the daily prayer service.
    5.   See https://en.wikipedia.org/wiki/The_Decameron

Eulogy for Avraham Yosef Weisenfeld

by Nachum Sokolov

(*Hatzefira*, 24 Kislev 5658, December 7, 1897, number 272)

Our comrade, Reb Avraham Yaakov Weisenfeld is no more!

One of the last survivors of the scholars of Galicia, one of the "early ones" has passed away recently in the city of Krakow. Weisenfeld has gone to his eternal world!

[Page 108]

This news moved the hearts of all who knew him. However, who knew Weisenfeld? Only those who were close to him. – – – There are wise people who do not wish to be known from up close, but rather who want that their books be read and studied. On the other hand, there are special people who are comfortable with being known from up close.

Weisenfeld was one of these special individuals. Those who knew him recognized that he was a flowering treasury full of literature. Those who knew him saw him as the symbol of a progressive *Maskil*, a living monument to the era of splendor and glory of the *Haskalah* of Galicia. He was a monument forged from the throne of honor of our leaders Rana'k[1], Geshi'r, and those like them. Those who knew him not only honored him in the splendor of his glory, but also loved him with exceptional love, not only for his expertise, knowledge, and ideas, but also for his sublime character traits, the grace of his soul, and the purity of his spirit. For this elevated man was a warm, pure *Maskil*, who warmed the hearts of all those near to him. He held the Torah, literature, and the Hebrew language dear and precious to him – with pure warmth, faith, enthusiasm, emotion, abundant pleasantness, with the same "grace of youth" and "marital love" of the *Haskalah*, with the same pleasant warmth and fierce devotion that we see in the splendor of the early ones of every faction, including the early ones of the *Haskalah*.

Such precious individuals, remnants of the great era, must be guarded as the apple of the eye from weakness, ageing, and death. But what can we do, for Heaven has decreed that even people of this sort must die.

However, even if we know that it was a decree that we cannot question, whenever one of our choice cedars falls down, we feel as if the death has ripped our hearts to pieces.

Weisenfeld of blessed memory was a native of Krakow, and of the generation of the greats who raised the banner of Hebrew *Haskalah* in Galicia. He, along with the finest of the *Maskilim* of Galicia, served the giant of the spirit, Rabbi Yitzchak Mizes of blessed memory. He carried the opinions and visions, the explanations and the feelings, the research methodologies and the paths of logic, the fine character traits, the mottoes of ideas and the regular conversation of those scholars in his heart throughout his life. Like all the early *Maskilim*, he was also pious. G-d fearing and observant of the commandments, with great patience and a calm heart. Like all the early *Maskilim*, he occupied himself in Torah for its own sake throughout his life: and included in Torah is wisdom and literature. He loved to deduce theories, and recall all the words of the excellent writers. He was always the paradigm of a man of friendship. He was always happy and joyous, devoid of sadness, devoid of pride, devoid of dryness, fully alive, feeling, enthusiastic, all pleasant – like a watered garden.

He was a modest, discreet man. Like the few *Maskilim* of the past generation, he did not aspire to write works. However, he exchanged a great deal of letters with the wise people of the generation. All of his letter were replete with Torah and knowledge.

From Krakow, Weisenfeld moved during his youth to live in the small city of Zgierz, next to Łódź, where he lived for many years, almost for his entire life, for we cannot count the final years in Krakow, which he endured in agony and old age, among the years of his life,

[Page 109]

after circumstances forced him to move there.

The elderly pass on without returning. Even we "young people" will soon be old, and what will the next generation be like? Will that generation understand his ideas and the burden of his soul, as we understand the ideas of our ancestors and rabbis?

I did not know Weisenfeld well, but – if it is possible to state such – "I felt him", the light within him, his good taste. I was sated with enjoyment from his works and conversations when I visited his home years ago. He was still planted on his heights. I also saw him about two years ago in Krakow, bent under the burden of old age, but still with his Divine sparks. Let those who were near to him, and who walked with him throughout the days and years arise and eulogize him appropriately!

May his soul be bound in the bonds of eternal life.

N. S.
Transcribed by W. Fisher – July 6, 1966.

———

Translator's footnote:

1.   Nachman Krochmal. See https://en.wikipedia.org/wiki/Nachman_Krochmal

Two Books about Two Eminent Men of our City

by Z. Fisher

Not long ago, two books were published, dedicated to the memories and activities of two Zgierz natives, whose names were known for praise throughout all of Polish Jewry and the entire Jewish world. As residents of Zgierz and heads of the community, they did a great deal for the Jewish community as they served as heads of the communal council of our city for many years. They excelled particularly in their successful work for the benefit of the community and individual. The elder brother, Reb Eliezer of blessed memory, also was elected to the city council, and later as a delegate to the Polish Sejm (Parliament).

One book is called *Man of Faith* by Pinchas Sirkis (300 pages). It was written in memory of his father, the rabbi and Hassid Rabbi Eliezer Sirkis of blessed memory. The book portrays his spiritual personality and full, fruitful life of communal activism on behalf of Jewry and Jews in all areas of life. All this was in the background of his large family, of fine pedigree in Poland, during the 18th century.

In the annals of that life, we survey the Jewish way of life in the cities of Poland, Wolhynia, and Podolia several generations ago. Indeed, Jewish life in Zgierz also passes by here, in the scarlet thread throughout the entire length of the book. Since Rabbi Eliezer of blessed memory used to record in his diary that which took place in his time and environment,

[Page 110]

it turns out that the scroll of his life faithfully and authentically surveys one of the most interesting and stormy eras in the life of the nation in the Diaspora.

When Rabbi Eliezer Sirkis of blessed memory arrived in the Land of Israel in 1935, he continued his important communal work (as one of the heads and leaders of Agudas Yisroel) with greater energy and dedication for the benefit of the public, and specifically for the benefit of the Orthodox settlement in the Land.

The second book, called *Zakuf Komah* [Upright Stature] by the aforementioned writer (200 pages) was written in memory of his uncle, the rabbi and Hassid Rabbi Daniel Sirkis of blessed memory, Rabbi Eliezer's brother – as they were the two children of the prominent Hassid, from the finest of the city, whose name preceded him among the Jews of Poland for his generosity and warmth of heart, Rabbi Shlomo Sirkis of blessed memory.

This book describes in part the youthful years of Rabb Daniel. After moving from one *cheder* to another, he finally received direction in Hassidism and the service of the Creator from an elder of the Kock Hassidim "who forged the personality of Rabbi Daniel in the spirit of Kock." Indeed, his opinions were always strong and his stance powerful in his struggle for truth without missing the mark... These characteristics exemplify him, his ways, and his activities throughout his entire life – including his sharp turn from Ger Hassidism to the Mizrachi movement, for he became one of the founders and leaders of that movement in our city – as well as his role as a leader of the communal council of Zgierz, where he imbued his spirit upon the council, introduced an atmosphere of the Land of Israel to the communal leadership, and enacted regulations that were always for the benefit of our townsfolk who were making *aliya* as pioneers to the Land of Israel.

His primary, widespread communal efforts found a living echo and great content in all strata of the Jewish community of Israel from the time that he arrived in the Land, the desire of his heart, in 1925. There, we find Rabbi Daniel as the head of the fighters an strugglers for the whole Land of Israel, for religious national education, for dedication and purity of character for the nation. He wrote passionate articles in the pages of newspapers, and reacted strongly and steadfastly to anything that took place within the Jewish community of the Land. Thus, he stood on his guard faithfully and with dedication for the nation, the religion, and the homeland.

Two of his books were published in the Land: *Zionism in the Straits* (260 pages), and with an *Upright Stature* (450 pages). The latter book especially received a broad, positive echo among most circles of the Jewish community of Israel.

In summary: two important books, full of content and great value, about two great Jewish personalities who were natives of Zgierz.

[Page 111]

The Confession of a Jewish Large-Scale Industrialist
(From his booklet: *To the Son and Daughter*)

Woe, you Moshe Ejger, the small person
The great fool, you imbecile,
It is coming, night is falling soon.
So give a thought, give a ponder;
We must get ready to sleep soon...
Therefore, G-d will not punish you –

What have you done, what have you made
And with what have you spent your life?
Tell, to whom was this all necessary
Your constant thinking, your headache,
Always going around with your resentments.
You did not live and you did not enjoy,
But rather always thought, ruminated in your mind,
You wanted everything to be higher than was within your power,
You had great plans, many projects,
And how many of them did you carry out?...
Always cautious, busy, businesslike, interesting –
You have completely forgotten "You should not say, when I have time, I will learn"[1]
You always said: I will yet, I will yet, I will –
A war came, and made rubble out of everything…

_ _ _ _ _ _ _ _ _ _ _ _ _ _ _ _ _

And now again, say what type of a taste this had,
Your poems, your stanzas, your rhymes?
Is it worthwhile, therefore, to think, to ruminate,
Will something better come of this?
Fool, what can this have for action –
Your children do not even know how to read this…

by Moshe Tzvi Eiger

[Page 112]

The calculations now, when you are already going away:
What is the entire purpose, and what is the goal?!
The last line – only nothing, in the head as in the wallet –
Vanity of vanities, all is vanity![2]

Rabka, 1932

Translator's footnotes:

1. Pirkei Avot 2:5.
2. From Song of Songs 1:2.

Arthur Szyk in the Zgierz Business School
(As our Fabian Grynberg remembers him)

The well-known writer Sh. L. Shneiderman, in his recently published book "Arthur Szyk" writes as well about young Szyk's studies in the Zgierz business school, that took place specifically in the turbulent revolt year of 1905 in Russia and in Poland.

… "The eleven-year-old Artur Szyk also joined the strike committee of the business school of Zgierz, near Łódź. Specifically there, he made his debut as a political caricaturist. He drew the caricatures of the Czar and his ministers. Our students made tens of copies and distributed them through the classes, and even through a series of schools in Łódź itself. The teachers displayed a great deal of liberalness toward the rebellious students, with whose actions they quietly sympathized.

– – – One of the caricatures reached the school principal, and the young Szyk had to leave the school."

The well-known business school in Zgierz (see Book of Zgierz, pp. 120, 275-6), with its large number of Jewish students from all parts of Russia and especially from Poland, in time became a warm nest for all sorts of ideological streams, which were nurtured at that time in the underground of political-societal life. An entire row of later famous societal activists and leaders of political parties – primarily of the left – emanated from there.

Our important fellow townsman, Fabian Gryn-Grynberg, who lived his latter years in America and was in literary contact with the Forward, sent us the following letter regarding Shneiderman's article in that newspaper:

[Page 113]

"Esteemed editor,

Every Sunday, I read with great interest your wonderful chapters about the world-famous artist and warm Jew, Arthur Szyk, written by the talented writer Sh. L. Shneiderman.

Szyk was my friend in the Zgierz business school. We sat on the same bench. I observed how he masterfully brought forth the characters of the teachers, which he drew with his caricatures. However, when the teacher caught him, he was in trouble.

I recall how Szyk, with his studious nature, would always bother the brake man in the tram that brought him from Łódź to Zgierz every day. The brake man "got angry" and hit him in the head or the face. My friend was heavily bandaged for several weeks.

I am very grateful to the Forward and the writer for portraying the wonderful personality of Arthur Szyk, who remained faithful to his people and strongly defended the honor and interests of his people, often risking his life and career. Few world-famous artist are left among us.

With respect,

Fabian Gryn, Forest Hills, N.Y.

In the Forward, July 25, 1978.

The Professor of "Zakon-Bosza"
(In the Zgierz government *gymnasja*)

by Zeev

The great, famed writer, Sholem Asch, had a bit of closeness with Zgierz. We know of his frequent visit to the Zgierz *Maskil*, writer, and scholar Reb Isucher Szwarc, whose home was known as a meeting place for scholars. Almost every time that Asch traveled through Zgierz on the way from his home in Kutno to Łódź (in those years, the railway line from Łódź to Kutno did not yet exist), he would stop in Zgierz and visit the Szwarc's, to whom he also showed his first manuscripts.

In the large, already bustling city of Łódź, Sholem

[Page 114]

Asch's father-in-law already lived. He was the Hebrew literaturist M. Ch. Szapira, whose daughter Matilda had, as is known, a great influence on Ash's artistic creations.

It seems that his father-in-law as well, the aforementioned Szapira, was very closely connected to our former hometown, for he had a position in the Zgierz government *gymnasja* before the First World War as a professor of "Zakon-Bosza" (Fear and Law).

This is what I found in an article in Di Zukunft. That journal (January 1982, pp. 25-29) was sent to us by Yitzchak Scharansky. The article was written by Meir Ber Gutman under the heading: Leibush Magid and the Professor of "Zakon-Bosza."

Unwillingly, we come here to the possible idea of a point of connection between the father-in-law's teaching position for "Zakon-Bosza" and the son-in-law's "Nazarene novels" that, in their time, so jolted the Jewish cultural world[1].

Shia Plocki, the Veteran Firefighter of Zgierz

After the First World War, many Jewish volunteers joined the ranks of the "*straż ogieńowa*" (firefighters) in our city. The need to protect Jewish property, especially the Jewish-owned factories of the city, became vital after the expansion and development in the city of the textile manufacturing and the sale of its products, from which most of the Jews earned their livelihoods. This step was also a matter of national pride – that is, that even we Jews, and not only the Polish and Germans who had exclusive rights in that area until this time, were capable of protecting and defending ourselves in times of danger. The first pioneer in such matters was Karol Ejger. Following him were Yaakov Skosowski, Zeinwil Kohen, Shmuel Feldman, Yehoshua Jakir, and others.

From our childhood years, we still remember the elderly, plump Shia Plocki, with his small, greyish beard adorning his red face. He wore a motorcycle helmet with a sparkling visor. He had a shop for writing implements and toys on the Long Street (later called Piłsudski Street). He was a unique character in his conduct and his relation to Jewish communal life, but he had a warm, Jewish heart. He raised and educated an orphan girl, from a far-away family, in his home. He was also charitable, and never withheld his hand from giving to the needy, even though rumors spread that his kitchen was not kosher to the highest of standards. It seems that this was merely slander.

It is told that he was among the first in the firefighters from the time of its founding, and he was one of the chief activists in its development. Nevertheless, there was something comical and humorous about seeing this elderly man among those running to a fire that broke out in some village around Zgierz, whether in Dąbrówka or Piaskowice,

[Page 115]

Brużyczka or Stępowizna, Proboszczewice or Lućmierz, Krogulec or Łagiewniki. He, the elderly Jew, in uniform, with the helmet on his head and the sledgehammer on his belt, would run to protect and save, even though he could barely carry himself on his feet. However, when he passed by the extinguisher or the ladder apparatus, they would always stop on the way to take him along. They, the firefighters, honored him and related to him with appreciation – perhaps because of his past merits, and perhaps because of his strength of heart to volunteer as the first Jew of the city firefighters.

However, anyone who did not witness Shia Plocki, marching proudly in the parade of the firefighters on the occasion of some national event or festive occasion, along the entire length of Long Street, with people watching along the sidewalk as their band was playing – and he was in the front ranks, in the shadow of the flag raised high – with an upright posture, and a shiny helmet on his head, to the beat of the marching music, along with everyone else – never saw Jewish pride in the lands of the Diaspora.

Translator's footnote:

1.   See https://en.wikipedia.org/wiki/Sholem_Asch

My Father Yehoshua
the son of David Baniel (Berliner) of blessed memory

by Dr. Shmuel Baniel

Reb Yehoshua of blessed memory was one of the prominent personalities of Orthodox Zgierz. He spent all his days engaged in Torah and Divine service. He was a Hassid with supreme grace; He stemmed from an old, wide-branched family, whose sons excelled in their deeds, and national and intellectual achievements, to the glory of the Jews of Zgierz.

Yehoshua Baniel Berliner

Father, peace be upon him, made *aliya* to the Land in 1934 along with Mother, my sisters, two young brothers, and me – the baby. Thanks to his Zionist activities as one of the leaders of the Mizrachi movement in Zgierz, he succeeded in receiving a certificate and making *aliya* to the Land.

Father occupied himself in commerce to earn a livelihood, but he lived from spiritual sustenance. He led and supported the *shtibel* of Polish Hassidim for 40 years, and continued the life of the *shtibel* here. I cannot forget the salted fish tails of the third Sabbath meal. Nor can I forget Reb Yankel Baum, Reb Gershon Szpilberg, and all the others who have already for a long time exchanged the anteroom for the banquet hall.

[Page 116]

During his last twenty years, father invested most of his time in the study of Kabbalah. He especially dedicated himself to the *Sulam* commentary of Rabbi Ashlag. He financially helped the publication of the commentary, and also conducted classes about it.

He wrote many innuendoes about matters of the redemption, and spoke a great deal about the Messianic era, but he refused to put such matters in writing. His Hassidic stories were well-known in the neighborhood, and tens of his followers would soak them up them with thirst, especially on Sabbaths and festivals, when the *shtibel* was filled to the brim.

He stopped his business activity in the final decade of his life, after his children had married and established their own families. He would study with the grandchildren, especially the Oral Torah, as he influenced them and imbued his spirit upon them.

He died of a heart attack at the age of 83. On the final Friday of his life, he told me that he had finally agreed to move to Bnei Brak, where the atmosphere was quieter and more religious. However, it apparently, it was decreed in Heaven that he would not leave the Montefiore neighborhood during his lifetime. All that we could do was to bestow final honors upon him. He is buried in Bnei Brak in the vicinity of the Chazon Ish and other luminaries.

We always loved hearing his stories about the town of Zgierz and its people, about the vibrant business life there, and the atmosphere in the *Beis Midrash* and various *shtibels*, and about its sages and scribes.

It pained us deeply to part from such a dear father, but we were comforted in his faith. Father believed in the coming of the Messiah and the resurrection of the dead with pure faith, and he instilled that faith in us as well – and with that we were comforted.

He died on 16 Av, 5737 (1977).

Yehuda Leibusz Wajnsztejn

by Zeev Fisher

Yehuda Leibusz Wajnsztejn

Yehuda Leibusz Wajnsztejn was strongly connected to Zgierz and its people. There was no event in Jewish life in the city that was foreign to him. He was involved in communal life, and took interest and followed every that that took place in the Jewish community. He was always prepared to help his fellow.

He was one of those types of activists who related to their communal tasks with full seriousness and responsibility. In this manner, he earned the trust of the heads of the community and the organizations in our city. Thus, we see him as a faithful delegate to the communal council and various organizational committees, whether factional or financial, in our city. His work always excelled in activity and dedication.

[Page 117]

From his early childhood in the company of his friends and acquaintances, he absorbed dedication, good traits, boundless love for his nation, and deep longing for the complete redemption.

The life of Y. L. Wajnsztejn is bound with chapters of the history of the Zionist movement in Zgierz. His Zionist path began with "Agudat Hatzionim," in which the love for Zion was boundless. The first Chovevim (lovers of Zion) were: Reb Tovia Lypszyc, Isucher Szwarc, Moshel Ejger, the Richters, the Berliners, and others. Y. L. Wajnsztejn followed in their paths and immersed himself in Zionist activity in our city. He immediately found himself standing among their leadership.

He brought his national pride, energy, and warmth of spirit to the Revisionist movement. He headed that chapter in Zgierz until the outbreak of the war. He remained faithful to that movement throughout his life.

As one of the Holocaust survivors, Wajnsztejn found himself active in the Organization of Zgierz Natives immediately after its founding in Poland following the Second World War. He later was one of its first organizers in the State of Israel, and was one of the most active members of the committee of our organization. His activities touched on all areas of the lives of the Holocaust survivors, both materially and spiritually. His role on behalf of the Book of Zgierz was great.

His heart and home were open to anyone in need, and anyone in difficulty. He involved himself in concern for assistance in any endeavor. When we founded the charitable fund, he was not only one of the founders, but also one of the first donors of his own money.

The joy of life, friendship, and culture pulsated from is essence. He was especially diligent and faithful.

He died on Av 10, 5736 (August 6, 1976). His memory will be guarded for a blessing.

David Berger

by Zeev Fisher

David Berger

With the death of David Berger, a personality wonderful in its uniqueness and full of fine traits departed from the stage of our lives. His heart was sensitive to the vicissitudes of life and suffering of the individual and community. How strong was his national spine! He was a faithful and dedicated activist in all realms of Zionism. He also displayed great organizational talent.

He drew his desire toward communal activism from the upper compartments of the soul. His developed esthetic taste and good heart captivated us. A great deal of desire of life radiated from him. In his presence, we were willingly calmed from the difficulties of life, and we dreamed of a better future.

[Page 118]

There was something particularly personal in his way, full of spirit and simplicity in his manner of speaking. We always felt that there was a great man in front of us, great in knowledge and spiritual content.

He was an orator who exerted influence on his audience both through his levelheaded intellect and his sensitive heart. Therefore, his opinion was decisive in all committee meetings and conferences in the institutions of culture and charity in which he took place among the first of influence and activity.

His home, abundant with light and warmth, was open wide to all in need. I often found myself at his home, and always enjoyed the spirit of friendship that pervaded. He excelled in his love of his fellow, whether in the eyes of the of the public and society, or in matters of charity for the needy and the daily difficulties of those with bitter lives. He inherited his feelings toward the suffering of his fellow from his father, Reb Aharon Yosef of blessed memory, a communal activist, a man of society, and a man of friendship. Like the father, his son David loved benevolence and charity, and was similar to him in his pleasant mannerisms and calm relations with his fellow.

Activities in the realm of sport were very important to him. He was the vice chair of the Maccabee organization in Zgierz, and dedicated himself with full enthusiasm and energy to the necessary actions to instill a sporting spirit in the strata of the youth. The roots of his connection to Hassidism did not dry up even with his immersion in communal activity. Anyone who knew him from up close absorbed the echoes of his soul from his words.

From Zgierz to Tel Aviv, he bore the vision of destiny, and dedicated himself to his work on behalf of the public and the individual.

The heart does not want to be comforted over the death of a friend, a man with an upright heart and a straight path. This is how his image will remain for many years in the memories and hearts of his many friends and acquaintances. He died on Cheshvan 2, 5740 (October 23, 1979)[1].

———

Translator's footnote:

1.   The text has an error in the Hebrew year. The text says 5702, but from the secular date given, it is 5740. (an interchange of a *beit* with a final *mem*).

Fabian Grynberg-Green

by Zeev Fisher

Fabian Grynberg-Green

All natives of our city remember well the noble image of Fabian Grynberg. He was a Zgierzer with all the limbs of his body. He had a sense of community, and a grasp of popular attitudes. Everything that took place in the city was close to his heart. He took interest in the state of the Jews of the city ,and did a great deal on their behalf, especially during times of trouble and tribulation.

This double love for our city and its Jews was etched very deeply in his blood. More than once did I see him with his wide heart in his communal activities. Not many of the communal activists of his stature were so humane in their activities, and so publicly conscious in their day-to-day lives. In his work as a member of the city council, he never for a moment stopped seeing

[Page 119]

the actual person, for whom and on whose behalf all communal matters existed. The community and communal activity were seen in his eyes as service of the living individual, who suffers and aspires. He served the Jews of Zgierz with all his energy and talents. His primary aspiration was to help everyone suffering and downtrodden.

Grynberg was the living spirit in every communal and charitable institution of our city. It is no wonder that he earned great trust from all who knew him as a man of conscience, who suffers the pain of the individual and the community, and hastens to their aid.

In his conversations and writings, he hates empty rhetoric and loves simple, populist talk that creates moral obligation, the will and possibility of actualization, seriousness, and the burden of bearing the yoke.

Fabian Grynberg loved discussing his memories of Zgierz. In his memoirs that he published in the *Der Tog* daily that was published in the United States, he also portrayed events and people of our city. He did not pass over the simple folk, and portrayed them with appreciation, warmth, and great faithfulness of the heart.

When he arrived in America, he immediately entered the forefront of the many, variegated branches of communal activity. His personality was enchanting, his mannerisms and way of speaking were pleasant. His levelheadedness and culture forged his path in the front ranks of service.

G-d gave him an abundance of life and talent – and he did not deal with them selfishly. On the contrary, he spread them with his light hands and generous spirit, in accordance with "his heart and flesh shall sing."

He died on Av 3, 5744 (August 1, 1984). His memory will never depart from the hearts of his friends and admirers!

The Eminent Writer Yehuda Elberg
(Visiting old friends from among his fellow townsfolk)

When he spent time in Israel on the occasion of receiving the Prime Minister of Israel Prize, Elberg expressed his desire to meet friends on are organization committee.

The meeting, organized by Mrs. Halperin, took place in the home of our comrade Zeev Fisher. It was a modest, social, friendly meeting.

Comrade Fisher highlighted the important contribution of the Jews of Zgierz as writers and thinkers to the splendid culture of Polish Jewry, and especially to its rich literature, in two languages, until the Second World War.

The banner is for us, the Holocaust survivors, that even after the war of annihilation against us, writers arose who continued on and succeeded in producing exemplary creations worthy of praise. One of them is our friend, our fellow townsman, Yehuda Elberg. The prize awarded to him by the state is also an honor for us, the survivors of the community of Zgierz.

[Page 120]

I bless you – the host concluded – that you will continue going from strength to strength, and wish you success in all the works of your hands. May your literary creations enrich the spiritual treasures of our nation in Israel and the Diaspora.

Those gathered spent several hours in the warm, homey atmosphere as they discussed memories of the recent past, of a world that was and is no more…

Our Accolades
(Excerpts from his memoirs remaining in his legacy)

by Nathan-Nota Netritz of blessed memory

" – – – Anyone who spent time with our fellow townsman, Wolf Fisher, in preparing the Zgierz Yizkor Book, must feel the greatest respect to him. The term "respect" is possibly too weak. The term "esteem" may be more accurate, and is indeed what I feel toward Wolf Fisher[1].

"We owe him a great thank you and a hearty congratulations for his energetic work for in perpetuating our destroyed community. Leibish Weinstein and I traveled with him to Jerusalem on more than one occasion to rummage through the archives of the university and Yad Vashem. We were astounded by his tireless searching and rummaging, and his joy upon finding traces of Jewish life in our city.

"With boundless love, awe and respect, Wolf Fisher visited the son of the famous writer David Frischmann, a renowned fellow townsfolk, whose works are a treasure in Hebrew and Yiddish literature. Wolf Fisher preserved his memory in the Book of Zgierz.

"This is what Fisher also did with the great Hebrew poet Yaakov Cohen. He often visited him and discussed with him the events of our town, in which the great poet grew up and studied in the business school, and where his poetic abilities were awakened.

"Wolf Fisher's greatest efforts were crowed with success. We, the survivors of Zgierz Jews, appreciate his incessant efforts, and feel a great sense of gratitude toward him."

Translator's footnote:

1.   The first term, *derech eretz,* means respect. The second term, *farerung,* is a stronger term of respect.

[Page 121]

E. Events and Folklore

[Page 122]

Way of Life

by The editors

… For decades, our ancestors forged a modest, populist way of life. They were always whole in soul and calm in spirit. Indeed, the six workdays had a grey appearance, but in truth, the special essence of tradition, and orthodoxy was felt with vigilance for what took place in the "Tents of Shem"[1]. Even a verse of the *Chumash* or a rabbinical statement spread out and took on a form. Many bright minds would think well and discuss, as they toiled to clarify that which was hidden and obscure in life. The melody of the *Gemara* would pulsate extensively, and stick to you with parables and innuendoes. The commentators of the nation would produce a multitude of adages. Thus, the folklore that typifies the atmosphere of the city was formed.

Translator's footnote:

1.   A term for the halls of Torah study.

[Page 123]

Zgierz Folklore

by W. Fisher

Like many Jewish towns in Poland, Zgierz also had its own folklore, its own adages, anecdotes, wise sayings, and stories that are perhaps sometimes similar to the folklore of other towns. But they always have motifs that belong to the Zgierz way of life, and were a part of the reality of Jewish life in Zgierz.

The rich folklore of our city was perhaps not so rooted in traditions of the previous centuries and in old, half–forgotten places of life. However, it was a result of the various incarnations that took place over several generations of Jews in Zgierz, and were deeply rooted in the spirit of the Jews of Zgierz. It shone with the wisdom, human understanding, and fineness that Jewish life in Zgierz possessed.

The specific charm of a relatively young settlement with a way of life that stemmed from the events, experiences and personalities that influenced the unique spirit of the population – poor and rich, scholars, Hassidim, Maskilim, merchants and tradesmen – is present in the folklore of our city.

Jews from all over Russia, especially from White Russia, Lithuania, and Podolia, came to Zgierz. They arrived in waves since the first half of the 19th century until after the First World War. They brought with them their local modes of speech and pronunciation, as well as their local customs and local mannerisms. However, this did not prevent them from feeling like a homogenous community, in accordance with the ancient style of Jewish community. Jews in Zgierz felt and thought in a communal fashion.

[Page 124]

In time – and times were diverse, as there was no lack of bad and even worse, especially during the times of Russian rule – the Yiddish language became enriched. New slang words, expressions, anecdotes, wise witticisms, word plays, naive and sharp expressions were created. There were flashy jokes or comical pursuits, at times accompanied by laughing at oneself, and through that at everyone, of one's own and other's difficulties, mocking the realities, laughing at human intellect and human experiences. Until the present, no wisdom in the world can surpass the wit of a folks–word of folk humor.

Thus, the local folklore that was characteristic of Jewish Zgierz was created from all this. To this day, in a certain sense, it can serve as a key that opens the door for us to the entire dynamic of Jewish life in Zgierz, to recognize the spirit of the community and the individual from the simple folk and the exceptional personalities and characters.

In this way, that folklore helps to draw a fuller picture of the very active and lively Jewish settlement in Zgierz.

A great deal of Zgierz folklore can also be found on the pages of the Book of Zgierz, especially in the excerpts of the creations that we have included there from the renowned Zgierz writers, such as Yaakov Kahan (from his memoirs *Minetiv Chayay*, pp 189–203), and Pinchas Bizberg (from his book *Sabbath and Festival Jews*, pp. 235–255).

About Two Sabbath Gentiles
(Wawzyn and Peter the Great)

by Z. F.

The position of the Sabbath Gentile [Shabbos Goy] in the Jewish experience, and his importance is well–known, especially those who came from the shtetl. Indeed, Jews knew how to relate to him properly and even to honor him. For there is no Jewish life and no Jewish community without a Shabbos Goy, especially in

[Page 125]

the Diaspora lands of Eastern Europe in times gone by. Indeed, through the generations, he became an inseparable part of the Jewish experience, and a recognizable and accepted concept throughout the entire Jewish Diaspora.

The Shabbos Goy was not exactly that gentile from among the gentiles with whom we lived and with whom we came into daily business contact. In general, they were elderly men, most of whom belonged to the poorer strata of the city. They found some sort of small but regular support for their meager sustenance from the Sabbath work for the Jews. In truth, not every gentile with self–respect (and especially the Poles, who were known for their puffed–up sense of national pride) was prepared to enter a Jewish house and engage in housework that was not considered honorable in his eyes. Therefore, the Shabbos Goy was a unique personality: in character he was modest, he did not lord over his fellow, he bore his burden quietly and patiently. Especially, he was a gentile who was comfortable with the Jewish spirit. He did his work willingly and accepted the compensation with gratitude.

When the gentile man (or woman) entered a Jewish home, clean and polished in honor of the Sabbath, with the festive spirit of rest enveloping everything and everyone, with the sparkling candlesticks on the table covered with a white cloth, with the children washed and wearing clean garments, etc. – all these undoubtedly left a feeling of honorable awe and respect for the Jewish family. Often enough, they expressed their feelings with words of praise for the Jewish family and their customs.

We will now bring two descriptions of Shabbos Goyim who were known in the city, who were woven with the Jewish reality in the city, each in his time. Thus ,for example, Peter (Pietryk in Polish) is still remembered from our childhood years. He was tall, but already under the burden of old age. He limped with heavy steps and a unique rhythm. This gave us children in the vicinity of the old marketplace the impetus to wait for him and hum from behind him in accordance with the rhythm: *Etshe–Petshe, Gdze–Idzetshe…*

The poet and writer Yaakov Kahan mentions him with respect in his autobiography *Minetiv Chayay* [From the Paths of my Life]. We did not know the second gentile, Wawzyn, but we heard about him and his wit from the elders. The writer Pinchas Zelik Gliksman mentions him in his book *Tiferet Adam*. However, a more comprehensive description of Wawzyn the Shabbos Goy can be found on a single page that remained by chance from the letters of Yisrael Weinik, may G–d avenge his blood, under the title: the Elderly Rabbi, may the memory of the holy be blessed, and Wawzyn the Shabbos Goy.

We will now bring an excerpt from his letter, in his words (with light editing by Z. F.)

[Page 126]

The Elderly Rabbi, may the memory of the holy be blessed, the Sabbath Gentile Wawzyn (From the series: City Stories)

by Israel Weinik

– – Wawzyn was the former Shabbos Goy of our town. Everyone, young and old, knew Wawzyn, who used to walk around barefoot, with a strip around his pants, which drooped a bit lower than his belt. By nature, he was a very good gentile. He spoke Yiddish like any Jew in town, and was involved in all Jewish matters. He knew all the laws. Were it not for his gentile traits, such as shaving his folksy, yellow, constantly growing beard, sipping the "four cups" ten times a day, and various other trivialities, he could be a considered a perfect Jew.

It is superfluous to mention what type of position Wawzyn had in our Jewish life in our town. Wawzyn knew very well that the community could not function without him, and he sometimes perpetrated various pranks. The old rabbi, of blessed memory, would tell about his pranks with a loving smile on his lips, and praise for Wawzyn's smart mind.

For example, Wawzyn knew that at the sale of the chometz on the eve of Passover, after drinking the first cup, which had no connection to the Seder night, he should pay the rabbi a few additional copper tens, so that he would be able to get double after the holiday. Thus did he act from old times, even though the rabbi used to tell him:

"No, don't bother yourself, Wawzyn. Let our transaction be already, so long as I am certain about the act of acquisition…"

Wawzyn, however, would act innocently, as he quietly smiled and took the last coins from his tattered pockets, and put them on the table as business transaction.

Every Rosh Hashanah eve, Wawzyn would go around to the Jewish homes to collect donations. He would present himself to the Jews as the vice–beadle, and did not fail to mention his service for the benefit of the Jewish community and public. His services consisted of: placing the candles and lamps in the synagogue and the *Beis Midrash*, and bringing the heavy *Korban Mincha* siddur home for every elderly and important woman, wrapped in a kerchief, any time the *eruv* in the city was broken[1], which

[Page 127]

happened very often. Indeed, when was it not broken? His services to the Jewish public included lighting the Sabbath oven and other tasks that were part of his regular roles, and from which he lived very well. With the arrival of the Sabbath, one could even note a spark of the additional soul[2]…

Wawzyn lived not far from the *Beis Midrash*. Since grass grew near the rabbi's window, it was the best place for him to snatch a nap on Friday nights, until he sobered up from the emptied cups that he had received in the Jewish homes.

Once, in the midst of a warm, summer Friday night, the elderly rabbi, of blessed memory, suddenly exited his home very upset about what had happened a moment earlier: the lamp had suddenly gone out.

This upset the rabbi greatly. He was known as very diligent in his learning, and he loved very much to study on Friday nights until dawn. During those hours, he found some sort of special taste and contentment from his studies. It was calm in the town, and it was so good to delve deeply into G–d's Torah, but now the lamp had gone out, and the rabbi remained sitting in the darkness.

Upset, the rabbi went out on to the street, and not far from him, under the window, he noticed Wawzyn lying drunk on the grass. A restrained smile swept over the rabbi's face, as if he found a fresh idea in a difficult Talmudic passage. The hope arose in the rabbi's heart that he would soon again be able to sit at the table and enjoy his Friday night learning. Exhilarated, he approached the gentile, patted his shoulder, an called out:

"Wawzyn, would you like a drink?"

"Do I want a drink? A fine question." Wawzyn lifted himself off the ground and stood upright, moved his shaking limbs and barely dragged himself to the house of the rabbinical court. With an open mouth, he prepared to drink the promised cup.

The rabbi was happy with his idea. It was obvious that his plan had worked, and apparently preoccupied and partly upset, he began to pace over the room with shuffling steps , groping in the room, searching by memory for a cup for Wawzyn. Of course, the rabbi was very careful

[Page 128]

that his mouth should not, heaven forbid, mislead him and utter a word that could lead to a desecration of the Sabbath[3]...

Wawzyn's intelligent mind quickly understood that the elderly rabbi would not quickly find a glass in the dark. Wawzyn entered the kitchen to which he had been accustomed for years. He immediately found the matches and lit the lamp. His hands trembled impatiently waiting for the cup that the rabbi had promised him.

The rabbi was happy that his plan had succeeded, and that he had light. Without saying a word, he immediately gave him his cup, and wanted to return to the *Gemara*, but Wawzyn, already on his way out, blew at the lamp and put it out...

"Oh–woe, Oh–woe!" The rabbi remained standing despondent, and a heavy sigh rose up from his heart:

"What will be now, Wawzyn? Oh, what do we do now?"

"Nothing," Wawzyn answered, already standing on the other side of the door. "One lies down to sleep, and is free..."

He immediately lay down on the grass and fell fast asleep.

Translator's footnotes:

1.   The Sabbath boundary partition enabling one to carry on the Sabbath. See https://www.myjewishlearning.com/article/eruv/
2.   *Neshama Yeteira.* See https://www.chabad.org/kabbalah/article_cdo/aid/380636/jewish/The–Additional–Shabbat–Soul.htm
3.   One is not permitted to tell a gentile directly to perform work on the Sabbath. One can only hint.

Peter the Great
(From The Path of My Life)

by Yaakov Cohen

From when I first became self–aware, I knew him, Peter, the gatekeeper of the house. After some time I called him "Peter the Great" due to his height. Every Sabbath, he would come in the morning to take the candlesticks off the table, and in the winter also to light the oven in the dining room. In addition to the salary that was given to him on a weekday, he immediately received a glass of whiskey, which he emptied in one gulp, as well as a slice of challah, which he put into the deep pockets of his cloak. He was alone, without a family, and was already not particularly healthy. He lived in one of the rooms in the upper story in the left part of the courtyard. From there, the unfortunate man would come down time after time to the sound of the ringing of someone who was late in returning home. He would drag his feet, and pace his heavy steps in his tattered sandals. He would open the gate, and receive his money for drinks as a type of silent submission. He was honest in his purpose, working faithfully, and bearing his burden in silence. My father would praise him

[Page 129]

and say, "This gentile is truly G–d fearing." Indeed, in the afternoon hours one would hear a hollow sound coming up from the courtyard, like the humming of a prayer. One could see him sitting on the ground in his dwelling, reading from a book, and humming with a broken heart Psalms in Luther's translation.

————

In the Tipsiness of Purim

by Zeev Fisher

"One is required to get tipsy on Purim" (Megilla, page 7)

The Hassidim sat at the Purim party with the wealthy Hassid Reb Noach Mandelson. They drank in accordance with custom, and enjoyed all the good delicacies that were prepared on the table in ample fashion, as they discussed Hassidism and the issues of the day. Of course, the conversation was spiced with words of wit appropriate for the traditions of the holiday, and the spirits were high.

And when their hearts were merry with wine, Reb Noach turned to those gathered to ask them what type of drink they wanted, in order to fulfil that which is said: To do the will of each person[1]. Reb Noach specified, "Blessed be G–d, there are various types of wine, Okowita, strong liquor, and also sweet, and there is mead, and the house is full of beer – everyone will get what they want!" The master of the house ordered the servants, and every person got what they wanted.

Reb Yosef Sokolower also sat among the gathering. He was a veteran Hassid and a scholar, sharp in thinking and in speech. He knew his statements and various types of words. He sat and was silent. Reb Noach looked at him and said, "And you, Yosef, what will you drink?"

"I," responded Reb Yosef calmly, "I would prefer a "*Kalishekel sak, I mean karshensak*" (that is a cup of juice, cherry juice).

The learned Reb Yitzchak Eksztajn, who was used to teasing Reb Yosef, was already sufficiently tipsy. He called over to Reb Yosef:

"If that is the case, Yosef, why are you Sokolower? Would it not be better to call you Yosef Sak... It is fitting for your tastes."

Reb Yosef listened to Reb Yitzchak, and responded with a light smile:

"Indeed you are correct, Yitzchak. But we should also seek to change your name. Why do you have this Sztejn (stone)? Yitzchak, to you, Ek (tail in Yiddish), is more fitting)."

The gathering burst out in laughter. The Purim names were accepted by the community, and thus did they remain: Reb Yosef Sak, and Reb Yitzchak Ek. These names also transferred to their children...

(From *Hed Rachok* [Distant Echo])

Translator's footnote:

1.   Esther 1:8.

[Page 130]

Singing and Dancing
(From my childhood years in the Gerrer Shtibel)

by Zeev Ben–Shimon

I remember those years from the Hassidic past of our town, the years in *cheder* and in the Hassidic *shtibel*. The students and the Hassidim remain so clear and alive before my eyes. I feel them and see them singing and dancing with the pleasure of inner joy. The service of the Blessed G–d must be with joy, enthusiasm, and fervor, with full love and life. The joy bubbled up from deep faith in the Creator of the World, and from there, also the elevation of the soul, which did not allow for any sadness and certainly no despair.

Thus did they, the Hassidim of Zgierz, worship and study with fervor and fire in the hearts. The prayers, the words, and the devotions were conducted with great faith and belief, and with song, emanating from the depths of the soul. With the Hassidic melody that the Hassidim often hummed to themselves, one can hear the refined imprint of the soul of his mood and spirit, the spirit and sensation of a negation of materialism in his natural sense of understanding. In his spiritual world, however, a Sabbath and festival mood of exultation always pervaded. Song and dance ignited his soul, and was a source of spiritual delight and festive joy.

For us in the Gerrer Shtibel, on festivals between *Mincha* and *Maariv*, things lasted until deep in the evening. Around the long tables, adorned with white tablecloths, there were Hassidim, especially elderly ones, sitting bent over books and *Gemaras*, studying or simply delving into matters of the day. Others were involved in conversations, discussing memories of Hassidism of old, previous Rebbes. Their discussions were often accompanied by deep sighs. Mentioning things from times gone by made the hearts emotional... At the same time, the memories were so homey, joyous, and warm... Where do you find such Jews now? Where? Hassidim of old with great trust and faith... They mentioned names of sharp youth and grey elders whose Hassidism pervaded the entire town. They were fervent Hassidim and great scholars.

The shiny lamps shone everywhere with festive geniality and sweet hominess. Stripped of materialism, from day–to–day worries,

[Page 131]

people waited for the crowd that would soon arrive. As they waited, they hummed a Hassidic melody, a devotional tune of longing.

Then a joyous sound from outside came through, and the echo of homey singing approached. Youths were running noisily and warmly, with joy. They are coming… That meant that the crowd who had been invited that day for a drink at Reb Shlomo's, the Hassidic wealthy man, were already coming to the *shtibel* for *Maariv*. It was lively and warm.

They always arrived singing and dancing. The tall, rich–man's *streimels* were tilted to the sides, "Cossack style." The internal, warm and festive high spirits were accompanied with a joyous sound of the running youths. The dance actually began on the street, far from the synagogue. This time, the policeman walking around the city hall acted as if the singing did not bother him at all. He knew that it was a holiday for the Hebrews, and it was best to act indifferently to the noise, singing and dancing on the street. It will be worthwhile for him…

When the entire Hassidic gathering danced into the *shtibel* with a warm, Hassidic melody, those who were already seated around the table lifted their eyes from their books. They began to stand up, and closed their *Gemaras*. The thought that "You shall rejoice on your festival"[1] is a great commandment moved them, the good pious Jews and fervent Hassidim, from their places. They stood up and inserted themselves into the dance circle. The dancing became greater and heavier.

"Look from heaven, and see"[2] – the eyes overflowed with tears from great joy. Goodness shone from the eyes. It seemed as they were dancing and leaping with lightness, as if with wings. Soon Reb Yisrael Zaken jumped on the table, tipsy, dressed in his satin *kapote* with his silk *gartel*, and called out: "Holy sheep! Meeeh!" A proud chorus of children responded. The dance continued on again. Hand to hand, hand on shoulder, they went around the Torah reading table in a circle. Large, white, black, and blond beards fluttered around, with beaming faces and fervent glances. Reb Yisrael, above all, attempted to shout over the song to his calls to the children. His eyes caressed the children so goodly, so tenderly. He smiled and clapped his hands, and the dance blazed on further – a dance that was wholly in the service of the Creator. "Sing to Him, sing praises to Him, tell of His wonders"[3],

[Page 132]

the fervent song echoed throughout the entire Hassidic *shtibel*. It included the young and the elderly, joining everyone in the vibrant circle of song: *ay dy dy.. yadi, dadi, dy* – one tune merged into the next, and the clapping with the dancing feet was rhythmic to the beat.

Those who were originally standing at the side and clapping their hands became more involved in the circle, which became wider and broader. Yosel Baluter was already dancing, hand on the shoulder, with Chaim Yankel on the table. The enjoyment of the festival beamed from everyone's faces, and the light of the lamps sparkled over their dancing shoulders, covered in satin and silk.

The dance became sweeter, heartier, and more joyous. The hearts were jaunty and warm, and when the mouths opened, the feet began to move; and new Hassidim arrived, from the houses, from the street, and joined the circle. With hand placed on shoulder, and heart to heart, they joined together in the circle, with such goodness and enthusiasm, with devotion, to the point of the nullification of the soul. The room was full of joy. Everyone in the *shtibel* – children, adults, and grey elders – sang and danced and joined in a great, surging circle, carried away with the wordless Hassidic dance tune: *adi, dadi, adi dadi, adi dadi dy…* The warm song burst through the open windows to the outside. The tens of faces of the wives and the girls, who had come to watch the Hassidim rejoicing and dancing, were beaming with pride. They maintained themselves with modesty, a bit in the shadows, but clapping their hands, imbued with the joy of the Hassidim. The entire *shtibel* and the surrounding courtyard was full of song and dance, with light and joy.

The circle spun, swinging in the dance.
Already hopping with the elders, spinning in a garland.

They dance around, and around again:
It is such a dance for us, a dance with joy and good fortune.

Reb Tovia–Yosef jumps as high as the heavens in his dance,
Before him, within him, as if in the imagination dances Reb Mendel–Noach.

[Page 133]

Reb Leibel Lipa's with the white beard is also dancing already,
Hand in hand with the tall Elia Wirbel in the circle.

The lamp on the ceiling shakes, and the walls vibrate.
The children outside in their mother's hands also shake.

Adi dadi, adi dadi... adi dadi dy...

This dance would have continued on until late at night had not Reb Shalom Henech…

Reb Shalom Henech, was a cordial Jew, a Hassid who was fully gracious[4]. His biggest mitzvah was making sure the guests in the *shtibel* had a place to eat on Sabbaths and festivals with the Hassidic householders. At the peak of the heat of the dance, he would enter from the anteroom, sweating and tired after allocating the festival meals for the poor people. He broke through the dance circle, and called out to Yossel:

"Yossel, enough! The guests want to eat!"

He pushed his way to the reader's table, gave two bangs and called up."

"Let us pray, let us pray"

This was sufficient that the dance, which was at its peak, died down and stopped. Yossele's soft voice could be heard, singing "And those from afar will come," and the crowd responded, "and give You a crown of rulership."

Then, joyous calls to Yossele could be heard, "Well done, Yossel!"

Thus ended the festive dance, and soon Itche Meir's festive singing could be heard "*Barchu*"[5].

The congregation, still a bit tipsy from the fervent dance, began to sway prayerfully, and joined into the melody of the festival service.

————————

Translator's footnotes:

1.   Deuteronomy 16:4
2.   Isaiah 63:15.
3.   Psalms 105:2.

4.   Hassid and *chesed* (gracious) are based on the same root in Hebrew. There are lots of rhymes and allusions in this article, which are lost in translation.

5.   The opening word of the *Maariv* service on festivals.

[Page 134]

Let it be with a Weaver
(An old folk song from our region)

by W.F.

In memory of our dear, ardent mother Chana Fiszer the daughter of Reb Moshe Yaakov Kopel of blessed memory who always used to entertain us with a hearty folk song from her rich treasury of songs.

The lot of the Jewish handworker and board worker during the last decade of the 19th century until the First World War was difficult. They stood bent over the lathe from morning until evening, banging with their hands and feet toward the quota of a thousand for the meager bit of livelihood.

When the weaving guild, and shortly thereafter, the growing textile industry, took in more Jewish youth of the middle class, girls began to slowly abandon their romantic illusions and began to practically evaluate their situation, which was very often far from realizing the dreams of young girls. The following folk song circulated around at that time:

> O, Mommy, make me a wedding
> I want to be with a weaver already,
> But let us travel to the wedding
> In a coach with rubber wheels.
>
> He will travel in a top hat,
> I will travel in a hat
> And at our wedding
> Russian music will be played…

That folksong expressed the longing for a bit of good fortune, settling for the sad reality, as well as inciting fantasies for the delicate girly pride.

[Page 135]

Blossoms of Episodes and Folklore

Reb Nota Heinsdorf, the Kock Hasid in Zgierz, would tell:

When the Rebbe, Reb Bunim, may the memory of the holy be blessed, would pass through Zgierz in his time, he would say: "the evil inclination is dancing here on the roofs. It is necessary to bring it down and chase it away from here. It is clear to all that one does not chase the evil inclination away with sticks or stones, but rather with Hassidism and the study of Torah."

As a Kock Hassid, Reb Natan Nota of blessed memory worked together with his brother–in–law Reb Leibush Pozner of blessed memory in supporting the first Rebbe, the Tzadik Reb Shalom Tzvi HaKohen, may the memory of the holy be a blessing, in the arena of spiritual life of the community. The three of them traveled to Kock, where they absorbed Torah, Hassidism, and fear of Heaven, and disseminated them in the city, until the city of Zgierz became a proper scholarly–Hassidic city whose renown spread, especially due to the large, famous *Yeshiva* of the rabbi.

(from Rabbi Meir Sczaranski,may the memory of the holy be blessed.)

Honor of the Mother

I heard that from the time his father died, Rabbi Avrahamele of CiechanÃ³w, the son of Reb Refael of blessed memory, would travel every year to visit his mother, the righteous widow, the woman of valor Mrs. Roda of blessed memory in the city of Zgierz, to honor and gladded the soul of the widow. Every time, he made himself a new garment to wear I hear honor. Every time, all the rabbis and great ones around that city would gather together to greet him for the sake of his honor

(The Book of Hassidism by Reb Yitzchak Refael)

Matchmaking Issues

Reb Avraham Weicenfeld writes:

Blessed is G–d, Sunday of the Torah Portion of *Reeh*, 5718. Here in Krakow[1]

In honor of my wise friend – Shzch'h[2]

Your soul should be pleased to hear the news that I have entered into a marriage connection with the city of Zgierz, in Poland. The dowry is 1,000 R't[3]. The dear, intelligent, young woman guards the ways of the household[4], and the family is wealthy and Torah oriented, with some knowledge of the language of the country and the ways of the world. The additional benefit is that, immediately after the marriage, I have become a free person, and I do not need to depend on the table of others, for there is immediately a business to work at, which will provide all my needs, with the help of G–d. For this maiden

[Page 136]

is an orphaned from her father, and her aging mother has turned over her business to my bride, for she is the only daughter. Aside from this, she owns two houses that yield a great deal of rent annually. And I will cast my burdens upon G–d[5], for he has prepared this great step in my life.

Translator's footnotes:

1.   This would correspond to August 10, 1958 (or the preceding evening).
2.   There is a footnote in the text here, as follows: Shzch'h is the acronym for Shlomo Zalman Chaim Halberstam of Krakow, one of the Jewish scholars of the second half of the 19th century.
3.   There is a footnote in the text here, as follows: Ruble Taler.
4.   From Proverbs 31:27.
5.   From Psalms 55:22.

"The Agreement" of the Holy Community of Zgierz for the Coronation of Nikolai II as the Czar of Russia

One day during the 1890s, the administrators of the community of Zgierz were astounded that the representative of the kingdom in the local city council told them that in three days, they must arrange a festive service in the synagogue on the occasion of the coronation of his majesty Nikolai Alexandrovich as the Czar of Russia and Poland, which was taking place that day in the capital of Petersburg.

All the Jews of the community were obligated to participate in the festive service, and the rabbi was to deliver a sermon on the importance of this event to the Jews as well. The clergy, cantor, and administrators must also appear. Representatives of the kingdom, the city council, and the police would be in attendance.

Turmoil broke out in the communal council, for the rabbi was sick in bed, and his deputy, Reb Moshel the rabbinical judge was, albeit a scholar, a straightforward man who was not involved at all in worldly matters. The city administrators consulted as to how to direct Reb Moshel to appear at this important event, but the timeframe was tight, and the command could not be revoked. The law of the land is the law.

The sextons went out quickly to all the houses of worship to announce and inform that in three days, at 10:00 a.m., a festive prayer service for the wellbeing of the new Czar would take place in the synagogue, and the entire community was asked to attend. The gallery would also be open for women.

The city was simmering, and everyone prepared for the great day. There was certainly room to ask, why all this preparation? What is the character of the new Czar? Would he not continue, heaven forbid, in the ways of his father, a well–known anti–Semite? Will he be benevolent or harsh?

The number of people asking and wondering was indeed not small. Nevertheless, when the designated day came, the synagogue, that had been cleaned and polished, was full to the brim. All the chandeliers and candles were lit. Flags of the kingdom were here and there, and a festive atmosphere pervaded through the entire building.

The important people of the city were already on the stage. The police chief and his entourage were there in uniform, as well as Jurczenko the gendarme in his full stature and splendor. On the other hand, the rabbinical judge Reb Moshel was in his place, with his long, white beard, streimel on his head, and tallis over his thin shoulders. Reb Beinush the cantor looked tense, as if just before Kol Nidre (to differentiate). The members of the choir were standing, prepared.

[Page 137]

The head of the community gave the sign to the beadle, who quieted the congregation by banging on the reader's table. Silence pervade in the synagogue, and all eyes turned to the speaker. The head of the community and his administrators looked on with bated breath.

Reb Moshel placed his palm on his face and stroked his beard, as if delving deeply into a difficult section of Gemara. He then began, with the sing–song Talmudic melody.

"Behold it is known to everyone that the 'elder' died, may it not befall us. So, if he died – he died. And we, as is our custom, recite the blessing, Blessed is the True Judge… However, it is impossible to leave a country without a leader, and of course the country requires a Czar, so that the awe of the government will be upon us, as our sages of blessed memory have stated: You must pray for the wellbeing of the government, for were it not for its fear, etc.[1] Therefore, we now require a new Czar, and they, in the house of government, desire that we Jews of the holy community of Zgierz agree to the new Czar. Therefore, we give our assent, and we all state: we agree, we agree, we agree…"

Then, the lions voice of the cantor and the congregation sounded loudly:

"He Who gives salvation to Kings…"[2]

The entire congregation rose and stood in silence.

The representatives of the government did not leave their places until they warmly shook the hand of Reb Moshel the rabbinical judge in gratitude.

The head of the community breathed a sigh of relief, and there was a smile of satisfaction on his face.

Translator's footnotes:

1. Pirkei Avot 3:2. The rest of the statement is: everyone would swallow his fellow alive.
2. The opening words of the prayer for the government.

We Were Slaves
(From his book "To a Son – and a Daughter")

Then we were slaves to Pharaoh in Egypt
And we are now slaves seven times over.
For about two thousand years we have been eating the bread of affliction
Exiled from country to country, from host to host.
Persecuted incessantly, a life of shame and if only,
Begging for mercy from nations, in the stubble of the enemy and the cruel ones,
Every enemy of Israel became a head and commander.

[Page 138]

Hitler also became a leader and ruler of the gangs,
In the land of Germany, the enlightened nation, with philosophy,
By calling out: "Destruction to Israel, Germany rise up!"…
The nation of Kant found – "the clear understanding"…
To the life of Germany! To the life of Hitler! Let us drink the potion,
There will be no more citizen of Mosaic persuasion, he is strange and foreign,
A corrupt root of Israel, Marxians, the yeast of the dough,
Their hand is in everything, and their trap is spread throughout the entire world;
For Germany is revenge and recompence, for the Jews, horror and the fire pan
The blood of Israel shall flow from the outstretched sword!

– – – – – – – – – This happened in the 20th century, this was Germany in which they placed their trust,
Did they not kill you? Did you not learn your lesson yet? –

We and our grandchildren will be slaves forever
If we do not build our home in the Land of the forefathers!

Eve of Passover, 5693 (1933)

Janis
(Memories from my *Yeshiva* years)

by W. Fisher

In memory of our cordial sister Bina, may G–d avenge her blood, the daughter of Reb Shimon Fiszer of blessed memory, who so avidly read the novels and story books that I would bring her from Janis.

He would come to us in the city twice a year, always between the vacation periods. Once was between Purim and Passover when one could already hear the recognizable sound of the matzo bakeries on the Jewish street. From there, the Passover aroma of freshly baked matzos in the mild sweet spring

[Page 139]

breezes carried a melody from Song of Songs over the entire city[1]. Janis would come for the second time during the pleasant days of the month of Elul, when the skies looked upon us with such gentle blue sadness, and the trees already began to turn carmine, gold and saffron for the upcoming High Holy Days.

When the tall, round, covered wagon rolled into the courtyard of the *Beis Midrash*, it remained standing there for a while. The two Jews on the coachbox were bickering over something, perhaps over the income from the journey, and perhaps over the next trip onward. This lasted only for a short while. Soon, the wagon driver descended from the coachbox. He was a husky Jew with a tanned face, ending with a short, black beard. He took the hand of the second, very elderly Jew, and helped him descend from the wagon.

"Janis!" a lad called out from the window, "Janis has arrived."

The call echoed through the *Beis Midrash*, and the *Gemara* tunes were interrupted for a while. A strange excitement could be sensed, and a happy smile came over the faces of some of the lads. Before long, it spread over the entire Jewish street, through the *cheders*, *Yeshivas*, and Hassidic *shtibels*, until the news reached the old city:

"Janis has arrived…"

After placing the trough before the horses, he wagon driver himself had something to eat in the nearby tavern of Meirl Kalski. First, he "put down" a reasonable sized mug of Macewski's beer while his passenger unloaded his load – is G–d not still a father[2]… for the spicy aroma of the freshly broiled livers on the grill strongly ignited his wagon–driver's appetite.

In the meantime, a group of lads came out courtyard and immediately began to help the bookseller unload the heavy load of books from the wagon and bring them into the *Beis Midrash*. The sack carriers were actually quite happy with their run and with the tumult that they had created, for what would he himself have done alone with the heavy load, were it not for their energy? Then he, like a respected merchant, quickly entered into his customary role

[Page 140]

as a bookseller. He was strict to not allow any book to leave his hand, with the suspicion as people might come there to rip him off. He knew that the lads do not consider it a sin to take out a book. Therefore he would grab it from their hands and shout:

"Wait, do not grab… not this sack, but only from the sack that you book before…"

For the most part, he trembled in front of the sack that was the lightest to move, and from which he would not know how many books had "flown away." Therefore, Janis was uncomfortable, and his small, reddish eyes began to dart back and forth with anger and impatience. He did not know where to go first, whether to remain here at the unloading of the wagon, or should he hurry to the *Beis Midrash*, where the merchandise was laying unguarded at the time. Therefore, he expressed his anger with his hoarse, nasal voice, but the group was barely affected by his shouting and they did their work with great zest.

Finally, the entire load was inside, and Janis had his belongings under his control, which calmed him somewhat. Soon, he found an older lad who brought him a cup of coffee from the nearby mikva attendant. Janis took a bit of food out of his handbag to satisfy his hunger.

Around *Mincha*–time, Janis talked to two older lads, whom he knew from his prior visits, to ask them to assist him lay out the merchandise on the table after *Maariv*, in the order that he, Janis, will show them. As always, this was done without payment, as the enterprise was beneficial for both sides.

Janis' Organized Book Table

Both lads were from among the good learners of the city. In the *Beis Midrash*, it was said about them that they also studied other languages and had impressive knowledge of secular books as well. They looked among Janis' books for those that could not be found by other sack–carriers. For them, assisting Janis was a golden opportunity to obtain many of the books that they were looking for, and to read them without paying even a groszy. It was also worthwhile for Janis, for he was going to remain there for four or five days, and they helped him

[Page 141]

lay out the books on the table in good order, as Janis instructed them. He knew how important a well–organized book table was for business, for one would be able to find the books them wanted.

In the morning, the finely ordered table dazzled the eyes. The gorgeous colors that beautified the long table caught the eye. The table was organized with various colored book covers, and looked as if it was decked with a multi–colored mosaic. The eye was treated with the collection of colors. When the tall, semicircular windows caught the sun rays and they shined cheerfully on the table, it literally blinded the eye. Even the white beams above appeared shiny from the brightness of the colors, and smiled lovingly at the people:

"Indeed, Janis has come…"

This does not imply that Janis was the only itinerant bookseller who used to visit our city and bring spiritual food for the thirsty souls of young lads. On the contrary, not a month went by when such a bookseller did not appear Zgierz, placing on the table of the Hassidic *shtibel* or the *Beis Midrash* the bit of wares that he brought in a flashy suitcase. However, the little bit of merchandise from the other book sellers consisted primarily of Hassidic books from Rebbes. They were rabbis and regular booksellers who we already knew almost from the outside. We, children and older lads, students of the *Yeshivos*, *shtibels* and *Beis Midrashes*, were thirsty for a fresh book, which would clarify for us other matters that are outside the four ells of halacha; matters about which we heard unclear echoes from afar, the meaning of which we had meager knowledge. Those sack carries knew our city very well and knew that they had a good market for their merchandise. Zgierz had a larger number of youth thirsty for knowledge than other towns. Those youth who, like everyone, studied in the *Yeshivas* and *Beis Midrashes*, covertly sought a new book, which they could not find from the usual sack carriers. The striving for knowledge was also felt by the learners in the Hassidic *shtibels*. In truth, we knew that we

[Page 142]

could find such books in the city library, but few had the boldness to open the door of the library, which so greatly charmed us. We knew that we could find there a great collection of books in Yiddish, Hebrew, German, and Russian, but in those days, a *Beis Midrash* lad was not permitted to enter such a room, in which pictures of the non–religious, the Zionist and Socialists, were hanging, all with bare heads. If the *Rosh Yeshiva* or principal had found out about this, he would have a reckoning with such a lad.

Therefore, the only source from which we could derive the bit of knowledge was from the sack carriers who brought us a drink of "living waters" from time to time. This refreshed the languid souls that were so craving to hear a story, to read about the wonderful things that are taking place in the world, far from the town.

The Interesting Stories that we Devoured

For a long time, we followed the interesting stories, such as about Reb Yosef the unchaste, who took the sword from the Angel of Death, but was convinced to return it… Or the wonderful story about the Maharal, who created the Golem and placed the ineffable name of G–d within it, turning it into a mighty defender of Jews. We used to devour the stories about the red Jews who were found on the other side of the Sambatyon[3], the river tossing up stones all week, thereby calming the steps of the enemies. The stories about the wonders performed by the wonder workers, such as the Shpoiler Zeide[4] and other such people, captivated us. Later, we told them over among groups of friends who gathered in the Hassidic *shtibel*, in the dark hours of the Sabbath, at the time of the Third Sabbath meal [shalosh seudos], when the people around the table had finished satisfying themselves with their morsel, and the tune of Michael–Mendel's *Bnei Heichala*[5] was being sung in the darkness. Ah, we inserted our stories in the mysterious mood of those hours, when we were overtaken with the feeling of someone who sees, but is not seen…

We were not able to obtain from every bookseller the story books, with the woven stories, that would tell us about adventures of great

[Page 143]

people, wonderful events, which would enrich our fantasies and our desire for the wide, unknown, world.

It was completely different with Janis. His colorful table with books was incomparably richer than the others. Unlike the others, he did not come for one day. He would remain with us for at least five or six days, and the negotiations between us learners and him regarding a kopek would take place the entire time, but eventually we reached and agreement. For a "sixer" one could get a book from him to read, and then return it. There were also story books that one could get for no more than two kopeks to read. If one did not have the 15 kopeks that he demanded as a guarantee, it was sufficient to leave one's *gartel* with him, and which *Beis Midrash* lad did not have a *gartel*?! Of course, he recognized us all from previous years.

The fact that he always came during the vacation period, when the constantly cross rebbe was somewhat milder to the students, and the discipline was weaker helped the enterprise. It was easier to find a bit of time to go to a corner of the courtyard and covertly read a book or two.

Our Childlike Glances Behind the Partition [6]

Years and decades have already passed since those days when Janis used to come to us with his colorfully arranged book table. So many stormy and bloody experiences have taken place in my life during that time. Many personalities, beloved and august, have been etched in my memory during that time. Many became fuzzy and then arose again. However, throughout the entire time, the image of Janis the bookseller remained alive before my eyes, with a latent shine emanating from his tanned face, shining over the title pages of his books, from the books on morality and Hassidic stories, which took a place of honor on the table together with the prayer books, the large ones from the Ar'i and Rabbi Yaakov Emden, and the small pocket prayer books, *megillot*, books of Psalms, Selichot books, books of petitions; as well as the collections of letters and books of fate, resting in the shadows, as well as all the other touching stories that so teased our childhood fantasies.

[Page 144]

For all my life, I loved books, important, old and new, well–bound and weakly bound, literary and scientific, in which all the various problems of life are dealt with, matters of great importance in the world. However, I have never forgotten the enchanting curiosity and great influence that the soft–cover story books on Janis' book table had upon me, which I read with such suspense, and which filled my heart with indescribable longing.

In truth, for the most part, there were books for primitive readers, stories for yearning boys and girls with dreams about princes and princesses, about love and revenge, about poor orphans, about robbers and convicts. In those times, however, those were lofty and strong themes. they developed our reading and thinking skills to a large degree, and strengthened our humanistic opposition to injustice and our appreciation of human rights.

Reminiscences and memories from those wonderful stories go through my mind, such as: "The Story of Three Brothers," "Sanctification of the Divine Name by a Righteous Convert," "A Friday Night in the Forest," as well as the jolly stories of Simcha Plachta, Hershele Ostrolopoler, Efrim Greidiker[7] and Motke Chabad[8]. In those books, we laughed and made a racket with fantasy life somewhere in the wide world, and with the wit and wisdom of Jewish folklore. A desire to read many more of those stories remained in our hearts, until we became more mature and began to take interest in the literature of our classicists, with new books from Yiddish, Hebrew, and world literature.

In the *Beis Midrash*, among the regular learners, sharp minds and diligent ones, there were also those who desired to catch a glance of that which takes place behind the partition[6]. For them, Janis had a special sack of completely different books, those such as "The Book of the Covenant," "Pathways of the World," and others, even "Ahavat Zion" by Abraham Mapu[9]. To those books, which Janis hid from an evil eye, Yoel Linecki's "The Polish Boy" also belonged[10], which we obtained a bit later, and which captivated us.

The negotiations surrounding those books always took place in the late afternoon hours or after the *Maariv* service, when the crowd had already dispersed. It was seldom within our power to purchase those books, despite the fact that Janis

[Page 145]

did not ask for a high price for them. For the most part, we borrowed a few copies from him to read, and Janis' book thereby passed form hand to hand. Janis had the desired reading material for each of the youths.

– – – For long years, I, along with many other Zgierz lads, who later became regular readers in the secular library, had feelings of gratitude for Janis, who gave us our first knowledge of books, and thereby made our lives more interesting, poignant, and exciting, like the lives of the heroes in their respective books.

Translator's footnotes:

1.   Song of Songs is associated with Passover.
2.   A cryptic statement, probably referring to the fact that he is a Christian.
3.   See https://en.wikipedia.org/wiki/Sambation
4.   See   https://www.encyclopedia.com/religion/encyclopedias–almanacs–transcripts–and–maps/aryeh–leib– shpola
5.   A hymn sung a *Shalosh Seudos*.

6.   The term here is *pargod* – which refers to the mystical partition between G–d and the rest of the celestial realm – i.e. between the unknowable and the knowable.

7.   See https://en.wikipedia.org/wiki/Hershel_of_Ostropol and http://www.museumoffamilyhistory.com/yt/lex/G/greidiker–efrim.htm

8.   See http://www.museumoffamilyhistory.com/yt/lex/M/motke–chabad.htm

9.   See https://en.wikipedia.org/wiki/Abraham_Mapu

10.   See https://en.wikipedia.org/wiki/Yitzkhok_Yoel_Linetzky

A Wise Person is Better than a Prophet

by Shimon Kantz

Someone gave over a sum of money to Rabbi Mendel Weksler as a dowry for his daughter. Reb Mendel was a student of the Gaon Rabbi Avraham of Sochaczew. When his son, the Admor Rabbi Shmuel, set up his own *Beis Midrash* and Yeshiva, he appointed Rabbi Mendel Weksler as the head. Reb Mendel was also the head of the Beis Meir Yeshiva of Krakow. His noble appearance gave him a certain charm. He gave off the impression that he was someone who was very distant from all life wisdom. He was a man of the spirit, with fine character traits. Once, when he came home, his wife was waiting for him. She gave over the money, and he put it in the upper pocket of his coat.

A bit later, he noticed that the money was not there. The members of the household were distraught over this, but Reb Mendel was completely quiet, and expressed his faith that the money would be returned to him.

He immediately sent for a certain young man who was a frequent visitor to his house, and ordered him to return the stolen money.

At first, the young man denied this, but he finally admitted and returned the entire sum of money to the Rosh Yeshiva. This was a wonder to us.

Rabbi Mendel Weksler said to him: "I am not a prophet or son of a prophet, and I did not do this via a portent, but rather through logic."

To the amazement of all those listening, he continued and explained: "I remember that young man from when he was a lad, and he studied the Talmudic discussion of the four types of custodians in the Tractate of Bava Metzia[1]. That lad asked a question: 'How can they impose an oath on the custodian, given that he does not have the stolen goods?

[Page 146]

Perhaps the custodian earlier gave the stolen goods over to another person, so during the time of the oath, the stolen goods were not in his hands, and he did not take a false oath. In any case, he is a thief.' At that point, I had the thought that he would be a thief.

Then, his listeners understood that a wise person is better than a prophet.

*

Rabbi Mendel Weksler of blessed memory served in a holy position in the city of Krakow, as the head of the Beis Meir Yeshiva. His generous traits were as large as his scholarship. I learned a great deal of Talmud and its commentaries from him. The great principle that he taught us from the doctrine of Hassidism remains with me to this day: There is no desire as the desire of wisdom.

His image stands before my eyes: Short, with a higher than average forehead, a small beard, and a facial appearance that expressed decisiveness and certainty. Love, refinement of the soul, warmth, his essence, delight, and interest radiated from his face to us, his students. His interest was above all, for he was graced with a rare trait of broad view and exacting perception. He knew how to delve into the depth of every detail, while simultaneously grasping the whole with a general view. Therefore, his personality was so radiant, rich, and variegated, imbuing loving warmth onto his students. This is what bound him to us. It seems to be the same with the older people with whom he came into contact. Everyone revered his wonderful memory, both in Torah and in the matters of the world.

To this day, I regard him as the richest soul of any that I got to know during my studies. Above all, his Torah was only one of the components of his personality. Nobility of the soul and emotion testified to the greatness of this exceptional man. His natural modesty testified to the purity of his soul. Therefore, all of his students esteemed, revered, appreciated, and loved him.

Translator's footnote:

1.   Some background on the four custodians:
https://www.chabad.org/therebbe/article_cdo/aid/92294/jewish/Mishpatim–Four–Custodians.htm

About Everything and Somebody – In the Holy Tongue – A Fine Yiddish…

by Avraham Ch. Shapira

Blessed be G–d, Friday, eve of the Sabbath, 5631 (1871), Zgierz

In the honor of my dear son, beloved as my own soul, prominent and well–rounded, G–d fearing, a Hassid, and intelligent, Rabbi Rephael Yaakov, may his light shine; and his modest, intelligent, praiseworthy wife, may she live; and to my dear, pleasant grandchildren may the live Shalom and Yesha, all good things.

Your precious letter arrived this week, and I was very happy to hear of your health, and that of your proud family – –. Regarding the marriage suggestion [*shidduch*] in Komarno, I do not know what to answer the *shadchan*, for I do not know the man

[Page 147]

and his household, and especially his son. Regarding this, I ask you to investigate and inquire about the matter, and especially about his son. Since it is close to you, I am alerting you that you should be able to investigate that matter. You asked me to tell you about[1] men's clothing – as it seems now, three or four inches shorter, the suit is cut as it was before, with one Polish cut in the rear. The peyos are cut. And for women – their own hair or deep caps. Anything more, I do not know. Hersh Ber Szwarc was with me. He said that Shimon Waldenberg came and told him that he must move[2], an he wants to rent a dwelling from him. I do not know what to tell him. I told him that you will be hear after Yom Tov. I do not believe that he will return the 15 rubles to you. He also told me about the fathoms of Dobre, which is now 50–200 Berkne and 100 Dembowa, 50 Kiwena[3].[4] To this, write an answer by return mail as to what to do. I did not receive a response to the letter. There is nothing new. Your father sends you greetings and hopes for your success. He blesses you with the blessings of the Passover festival, to protect you, so that you may rejoice with your family and all who are with you as you see fit. Yosef Tzvi Kahana Szapiro

A.Ch."Sh

(A copy of a letter from my grandfather Reb Yosef Tzvi, may the memory of the holy be blessed, Kahana Szpira of Zgierz)

Translator's footnotes:

1. Here, the letter switches from Hebrew to Yiddish – hence the title.
2. Wording of this phrase is very unclear.
3. Here, the article switches back to Hebrew.
4. These are likely local terms for types of cloth. I could not identify them in a Polish or Yiddish dictionary, but they appear to be based on Polish names or places.

Capital and Livelihood

by A Ch " Sh.

My grandfather, Reb Yosef Hirsh of blessed memory, once complained to the Rebbe, Rabbi Henech of Aleksander, that he has no livelihood. The Rebbe told him, "Reb Yosef Hirsh, they say about you that you once earned a hundred thousand rubles from one business transaction, and you say you have no livelihood?" My grandfather answered, "It is indeed true, but the small change for daily livelihood is not always available…"

Connected to the answer, the Rebbe once said at his Sabbath table celebration:

"I once heard from a pedigreed Kohen that if one earns a great deal of money at one time, this does not mean that one has a livelihood, but only that one's capital has increased… From this we learn that we must do a great deal of mitzvot and good deeds, not only for the reward of daily livelihood here, but primarily so that our capital there (i.e. in the World To Come) will be greater."

(heard from Reb Avraham Yitzchak Szapiro of blessed memory)

[Page 148]

Three I Knew

by Z. Fisher

Every city has its crazies (an old proverb)

Chaskel the Fool

Uncannily, I will present to you the characters of the people who went about with wild shabbiness, with their craziness. Their lives, their silences, speaking, and deportment were incomprehensible to us. Often, we would think that they were carrying something sinister and dark within themselves. However, this thought evoked great pain within us. The disguise endlessly wove images of lost souls with sad experiences. They were not foreign to their surroundings, even in their complete shabbiness. On the contrary, they were moving shadows of the Jewish street, of the city. No, not shadows, but veritable human beings, unfortunate people.

There were three city fools whom we remember from our childhood. My childhood fear recalls the fool Chaskel, a man of average height and wide shoulders with a black, disheveled beard. He was poor, but whole and clean. His face was always tied with a red kerchief tied over a velvet hat. His eyes burned with a black fire, like a hungry wolf.

Through his black–bearded face, one could barely see his mouth, from which one always could hear a wild roar, like a wounded lion. The bit of face that could barely be seen through the beard and kerchief was twisted from tribulations. It was hard to know whether this was from constant tooth pain, or whether he was badly pained over the fate of a person, a type of melancholy... In fact, he did not stop making strange grimaces that instilled fear. Even though he never went through the street without his tallis bag under his arm, the children and young wives ran from the sidewalk when they encountered him. Nobody

[Page 149]

understood what the grimaces and roars from that bearded, taciturn man meant. Therefore, imaginations ran free regarding his experiences.

In truth, Chaskel was not a true Zgierzer, for he came to us from a nearby town. However, since his daughter worked as a servant for a Zgierzer household, he also had the privilege of being considered one of our own city fools.

The Fool Moshe

After Chaskel, I recall the crazy Moshe. We rarely saw him on the street. His time was in the summer, especially on the very hot days... He was an irritable person. He would always shout and scold, always with harsh complaints about the world. However, it was hard to understand what he wanted from the world, and what he meant.

We would especially hear him in the cemetery on Tisha B'Av, when he would wander among the gravestones, shout and threaten with his fist toward heaven, "They will slaughter me... will shoot me... they will hang me... and finally, I will be taken to the world..."

This was repeated every Tisha B'Av. His heartrending shouts resonated over the entire cemetery. Jews, righteous women, tried to calm him. However, he did not stop shouting with a shrieking voice for hours.

Yankel the Fool

Yankel came to our city after the First World War and remained with us. He had nobody here. He was alone, a stranger. People said that he had come from central Russia, where they had enough of his craziness, and sent him back to Poland. They also said that he came from a fine home, but one could not get from him any details of his past or previous life.

He was firmly built, and middle aged. His dark face with an intelligent appearance was covered with a short, black, prickly beard. He seldom raised his eyes. His head was always tilted toward the ground, as if he wished to peer into the depths, filled with secrets.

He would pace over the long street for entire days and beg for a groszy from

[Page 150]

the passers–by. Summer and winter, he wore a fur hat on his head, and a worn–out, long, heavy winter coat. The large, deep pockets were stuffed with spoons and pots. Tin kettles hung from around his belt, in which he cooked the collected products. He would cook in a corner of a Jewish courtyard and then share the food with the poor people in the poorhouse.

One can tell various anecdotes and stories about the crazy Yankele, which played out in grotesque, comical situations not only regarding Yankel, but also regarding those who laughed at him.

Among others, it was also told about how a wealthy, Hassidic lad once saw Yankel take a groszy from a gentile on the Sabbath. The lad lectured him, "Yankel, you take money with your hands on the Sabbath?"

"What are you talking about?" Yankel answered him with a question, "A groszy is money according to you? Are you the same beggar as I am…"

This repeated itself another time. Again, they saw how he took money in his hands on the Sabbath, and told him that this is a sin. He again answered, "This, Polish groszy, is money for me… is also a sin for me…"

Yankele never bothered anybody. Everyone would move out of the way, and therefore, he would always go in the middle of the street. He seldom talked. Only if someone asked him something, would he raise his head, look at the questioner with his dark, calm, perceptive eyes, and answer with a joke or a witticism.

One would not always laugh at his witticisms. Often, his jokes would leave one with a feeling of sadness, like a scorn on the heart.

Yankel fit in with the long street, for he was a living part of that street for many years. People got used to his witticisms and craziness.

Yankele was one of the first victims when the Germans occupied our town during the Second World War. He disappeared from the long street, and he was never seen again.

[Page 151]

Three I Knew

by Moshe Tzvi Eiger
(From his booklet "To a Son – and Daughter)

To the rabbi of Zgierz

Vanity of vanities says Kohelet[1] –
There is no benefit of wisdom over folly
Together the wise man, the fool, as well as the animal –
It is the same to the eye, and the same thing happens to them.

We are still occupied with this law
And there are many opinions and disputes among the halachic decisors:
There are those who say – and I shall rejoice with joy –
For the folly of the fool is better than wisdom.
For the more wisdom the more vexation;
And pain and bitterness – with understanding and knowledge.
The wise when they act turn toward the fool
And in reality, there is no person wiser than the fools…

And some say: there is some[2] wisdom for the fool
For is not the folly of the wise better than the wisdom of the fool.
Silliness rests upon the head of the fools
And loftiness and proper spirit for the person of the spirit.

The satisfaction of the wise for one hour
Is better than all the enjoyments of the fool. For he has the contentment.

And the wise say: To everything there is a time,
And if you cannot bear wisdom alone,
Say to folly: Behold you are my sister!
For wisdom is a bit better than folly.
I myself tend to the path
That the folly of the wise is better than the wisdom of the fool;
And since some say one way, and others say the other –
I ask of his honor to decide upon the law…

Intermediate days of Sukkot, 5692 (1931)[3]

Translator's footnotes:

1. Kohelet (Ecclesiastes) 1:2. The next few lines are paraphrases of various statements from Kohelet.
2. The word used is obscure, and the translation of 'there is some' is a conjecture.
3. Kohelet is read in the synagogue on the Intermediate Sabbath of Sukkot.

[Page 152]

The Jews of Zgierz

by The Editorial Committee

– – The common folk, as well as praiseworthy, dear people, families who struck deep roots in Jewish tradition, and whose character is – modesty, proper behavior between man and G–d, and no less between man and his fellow. They were quiet and modest during their lives, they occupied themselves with various types of livelihood, which encompassed the needs of their lives during those times. They loved the movements, and had a joy of life even though their livelihoods were as difficult as the splitting of the Red Sea. When they had a bit of rest from their labor and toil, they would sing with a full heart and proper emotion, "My soul blesses … You have garbed Yourself in splendor and glory."[1] When they recited "The Heavens tell"[2], their intention was that sky, the one above their heads.

They were G–d fearing and devoted to the traditions of their ancestors, but also happy with their lot in the life of this world. They were not overcome by oppression, and did not know the taste of despair. Even though they were prepared to groan at all times, the Jews of Zgierz still had happy faces. A taut thread of grace and pleasantness was upon the face of the Jews of Zgierz, even though they were almost always immersed in the tribulations of the exile.

The Jews of Zgierz encompassed all the various hues of Polish Jewry. The order of life of Polish Jewry was in the city, as well as the spiritual stance of Polish Jewry, with all its ways, ideas, and imaginations, all images of the spirit, of the human spirit and the spirit of Israel, as well as in the winds blowing with the understanding of the times.

Indeed, the way of life of the Jews of Zgierz was similar to that of other cities. All Israel are brothers. Nevertheless, brothers differ from each other in appearance, ideas, and nature. Even more so, Jewish communities differ from each other in ways of life and paths of the spirit. Every community has its unique extra soul[3]. It is impossible to explain everything, but neither are we exempt from explaining a little of the recognizable signs and uniqueness of the community and its members, with their personalities and images.

In truth, the internal essence of a person is one of the mysteries given over to the heart. Anyone who examines it in a simple way errs in practicality or with exaggeration, with switching important matters with unimportant ones, or by misrepresenting the essence of the matter. Nevertheless, we have permission to state that they city was beloved by its Jewish residents despite the bundles of tribulations that they endured there. Life there was bitter, the surroundings were inimical, there were decrees and persecutions, but the Jewishness was sweet. Livelihoods were difficult, but Torah flourished. The Jews fulfilled the commandments there in poverty. They lived a modest life, but nevertheless a vibrant life full of content, a richly Jewish variegated and wonderful life.

Our city was young, but we were able to build within it synagogues for prayer, schools and Yeshivas for Torah, as well as charitable and benevolent institutions. Jews of means and impoverished Jews – all found their spiritual nurturing in our square letters in which they studied and worshipped.

With all this, the people of Zgierz tell in this volume of noble, scholarly personages, as well as of those modest, anonymous people, in whose honor nobody delivers a festive speech. They are simple, poor people, but those who knew them and are expert in their way of life can tell about them and describe the wisdom, morality, the holiness, and all the sublime traits that they possessed and that come to the memory in splendor, kindness, and glory.

Translator's footnotes:

1. From Psalm 104.
2. Psalm 19.
3. The extra soul generally refers to the additional soul granted to a Jewish person on the Sabbath. Here it refers to a unique spirit, over and above the common spirit of all Jewish communities.

[Page 153]

F: Holocaust and Destruction

" Wagons, tell me, empty wagons: to where is this journey?"

[Page 154]

From the book "Last Letters"
published by Hakibutz Hameuchad, 1956

by Yitzchak Katznelson

Sections from "The song of the Jewish nation that was killed"

A section from the poem:

"Here they are again, the wagons of the train!"
"Empty wagons! They had just filled you, and you are again standing empty,
Where did you put them, the Jews? And what will be with them, and happen to them?
A myriad were counted, and then it was sealed – and how did you come back here again?
Wagons, tell me, empty wagons: To where was this transport?"

―――――――

[Page 155]

The World that was Destroyed

by the editors

– – The section on the Holocaust and destruction in this additional volume is joined as a continuation of that section in the Book of Zgierz. We know that the things written in the book and in this additional volume are only a small amount of what took place, a drop in the sea, the sea of tribulations and torment that the Jews of Zgierz suffered.

However, one who leafs through all the chapters of the book and this additional volume, and considers them together, with the realities, personages, material and spiritual communal life, their struggles and agonies during the years of the Holocaust, will get an essence of a fundamental Jewish reality, infused with love of one's fellow Jew and national honor, which was created and existed under the most difficult of conditions. The Holocaust era, the years of gradual liquidation of the community of Zgierz, the persecutions and murderers perpetrated in cold blood and cold calculation in all its details will rise before the eyes of the reader.

The hand writes to give over knowledge and memory, so that we can collect the boiling tears over the loss of our community into the vast flask of tears of our nation.

May G–d avenge their blood!

[Page 156]

Jews of Zgierz
on the Sixth Day of the Second World War

by Dr. B. Gelbfish

The sixth day of the Second World War was a critical day for the residents of Zgierz. On the night of the 5th going on the 6th of September, the announcement was made that men of military age must leave the city, without their families. To this day, it is hard to figure out from where the announcement came, because the authorities had left the city on the first day of the war.

On Friday, September 1, the population of Zgierz, as in the rest of Poland, understood that something terrible was about to happen. Everyone sensed the misfortune. However, in the state of deep fear, nobody did anything to deal with the impending misfortune. People were in a panic and a state of discomfort. The enthusiasm for the military leaders suddenly disappeared, and people stopped talking about mounting a resistance against the enemy.

Hitler's promise that, irrespective of the result of the war for Germany, Poland would lose its independence, evoked an oppressive feeling. However, Jews believed Hitler's threats of liquidation and annihilation.

Starting from Sunday, September 3, the Germans began, with their German punctuality, to incessantly bombard the city, the railway station, the chemical factories, and the like, from the air daily at 3:00 p.m. On the fifth day of the war, they bombarded the center of the city, intending to find Pastor Falcman, esteemed by everyone, in his home, for the sole sin that he conducted himself

[Page 157]

as a loyal Polish citizen. It was clear that nobody could avoid the misfortune. The weather helped the Germans. There was a fine blue sky, without rain or wind, the entire time. The clear, blue sky over Zgierz was as if to vex us, for it allowed the Germans to freely bomb the defenseless residents.

The mood became more oppressive from day to day. Even the news that England and France had declared war on Germany the third day had no effect on us. The greatest optimists lost their strength. The chatter regarding the retreating Polish army leading the Germans deep into the country in the areas of the Pinsker marshes so that the enemy could be defeated there – was believed by nobody.

In this situation, almost everyone followed the order to leave the city. Many men did not want to leave their families, so they took their wives and children with them, leaving their belongings open for the taking.

The way was very difficult, for almost nobody had any communication means for leaving the city. Many people went a few kilometers, and then returned. Some barely reached Stryków or Głowno. A small number, however, traveled day and night to reach Warsaw, and from there traveled further east to the Zaleszczyki region, at the Romanian border. Unfortunately, they arrived too late, as the district had been taken by the Soviets on the 17th day of the war.

More so than the Poles, the Jews obeyed the order to leave the city with full strictness. Not only did men of military age go, but also those younger and older. They fled, driven by fear of Hitler's army, which promised destruction and death.

The Jews of Zgierz left everything behind, and set out on their journey, full of pain and suffering, accompanied by the hatred of the Poles toward them, overstuffed with the anti–Semitism that had become so prominent during the last years of the Polish regime. They remembered very well Składkowski's *"Owszem Politik"* [Politics of certainty], the law against ritual slaughter by Madame Prystor, the beating of Jewish students at the universities to the point of blood, the boycotts of Jewish businesses, the pogroms in Przytyk and Minsk–Maziowiecki – deeds that they were not able to forget.

[Page 158]

As in the rest of Poland, the Jews of Zgierz endured the tragic reality – the Polish Sanacja regime prepared the ground for the shedding of Jewish blood, for enthusiastically receiving the Hitlerist venom, and they themselves fell under the hatchet of Nazism. The Jews felt already at the beginning that many Poles helped the Nazis in that terrible aktion, for they had been fed with anti–Semitic propaganda, and played a significant role in the persecution of the Jews.

As I have already mentioned, the refugees did not succeed in reaching the Romanian border. The vast majority returned back along the way. A smaller proportion remained in the occupied areas of western Ukraine. Very few returned home at the end of the war. There were only Poles there. Jews remained in the Soviet Union, endured hunger and pain, and survived the war there. When they returned to Poland, they found almost none of their kin.

The Jews of Zgierz were murdered in the ghetto and in camps. Zgierz refugees in Slonim were killed in that manner – among others, the Horowicz family, the Konows, Dr. Wolkowicz's family, may G–d avenge their blood.

One shudders when studying the balance. Barely 300–400 people survived out of the 5,000 Jews of Zgierz. The majority settled in Israel, and the remainder in various countries of Europe and America.

The Jews of Zgierz did not return to their homes, where every stone would remind them of the suffering of their dearest; where one could barely find the cemetery; where they tortured and murdered their nearest and dearest.

The heart weeps over those who were tortured and lost. However, their bright memory demands us to have a strong and brave heart, so that their terrible deaths will be the cause of a rectification in our further, bright upbuilding. We, who merited being saved from the great conflagration, will always have the old adage etched before our eyes, engraved with letters of fire and blood: Never forget!

Montreal, Canada, September 1949

———

[Page 159]

In a Struggle with the Angel of Death…
(from my experiences during the war years)

by Wolf Kleinman

In 1939, after the outbreak of the war and the entry of the Germans into Poland, Jews, including those from Zgierz, began to flee to Russia, the only country in which one could hope to find a temporary refuge. I was also among those who escaped, and that is how I reached Białystok.

In Białystok, I met many Zgierzers in the well–known "cellar" and I realized that the expulsion of the last remaining Jews of Zgierz was not far off. I had left a wife and a four–and–a–half–month old child there. Then I decided to return to Poland, where my eventual meeting point with my family had been designated as Warsaw. We immediately met up there.

I also met many Zgierz Jews in the Warsaw Ghetto. My sister and her child were also there. I lived on Zamenhof. My former manufacturer, Brafman (the son–in–law of Yisrael Jakubowicz) lived not far from me, on Meizels Street. The Zgierzer Rabbi also lived with Brafman. He comforted us, encouraged us to not lose hope for better times, and to live with the faith that G–d will send a salvation for the Jews.

Life in Warsaw became more constricted from day to day, and my sister decided to go to Głowno, for in Głowno, life was still easier than in the Warsaw Ghetto. At her request, I went to Głowno along with my wife and child. I still found many Jews there who had remained from the deportation from Zgierz. Among them were the Szajnholtz and Ofenbach families, along with many others whose names I no longer remember.

After a month in Głowno, they also deported us from there together with the rest of the Jews. Thus did I, along with my wife, my sister, and my child

[Page 160]

return to the Warsaw Ghetto. My sister, who resided with her husband's family, went from there to Luków, and I never heard from her again after that.

When the Germans began their war with Russia, life in the ghetto became more unbearable. The hunger was great, and the death rate was even greater. They I decided to escape from the Warsaw Ghetto. Earlier, I had sent my wife and child to Częstochowa. Shortly after that, in July 1941, I was transported by a gentile, and also traveled to Częstochowa.

The Jews of Częstochowa, as everywhere else, were going through unbearable times. As in all other cities, they were living there outside the law. Every German tyrant would shoot and torture. The old synagogue was vandalized and destroyed already at the outset. Each day brought new tribulations.

We worked for the Germans until the large deportation from the Częstochowa Ghetto in September 1942. Over 60,000 Jews were deported during that expulsion. Only about 3,000 remained. My wife, my child, my mother–in–law, her four sisters, and the rest of her family were among those deported.

The deportation took place in accordance with their well–known murderous formula *"Rechts" "Links"* [Right, Left]. Naturally, we did not know that those sent off to the right were being sent to annihilation. My way was with those sent to the left, and we were sent to various workplaces. A small ghetto was created at that time for the few remaining Jews.

Zgierz Jews in Resistance

After we lost our special unique people, life here, in our small ghetto, also lost all its worth. When the news of the Warsaw Ghetto uprising reached us, we, a number of dedicated

[Page 161]

members of our workplace, decided to organize a resistance group, to conduct self–defense against the frequent snatchings and shootings. We succeeded in purchasing a bit of light weapons from Poles, paying with valuables that we had taken along at the time of the cleaning the Jewish dwellings after the large deportation.

Once, during a secret conference of our group, the Gestapo followed our tracks, certainly due to an informant. They then closed off the small ghetto and went to the house where we were gathered. Our watchperson then informed us that we were surrounded. A panic ensued as we started running in different directions. Most of us were captured as we were escaping. I succeeded in sneaking into a gate. At that same moment, I noticed a fleeing youth from our group who was being chased by an S.S. man. That youth still had the energy to grab his Sten, aim it at the German, and shoot him. I saw how the S.S. man fell. The youth ran further, and went over a fence. At that moment, he was hit by a volley of bullets and fell on the ground. Immediately after the Germans led out all the captured people and left the Ghetto, I went to clear out the dead and wounded. I went over to the fallen youth, but he was already dead. The next morning, I found out that the youth was the son of Menashe Szwarcbard of Zgierz.

A short time later, in 1943, the "Small Ghetto" was also liquidated and the remaining Jews were sent to three work camps: Hasak Warta, Hasak Peltzeri, and Hasak Rakow.

In January 1945, the Russians entered Częstochowa, but the Germans still appeared that same day to transport those remaining in the work camps to Buchenwald. I was in Buchenwald for about one month, and I worked at various cleaning operations in Weimar. Later, they sent us to a work camp in Colditz. Shortly before the end of the war, the Germans sent us out of the work camp. We marched 40 kilometers a day. That death march ended in Theresienstadt. The Germans still ruled there, but the International Red Cross already had full supervision of us.

At 5:00 a.m. on May 8, 1945, the Russians entered and liberated us. Our situation changed radically, but a new catastrophe threatened the survivors and starving masses. The spontaneous voracious eating led to dysentery, typhus and other illness that spread like an epidemic.

At that time, I became involved, with some others, in getting help for the sick. Once I entered a house where a youth was lying half dead with typhus. He was familiar to me. To my question about who he was and from where he came, he responded that he is Szternfeld from Zgierz. He was a grandson from the old Zajonc and a brother of Moniek Szternfeld.

If that youth, who is today certainly a father and perhaps even a grandfather, reads these last lines, he will certainly remember who it was that brought him the first aid and encouragement, so he could strengthen himself and overcome his illness, and be able to tell over what he endured.

[Page 162]

Through the Small Bridge Between Life and Death
(Experiences of a Jewish woman during the years of annihilation)

by Mania Jakubowicz–Gothelf

Mania Jakubowicz–Gothelf

Mania Jakubowicz–Gothelf (nee Mondraj), the wife of Mendel Jakubowicz (killed in the Soviet hard labor camps in far–off "Sever"[11]) tells us, in brief, about her experiences since the outbreak of the Second World War until her liberation from the German death camps.

On September 7, 1939, the German army captured our city and immediately began to pour various decrees daily over the heads of the Jews of Zgierz, and held us in

[Page 163]

constant fear of death. The sophisticated decree to wear the yellow patch immediately segregated us and put us in a wanton state in the eyes of the inimical Poles and the local Germans. Almost all of the latter group immediately began to wear swastika bands on their arms, and placed themselves at the service of the new authorities, primarily engaged in the persecutions against the Jews.

In December of the same year (my husband was not at home, as he had left Zgierz with many others), several Volksdeutschen entered my home, removed the furniture, and loaded it upon wagons. However, while inside my house, they consulted together and demanded the key to the dwelling from me. In the end, I was simply expelled from my house. I then took my three–year–old Eliush and went to my parents in Łódź.

At the beginning of 1942, I was sent into the ghetto, along with all the other Jews of Łódź. For almost five years, I endured the hell, about which a great deal has been written. In the ghetto, I met many Jews of Zgierz who joined in our suffering. I often met the following Zgierzers: Kuba Czernikowski, Leibush Waldman, Shimon Fiszer's daughter Bina, as well as Ruta, the wife of Wolf Fiszer, and others whose names I no longer remember. Among them was the daughter of the upholsterer from Zgierz Moshe Wajnbaum, who helped save my child during a life–threatening moment.

I went through an especially sorrowful chapter in the Łódź Ghetto with my six–seven–year–old child Eliush. I endured with him all the hardships, hunger, and various illnesses. I cannot bypass and neglect to mention here at least one of his many questions that he asked me, which echo to this day in my ears and which let us understand what our small children went through at that time, as their child souls were deeply affected with the fear and suffering of their helpless parents, and how this came to expression during the dark days of destruction and annihilation.

Once when we were looking out the window at the street toward the other side of the barbed wire, and saw a civilian carriage passing by, he asked, "Why can those people, over there, travel, and we cannot?" I answered, "Because they are Germans, but we are Jews, and are not allowed." He thought a bit and asked further, "Could it even happen that they would be Jews and we would be German?"

[Page 164]

We would receive a morsel of bread for working at night in the resort. I hid it for my child. Once when I came home at dawn, I showed him the morsel of bread while I was still on the doorstep to cheer him up. However, the child turned away from me with his shoulder. I stood there and asked, "What happened? Why are you angry with me?" And Eliush answered me, insulted, "You work an entire night and are starving, and you bring me the morsel of bread that you should be eating?!"

He loved it when I would sing him to sleep with a lullaby, often when he was hungry. He especially loved the popular song in the ghetto, "Mein Shtetle Beltz"[2]. One day, he asked me, "Mommy, can you also sing to me 'Mein Shtetle Zgierz'?" I was without words…

Let these few lines be for him a good memory, and for me, the sole comfort…

*

On August 12, 1944, during the day of the liquidation of the Łódź Ghetto, I was deported to Auschwitz together with my sister Sonia and her two children. I have no energy or words to describe what we endured in Auschwitz. There, they took away our children, and they also took away my sister during a selection.

The picture of that day at the end of August remains etched in my mind, when Chaim Romkowski came into the camp accompanied by the entire entourage, including the Jewish police in their uniforms. They went around with certainly, seemingly unaware what was awaiting them. Naturally, their appearance aroused various commentaries among us.

In October 1944, I was transported to KZ Stutthof. There, we were placed into groups of five, from which the Germans selected those that they desired and sent them off. Only later did we find out that they sent them to the sea and drowned them[3].

From Stutthof, we were sent to Zall–Batten, near Thorn (Toruń). We arrived at night. They ordered us to jump off the wagon, and we – jumped into the water. We had to raise our heads over the water, so as not to drown. Then they chased us into stables, meant for animals. The crowding was literally suffocating.

[Page 165]

At dawn, after the selections, they took us 16 kilometers away, and gave us spades and pickaxes (the ground was already frozen) to dig pits. Some of us believed that we were digging trenches, and others believed that we were digging graves. They brought us back from work when it was already dark. Hellish scenes took place as we were dividing up the bit of soup. In Zall–Batten, we saw high heaps of dead bodies through an opening in the fence. We spent two full months in such conditions.

From there, they prodded us on foot to Zall Melch in January 1945. There, we worked in the forests, carrying cut down trees to the river. Finally, they made it clear that they will forcibly send us on a death march, which they planned for us. We were placed under the control of a military officers group. They chased us over hills and valleys, through deep snow, over rivers and bodies of water. It is impossible to understand how the layer of ice did not break under our running feet. Anyone who could not persevere this was not among those who returned. On the other hand, we did later see their clothing, which we were able to wear for the difficult march "to Germany."

At dawn on January 19, we set out on the march, which was called "To Germany" so that we would not fall into the hands of the enemy (the Russians). That is what an officer, and S.S. man, told us in a speech before we set out. He turned to us with these unbelievable and amazing words, "Dear children, we will also be saved!" He said that we are going on foot due to the fact that the trains are all occupied with the military… "And I call on you to obey and cooperate" etc. We were all surprised and frightened: are they not preparing for us a new death trap? However, at that time, we were so isolated and hidden from other people that we had no inkling that the Russians had already taken Warsaw and were marching onward.

Hungry, frozen, barefoot and in rags, we – a camp of 2,000 women – dragged onward with our last strength over snowy back roads in unknown area. Every day, people died of hunger and exhaustion. On the seventh day of the march, I felt that I could not go on any further, and I lay down in the snow in resignation. The "*blokowa*" (barracks leader) ran by and

[Page 166]

tried to encourage me to immediately stand up, for I could be shot on the spot. However, I was indifferent to everything, and I answered her in that fashion. Nevertheless, she stuck with me, and told me that if I get up, she would help me. She said I should grab her shoulder and hang on to her. Thus did I succeed in dragging myself along until nightfall, until we reached the next resting place in a stable. Thus did she, Ella, a Czech girl, save me from certain death.

There, in the darkness of the stable, I met a girl from Łódź named Rozhka, who was quite exhausted and resigned. I called to her, and lay near her to warm her up. After that, when the S.S. men dragged out those who were half dead and weakened, I heard shots from the outside. Later, I found out that all of those who were dragged out of the stable had been shot.

The march set out again at dawn. Rozhka, and two or three other women and I felt that we could not continue on with the march, so we snuck into a corner of the hazardous stable. With fear of death, we heard how an S.S. man searched for those who remained behind. We lay there as corpses.

The day passed in silence, but we could not move from the place.

The next day, Germans entered again. However, this time, they found us with the light of their lanterns. To our good fortune, they were not S.S. men, but rather soldiers from a Wehrmacht division who were retreating from the front. To their questions about who we were and who were the corpses behind the table, we answered that we know nothing about the dead, and that we had just come from a far–away village to seek food. The soldiers then quickly brought us food.

After they marched on, we looked around and saw an abandoned house not far from us, without windows or doors. With the hope that we could perhaps find something there with which to warm ourselves up, we dragged ourselves over there on our hands and feet.

After having unbelievable and miraculous encounters with retreating German soldiers in that hovel, one early morning we heard the detonation of bombardments, and we understood that the front was approaching.

[Page 167]

A new time of fear fell upon us. Now, as the liberation approached, we might be killed by Russian bullets. We found a small cellar in the house, and went down as we heard the bombs and grenades fall closer and closer.

Suddenly, everyone shuddered – a bomb fell into the house. We felt that we were at the end of our lives.

I do not know for how long we remained in shock. It seemed like the hours stretched for an entire night. Then, a group of Russian soldiers found us while searching for hiding Germans. They took us out of the cellar, barely alive.

Then, a curious event took place with us. Together with us there was a Polish Christian, who, like we did, found temporary refuge in the abandoned house. The oldest of the soldiers, a Tatar, who continuously looked at us with suspicion, thought that we were disguised German spies. We began to explain, but it did not help. He led us to a room, and put us in front of the major. The Christian declared in broken Russian that he was a Pole, but that the others are Jews whom he found in an abandoned house.

"What?!" says the major, to our great amazement in Yiddish, "You are Jewish children? From where do you come?"

"We come from all the death camps," we responded, "Where are we?"

"You do not need to be afraid anymore," he calmed us, "you are now free people. Nu, nu, I will look after you – – –."

They took us aboard one of the loaded ammunition trucks and immediately drove us away from the front. Then, we arrived at a second military division, which also received us in a friendly fashion and once again sent us to another division, where the officer, also a Jew, permitted us to travel to Łódź, which had already been liberated a few days earlier.

*

Neither Rozhka or I found any surviving members of our family. Our homes had been taken over by Poles. There was no place for us there. I told Rozhka, "Come, stay with me. We have gone through so many experiences together. We also can live together. I am traveling

[Page 168]

back to Zgierz. There I left my home and dwelling, and there I will wait for Mendele. He will certainly come home soon together with those being repatriated from Russia. They will receive me better in Zgierz."

Rozhka remained with me for many years, and we also made aliya together in Israel. I no longer expected Mendel. Fate destroyed my hopes and plans.

Translator's Footnotes:

1.   Siberia
2.   See https://www.yadvashem.org/yv/en/exhibitions/communities/balti/mein_shtetle_belz.asp and listen to https://www.youtube.com/watch?v=YU4oNZVqcaE . There is a debate as to which town this song refers, Belz Poland, or Bălti (Belts) Moldova.
3.   Stutthof is now the city of Sztutowo, Poland, on the Gulf of Danzig. There is indeed documentation of prisoners being drowned in the sea.

During the Events of the Holocaust

by Fela Gotlieb–Rosenblatt

As we hear the voices of the neo–Nazis reaching us lately from time to time from "new" Germany, words that arouse in us both disgust and fear, and this is while some of the Holocaust survivors are still alive – I thought in my heart: Have I, as a brand plucked from the fire[1], have I fulfilled my duty to my conscience and to my nation without giving eyewitness testimony to what I endured in the death camps, and on the atrocities that I witnessed with my own eyes.

They say: better late than never. Therefore, I have decided to perpetuate, at least in this small chapter, that which took place to me during the terrible years of the war, to remember and remind about the events that should never be forgotten. This will also be a token of remembrance for my entire family who perished in the Holocaust. I, the sole survivor, regard it as a command from On High, to tell and perpetuate, so that the future generations will know.

*

From the beginning of 1940 until August 1944, we lived (if it is at all possible to include these years in the number of years that we have lived upon the earth), my mother, my brother Raphael Mendel and me, in in the Łódź Ghetto. My father, brothers and sister had been deported to Piotrków.

Toward morning on August 24, 1944, a date that will be etched in my memory forever, we were forcibly removed from our home by the Germans. We were taken to the Łódź railway station along with a large group of Jews. There, we were loaded onto the transport wagons that were meant for cattle, by force and accompanied by beatings. The Germans told us that we were traveling to Germany for work, that we will work, and that there will be no danger.

[Page 169]

Approximately one hundred people were crowded into a single wagon of the train. Already at this stage, men were separated from women, brothers from sisters, children from mothers. The wagons were locked from the outside, and we were left standing in terrible, cramped conditions, without air to breathe, and without water or food. A single bucket was placed in the wagon to serve as facilities for us all.

After hours of a suffocating journey, in hunger and thirst, having no choice, we pressed ourselves against the windows of the wagon with our last strength, and snatched a bit of the cold mist that accumulated on the windows in order to wet our lips and assuage our terrible thirst.

The train suddenly stopped after a journey of approximately 20 hours. The doors were opened, and the Nazis boarded the wagons and removed the people who had fainted or who had appeared weak. Then the doors were closed, and the train continued on its journey.

Toward morning of the next day, we arrived to what we later found out was the Auschwitz death camp. When we got off the trains, we saw a gigantic sign on the entry gate, greeting us with the motto "Arbeit Macht Frei" [Work Sets You Free]. As we passed through the gate, we saw pillars of smoke ascending skyward.

A group of people with shaven heads and wearing stiped clothing greeted us. From mouth to ear, we heard the rumor that we had not been brought there to work, but rather to be killed. At this point, they also told us that there is no reason to take the small suitcase that we brought with us, for we would not need it.

We did not believe that our fate was sealed and that we were being taken to annihilation. We still had hope that they were talking about only hard labor and a prison camp. However, this hope disappeared immediately after that, when the Germans already separated the men from the women, and the youths from the adults, via the well–known selection.

At that point, I was separated from my mother, who was taken to a different direction with hundreds of others. I neve saw her again after that. My brother was separated from me, and was taken with a group of men and children in a different direction. I never saw him again either.

Thus, in one moment, I lost my mother and brother, and I also lost my hope.

From the train station, we were taken by foot for a one hour walk to the area of the barracks. There, we were placed in rooms, with a group of five people to a room. As soon as we entered the rooms, we were ordered to strip naked, and the S.S. soldiers shaved all the hair from our bodies. When we went outside, we no longer recognized each other, for we all appeared as images from a different world.

It was now evening. After being without food or drink for two days, we were ordered to lie down on the ground naked. Thus did we lie all night.

In the morning, we were taken to the showers, from which ice–cold water flowed. Then, we received our torn rags as clothing.

[Page 170]

In the morning, we were divided into groups of about 50 people. We stood in a circle, with a pot of food in the center. Everyone was given a taste from the pot. The first ones burnt their mouths because the foul soup was scalding, and the latter ones, for whom there was nothing left, "dried" the pot with their fingers to obtain a few morsels.

After the "meal," we were taken to the edge of the camp, where the crematoria stood. Two S.S. captains suddenly appeared and told us in German – today the ovens are not working, for a mishap had occurred. Then we were all returned to our barracks, where the S.S. commander, Frau Müller, waited for us. She stood on a chair in the middle of the room with a whip in her hands, and anyone approaching the chair got a whipping on all parts of the body, especially on the head. This is how things continued daily, for three weeks.

An additional torment that the Nazis enjoyed was to awaken the entire group at 3:00 a.m. to go to the washroom, which was actually an open field, and then to stand us in a silent formation. They then command us to shout, "The Jews wanted the war." This repeated itself nightly.

After three weeks, without knowing why we "merited" to not be sent to extermination, they took us out of Auschwitz on trains and brought us to various labor camps in the vicinity of Hamburg: Altona, Sternschanze,

Poppenbüttel, and others. We worked there for half a year in the railway station, in building houses, in the cement factory, and other such hard physical work. We remained in this camp until the liberation by the allies.

Life in the camp was unbearable. We were placed into groups of about 500 individuals, with men, women, children, sick people, and pregnant woman all in one room. There was no place to stand, and we could only sit if we put our legs on the shoulders of those sitting in front of us.

This is how we lived for three weeks. We received a portion of soup once a day, which had to be sufficient for the entire day.[2]

Thousands of people, who lost their human form (Muselmen[3]) slept in the camp yard. There were also many bodies. This is how we lived the entire time.

In the final week before the end of the war, the Germans shut off the water intake to the camp, and we were forced to drink sewage and effluent to prevent dehydration and remain alive.

During that time, we already felt that the end was approaching. The incessant bombing day and night was our sign of impending salvation. Indeed, after about a week of non–stop bombardment, the liberating soldiers burst into the camp and liberated us from the hell. Virtually all of us had lost our human form.

Translator's Footnotes:

1.   This phrase is from Zecharia 3:2
2.   I suspect this paragraph is in the wrong place, and belongs a few paragraphs above, just before the author left Auschwitz.
3.   See https://en.wikipedia.org/wiki/Muselmann

[Page 171]

People who Became "Muselmen"

by Zeev Fisher

During the first postwar years, we often heard from people who survived the death camps a strange expression to describe a certain state of the prisoners of those camps – including acquaintances and natives of our city – who were together with them for a period of time. For example, as a response to the question, "Did you not meet so–and–so when you were there?" one might get the response, "Indeed, I saw him toward the end. He was already a 'Muselman.'" Muselman? What is this? However, from the expression on his face and the gesture of his hand, we knew that we should not ask more. During those days, we heard in this expression something strange, something mysterious, as if from another world, something frightening to the depths of the soul. No, we no longer know such evil, degrading, and disgraceful deathly torments, which are so ignominious and oppressive that they bring a human being to the threshold of loss of sense of self. This sometimes happened a long time before the person was taken to the gas chambers.

When I visited the Museum of the Ghetto Fighters[1] and chatted with the director of the museum Mr. Tzvi Shiner of blessed memory (incidentally, a descendant of Zgierz residents) on the topic of the "Muselman," he pointed to a miniature statue and said, "Perhaps this small statue, the handiwork of the well–known sculptor Marek Szwarc (the son of Isucher Szwarc of blessed memory of Zgierz) will best explain to you the concept of "Muselman," which you are interested in. I gazed at this small statue and was shaken by the expressive, frightening appearance of the image. Indeed, it no longer had any sign of the Divine image in which man was crated. Woe, how talented were those murderers in changing the human creation into a monstrous form from some sort of netherworld!

We found an extensive description, but moving to the point of pain, in the book "Stories of Hassidic Revelations" by Professor Fishel Schneerson, the well–known, famous psychologist of those days. Since the description is relevant to us, the generation of the Holocaust, and touches the depths of our hearts, I will bring here several paragraphs from the chapter, "Miracles with a 'Muselman,'" to learn, teach, remember, and remind:

– – – "There is no doubt that people did not yet understand the essence, full of secrets, of those people who were called 'Muselmen,' who numbered in the thousands and myriads among the prisoners of the Nazi camps. Certainly, none like them were ever seen in all of human history. These are the people in the camps whose force of resistance had been broken due to the multitude of various torments. They turned into people not of this world. Anyone who never saw a Muselman, has never seen the all–encompassing suffering that crosses the final boundary and is beyond the ability of a human being to feel, and certainly to contend with, due to its great depth. At first glance, a Muselman looks like a person who has died before his soul has left him, or, on the contrary, whose soul has left him before he died. However, when one looks at him from up close, one notices that the suffering left a small drop of life in the person's precarious existence. Nevertheless, the hylic essence that takes hold of the body, so to speak, forges the Muselman into an image of

[Page 172]

suffering that an eye has never beholden – suffering that gathers and renews itself every moment. The Muselman is shockingly thin, without a grain of flesh on his body. His weight is the weight of his bones. He cannot eat and does not sense hunger, as if he is already beyond the tribulations of hunger. Nevertheless, this living skeleton walks and moves, holding in his hand one of the "portions" of bread that he does not want to eat, but also is unwilling to toss away. It is not to eat and not to toss! Life and death act here in a secret blend, with the stubbornness of the will to live blending in a wondrous manner with the stony indifference to death. When the Muselman swallows and ingests something, he immediately gets thinner – – and nevertheless, he goes about without groaning and without crying out, as he holds "his" "morsel" of bread in one hand, and wipes up the moisture and dirt with the other hand, without groaning and without crying out! The Muselman was already sanctified with his torments. He was completely simplistic in body, beyond suffering and hunger. – One needed to speak a few times to a Muselman, until the words would penetrate his mind that had become plastered. Even so, he looks around his surrounding with the eyes of a baby, full of otherworldly, covert simplicity. – – – Only the "portions" of bread that he holds spasmodically in his hands are the last, late, remnants of life on earth." – – Then the day come when the camp doctor comes for an examination, as usual.

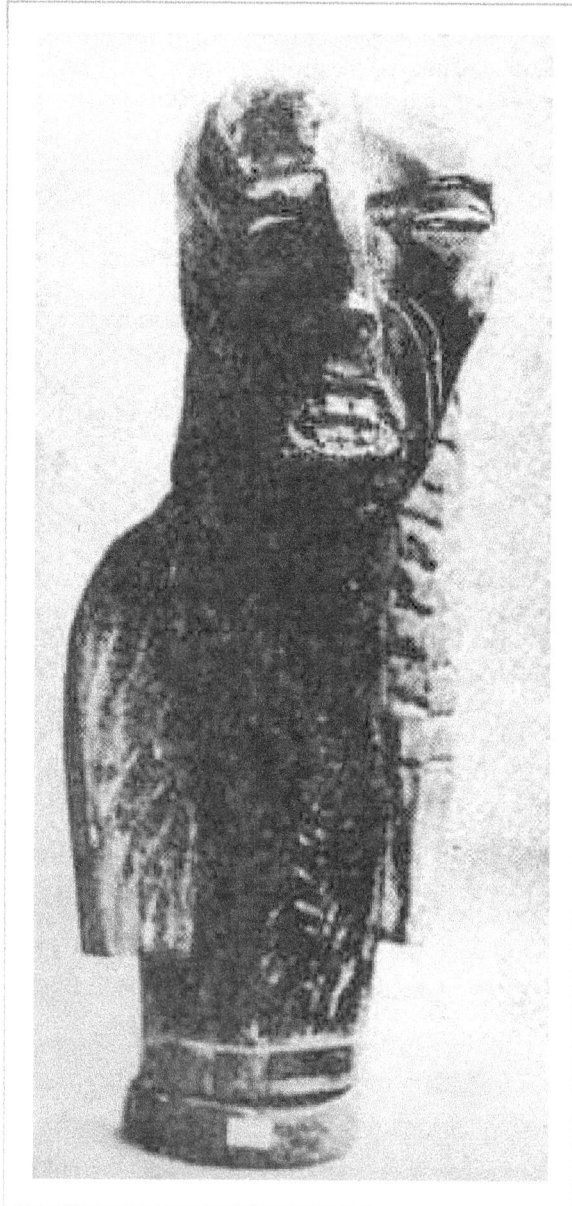

The wooden statue of Marek Szwarc – "The Muselman"

"The blocks close. The head of the block and house servants take their places with murderous wrath. The prisoners all stand naked. Every prisoner passes in front of the doctor, walking back

[Page 173]

and forth. The doctor immediately recognizes the Muselman, whose flesh cannot be found and is not seen on his body. – – The doctor simply gestures with his hand, and his scribes already know his intention. They would write down the numbers that were on the hands of the Muselmen, and gigantic transport vehicles would come after some time, call out the numbers, and the Muselmen from all the blocks would be hauled to the crematoria…"

I approached Aryeh ben–Menachem, a researcher of ghetto life (especially of the Łódź Ghetto) for information about the origin of the term "Muselman." I asked him to explain the source and meaning of this strange expression. The response that I received is based on large–scale correspondence with famous agents in Israel and the Diaspora, who are involved with all aspects of the Holocaust that require special research. We include here a few paragraphs that relate directly to our topic:

Translator's Footnote:

      1.   https://museums.gov.il/en/museums/Pages/lohamei–
hagetaot.aspx#:~:text=%E2%80%8B%E2%80%8B%E2%80%8B%E2%80%8BThe,the%20world's%20oldest%20Hol
ocaust%20museum.

About the Term "Muselman"
in the Nazi Concentration Camps

by Aryeh ben–Menachem

We will write about the origins origin of the term "Muselman." It is a known fact that any new phenomenon, whether actual or abstract, requires a name or a nickname so that it can be told over to others. Therefore, the prisoners of the Nazi concentration camps had to invent an appropriate term for a phenomenon that was unknown to them before their arrival in the camp. They had to invent some sort of name for those prisoners passing before their eyes in a state of utter despair and lack of energy, who were still moving about, but without any purpose in their motions, suffering but not capable of reacting to their pain or suffering, indifferent to everything going on in their environment. This nickname had to be granted not by academics and experts of languages, but rather by the prisoners themselves who were witnesses to this, or by the S.S. men who were the cause of this situation.

Many theories were given after the war regarding the topic of the origin of the term "Muselman," the actual meaning of which is nothing other than "Muslim" – i.e. a believer in the Islamic faith. According to the majority, this term was created as a reminiscence of the photographs that used to be published in the newspapers before the war of residents of India lying in the streets in a very lowly physical state, with definitive indifference. The simple folk thought that all residents of India were followers of the Islamic faith (in German, *Muselmann*). This was the source of the term in the concentration camps (but not in the ghettoes, where different terms were used, such as "*klepsydra*" in the Łódź Ghetto). The term "Muselman" apparently originated in the Auschwitz Concentration Camp, though this has not been established with certainty.

[Page 174]

We must note that the expression "Muselman," like all the other terms that we mentioned, was used against its bearers as a derogatory and mocking nickname. The S.S. men, as well as the various "service people" in the camp, used to arrange cruel "games" with the "Muselmen," to denigrate them, to beat them, and even to kill those who could not get accustomed to the conditions in the camp, or who became abhorrent in their looks, behavior, or the odor that the exuded.

The "*Przegląd Lekarski*" monthly of the organization of Polish physicians conducted a broad inquiry on the topic of the phenomenon called "Muselman." Summaries were published in booklet 23 / 1983. We will skip over the medical, social, psychological and other expressions here that the inquiry dealt with at length, and suffice ourselves with an excerpt from the description of the image of a "Muselman" as portrayed by combining the responses of the participants of the inquiry:

"The 'Muselman' is nothing other than a creature who was indifferent to what is going on in his surroundings, who functioned in a mechanical manner and attended to his needs in that fashion. His steps were weak. He did not lift up his feet as he walked, and tended to raise his elbows to balance his weight. He would sleep in a curled–up fashion, placing his blanket over his head. His voice was unnatural, trembling, and grating, and at times aggressive or wailing. His speech was slow and incomprehensible. His skin was covered with wounds, sores, and signs of lice bites and scratches, exuding pus and a foul odor. His head was covered with a cap falling over his wide–open eyes, peering as if looking backward. His skull was large and swollen, and his bones protruded. He would wear rags, and would sometimes enwrap himself with torn paper bandages, soaked with blood and pus. Hid would not react to what was transpiring around him, neither to the shouts of the S.S. men nor to the beatings and kicks that he endured. He was more reminiscent of a sick beast than a human being."

A separate chapter is dedicated to the relationship of "Muselmen" with each other, between them and other prisoners in the camp, and between them and the guards from the ranks of the S.S. All this is in addition to the view of many others regarding the topic. Here is not the place to give over the details.

Indeed, we can regard the phenomenon of a "Muselman" as the destruction of all humanity within the human being, but also as an instance of sublime heights, unique in its kind despite it being the most outrageous in the annals of interpersonal relationships. In his deterioration, the "Muselman" reached a state of complete equanimity of the soul, and therefore also – at the end of the matter – of superiority toward his murderers, as he became independent of their criminal will and everything going on around him. Thus, he reached a state of freedom and decisive calm, in contrast to his fellow prisoners, and certainly in contrast to his German murderers.

Nissan 5744. April 1944.

[Page 175]

From the Vale of Weeping
Impressions of a tour of destroyed Poland after the Holocaust

Published by the Chevra Kadisha [Burial Society] of Tel Aviv – Jaffa

by Rabbi Binyamin Sczaranski

Rabbi Binyamin Sczaranski,may he live long, the son of Rabbi Meir Sczaranski of blessed memory (see Book of Zgierz, pp. 500–501) was one of the members of the official delegation of Israel who went to visit the memorial places in Poland on the occasion of the 40th anniversary of the Warsaw Ghetto Uprising. The impressions of this tour were published in a special anthology entitled "From the Vale of Weeping" published by the Chevra Kadisha of Tel Aviv – Jaffa.

With the permission of the rabbi, we bring here a few sections of his impressions of his tour of post–Holocaust Poland.

The Great Outcry from the Vale of Weeping

"Throughout the years, I felt in my heart a strong pull to see Poland. I longed to visit the country which I left when I was one year old… Even so, it was part of my essence. I was bound to it with the latent bonds through which every person is bound to his ancestors whom he never knew personally."

He gave over and related his difficult experiences when he visited the death camps and also several cities in which large communities, important to Polish Jewry, were once concentrated; as well as small towns that are etched in the hearts of myriads of Jews with holy memories. These places stand desolate and empty of Jews. He then turns with a heartrending call to the entire Jewish world to remember, to remember forever!

Remember, Remember Forever!

Today, after my visit to Poland, I live with a strange sensation that many generations separate us from the generation of the destruction. The Jews of the eve of the destruction and the Jews of our day are so different from each other that fear takes hold in the heart and thoughts lest we soon cease believing in our past… The memory of Polish Jewry weakens and becomes cloudy. This Jewry, from which we live to this day – no longer has an influence on our mindset. The sole things that bind us to it are the stories and legends, as if all this was from the distant past that has disappeared, a golden dream that once was and is no more. The new generation indeed has frightful words: destruction, six million, death camps, ovens, crematoria, gas chambers. I am wary of asking aloud whether there are not other words from Jewish history that serve as descriptions for the crusades, pogroms, inquisition cellars, and blood libels? I am not able to quiet within me the question that torments me: From the brutal bosom of this world, is there not in our memory

[Page 176]

some element of cynicism and perniciousness, through which this Jewish world was erased from the face of the earth? Through our forgetting, have we not fulfilled in some strange way the goals of the wild murderers?

There is nobody who can contradict the fact that the decline in the traditional spiritual level of our generation is a direct result of the Nazi destruction, which threw Jewry into a state of definitive chaos. This destruction left its wake a terrible vacuum, from which arose perverse concepts and distorted ideas regarding life, a shallow secular life with all that we lost being covered over by a dangerous and perverse chase after the vicissitudes of times. Suddenly we all found ourselves hanging over the frightful waves of the stormy ocean of internecine hatred. We were like orphans, and it does not seem that our outlook today is a part of the terrible destruction. The eyes does not tear up and the heart does not burst when hearing the random number – 6,000,000. And who knows, may G–d protect and save us – whether the Holocaust will not rest on the recesses of history, feeding chairpersons and committees, serving as material for texts and mourning ceremonies, marked by the lowering of the flag and wreaths of black flowers…

The thousand–year–old Polish Jewry has been wiped off the face of the earth, and with it has disappeared a thousand years of the spirit. Only isolated survivors remain from the golden age of Torah, wisdom, Hassidism, and morality. Even the characteristic Jew, the modest, upright Jew, one of the "People of Israel" can barely be found anymore. The myriads who gave up their souls while reciting *Shema Yisrael* have left only one command to future generations, sealed in blood: to cleave to the faith of Israel and its holy Torah, the eternal heritage of the Jew.

Approximately 3.5 million Jews were murdered in Poland alone. After such a terrible destruction, the march of life of humanity did not stop. We all continue to live our lives through their daily course, immersed in personal forgetfulness, given over to the illusions that the excesses of the latter half of the 20th century has imparted to us. Even those who survived of Polish Jewry, and were miraculously saved from the destruction, have joined the march of life in a natural manner, with the stormy and exciting realities, which cause the past to be forgotten, and cover the memory of our dear martyrs, may G–d avenge their deaths, with a mantle of materialism. All of us "move to the daily grind" and the blurry shadow of the destruction recedes to the recesses of our lives.

Jewish brethren! Rise up and do everything that we did not know how to do so that forgetfulness does not place dust over this most terrible chapter of the annals of our nation, so that the memory of the Nazi Amalek will not depart from our midst! Rise up and let us gather all the material in writing and through word of mouth that relates to Jewish life in Poland before the destruction and during the destruction. Let us rummage through the sources, search for documents, expose forgotten letters and abandoned pages, and inscribe in the hearts of all the coming generations that which the Nazi beast perpetrated upon us, so that our children will remember until the end of all generations. Our daughters will tell their children, and it will never be forgotten. A holy duty rests upon all of us to multiply the descriptions and stories of the Jews of pre–war Poland, so that their shining images will stand before our eyes, illuminating our paths of life before us, and strengthening our hearts in all the trials, so that we will cleave to the Torah forever.

[Page 177]

Elegy for Jewish Towns

by Antoni Słonimski[1]

Translated by Jerrold Landau

There are no more Jewish shtetls in Poland. The
Hrubieszóws, Kurczowas, and Połaniecs have disappeared:
One no longer sees the candles burning in the windows.
One no longer hears the singing from the wooden synagogue.

Gone – the last ones with Jewish garb. Covered
With sand is the blood, the vestiges, and the blackness of the
conflagration;
The walls and the floors have been whitened and cleaned with lime,
As if it was for a holiday, or – because of an epidemic.

A strange, cold, pale moon lights up –
When everything from the night attacks from behind the shtetls.
And they, the poetic Jewish children – they will
Never see the two moons of Chagall[2].

They are already going, golden, over new planets –
Fugitives, dismal, disheveled, silent–heavy.
The shoemakers who were poets are no longer here,
The troubadours among the barbers are no longer here.

The shtetls where the Biblical songs once were are no longer here
They have united with Polish songs and with Slavic sadness,
Where Jews, in the shadows of the orchards – already old and worn out –
Used to weep for Jerusalem's sanctified walls.

Translated from Yiddish: Y. Papiernikow

Translator's Footnotes:

1. See https://en.wikipedia.org/wiki/Antoni_S%C5%82onimski
2. The moon was a common theme in the paintings of Marc Chagall.

[Page 178]

Our Way to the Land of Israel

by Fela Gotlieb (nee Rosenblatt)

In 1945, at the end of the war, I was brought to Sweden along with a group of survivors of the camps. I participated in meetings of the Jewish community while I was in Sweden. There, I first found out about the existence of an organization dealing with illegal immigration to the Land of Israel.

Despite the fact that I had a permit for entry to America, my entire will was to arrive in the Land of Israel after all the tribulations and suffering that I endured along the way.

We were about 500 girls in the *aliya* group, and it is superfluous to note that all the proceedings of the organization were conducted in secret, out of a concern lest the activities of the organization be revealed.

A group of Zgierzers in Cyprus, 1947–48

They came from various gathering places, including: Poland, Germany, Sweden, and Italy. They met in Cyprus, and remained there for 1 – 1 ½ years.
Standing: P. Rozman, Y. Adler, R. Himel, P. Chaimowicz, Y. Wojonski, Y. Konski, A. Praszker, Ch. Wajonska.
Sitting: Z. Kleinman, F. Rosenblatt, Kuza, Kuza, unknown.

In the month of January, a group set out from the shores of Sweden to the direction of the Land of Israel aboard the Chaim Arlozoroff ship[1]. When we arrived in Italy, a group of about 1,000 lads boarded the ship. Thus, we were a group of 1,500 people aboard a ship that was shaky in any case, and that had a capacity of about 700 people. The crowding

[Page 179]

was great, there were no sanitary conditions, but there was joy in the hearts of all of us because our journey was reaching its end.

The journey lasted for about six weeks. The name of the ship changed several times during the journey in order to escape the tracking of the British Army, which was searching for ships of immigrants.

When we arrived opposite Atlit[2], the ship was suddenly attacked by two destroyers of the British Army. The ship was forced to stop, and British soldiers boarded the ship to take us off. The soldiers met fierce resistance from our side, and in essence, a war of life or death took place. Our weapons were boxes of canned food, bottles, and any other object that we had with us. Against us were soldiers armed with weapons and tear gas. After a battle that lasted for hours, during which a number of soldiers were injured, the British overcame the resistance and removed us by force, placing us onto a British ship waiting alongside.

When we were placed on the ship, we mounted a hunger strike. Nothing helped, however, and after a short journey, we were brought to an unknown place. Later, we figured out that we were on the island of Cyprus.

From the coast, we were taken by trucks to a camp in an open area, surrounded by a barbed wire fence and guard towers manned by guards.

The scene that unfolded before us was like a continuation of the frightful scenes from the death camps. These were scenes that we thought we would never see again.

We were placed in a prison camp, with only the clothes on our back. The accommodations were in tents. The heat was unbearable during the day, and the cold was searing at night.

The relations of the British toward us were difficult, taking the form of oppression. Despite this and perhaps because of this, we all united without discrimination between country, origin, and sex in our opposition to this foreign, oppressive regime. In essence, an underground was formed in the camp.

One of the daring actions of this underground was digging a tunnel in broad daylight under the nose of the British. It led to the sea. Several people escaped through this tunnel. Their mission was to inform the Jewish institutions in the Land and throughout the world about our fate.

Slowly, we organized a community in the camp, and created the basic infrastructure of "normal" life. Everyone gave their part based on their profession and trade. Similarly, in order to preserve the high morale, and with the intention of irritating our oppressors, we would dance the Hora and sing Hebrew and Yiddish songs even at night. This aroused the ire of the British, but it continued on nevertheless.

After several months of imprisonment, a number of emissaries arrived from the Land. We also merited the investigation of Mrs. Golda Meir, which was a deep, emotional experience for all the residents of the camp.

[Page 180]

My uncle Yosef Gotshel from the Land of Israel was among the visitors who arrived in the camp after he found out that I had survived. He stayed in a hotel in Nicosia, and came to the camp daily with his hands full of packages of food. We divided them amongst ourselves. In addition to his donation, my uncle collected information, greetings, and hundreds of letters from the camp residents to give over to relatives in the Land.

Having no recourse, we had no choice other than to get accustomed to this "manner" of life, even though we never stopped awaiting the day of our liberation.

I was in the prison camp for 13 months, but it seemed to me like 13 years. After 13 months, the turn came for my group to be freed from the camp. When I was informed of this, I did not believe that the end of my journey that had begun ten years earlier was at hand. Even when I was already on the ship, I did not believe that the Land of Israel was in front of us.

Only when I disembarked from the ship with my friends on the coast of Atlit, and when I set foot on the soil of Israel and heard the Hebrew language around me, only then did I understand that my terrible journey had concluded.

Candle lighting during a memorial gathering of Zgierz natives in 1982

Standing (right to left): Pinchas Sirkis, Yosef Katz, Refael Katz, Zeev Fisher, Chaya Halperin, and Yisrael Malkieli

Translator's Footnotes:

1. See http://www.palyam.org/English/Hahapala/hf/hf_Arlozorov.pdf
2. See https://en.wikipedia.org/wiki/Atlit

[Page 181]

Memorial

by Esther Krol–Jakubowicz

Another memorial for our native town of Zgierz
Another sad meeting in memory of our dear ones
The hall is almost half empty,
For many of us are no longer alive,
They have joined their martyred relatives,
And we are here with our memories
For those who once were and are no longer.

Darkness. All the lights have been turned off.
Only six candles are burning
As a sign for the six million
The melody of "*Kel Malei Rachamim*" weeps.

.Images hover in the darkness –
Fathers, mothers, brothers, sisters,
Children, relatives, neighbors, acquaintances,
Passing by in large numbers with closed eyes –

And blurry pictures of the city –
A Garden of Eden[1], with lilac and jasmine flowers
The pond, the forests around the city – –

The *Kaddish* prayer has concluded
Silence…
The lights are turned on again –
The images disappear

The images disappear – but not from our hearts
They will continue to accompany us until the end of our days –
Perplexed, wiping tears, clasping hands,
Exchanging a word and another word, or two – –
People bid goodbye – this one weeps and that one weeps,
Each one with the grief and pain in their hearts.

Tel Aviv, Tevet 5745 (1984 or 1985)

Translator's Footnote:

1.   There is a footnote in the text here: "Garden of Eden" (*lustgarten* in Yiddish): That is how they used to call the garden, which was later called Park Sienkiewicza.

[Page 183]

G: The Book of Zgierz through the Eyes of Personalities and the Press

[Page 185]

Excerpts from Letters About the Book of Zgierz
(From a letter to Wolfe Fisher, October 1, 1975)

The Book of Zgierz is literally a treasure. I know how much effort and work you have put into the book. You must indeed have great satisfaction. It has a bounty of interesting material. It is very well written and very well constructed.

Malchieli excelled in translating the material that I sent you. He has a wonderful style and a poetic language. It invokes a desire to read more from his pen, especially from his original writings.

Once again: the Book of Zgierz is one of the best Yizkor Books, written and constructed with talent and love. Congratulations are due to you and to all who were the emissaries of the survivors of Zgierz. It is a pleasure that your effort resulted in such an excellent result.

Yours, with closeness

Yehuda Elberg

(A section of a letter to Zeev Fisher, May 22, 1977)

I received the volume of The Book of Zgierz a few days ago. I dedicated yesterday, the Sabbath, to reading the book that portrayed the image of that holy community. Indeed, Zgierz has received the perpetuation due to it.

Even though I left Zgierz when I was a young child, I was connected to our shtetl. A respectable portion of my family lived there until the beginning of the Second World War.

I read the book with great emotion. All those who concerned themselves with the publication of the monumental book on the community of Zgierz should be blessed.

Once again, thank you for the important work that you performed in perpetuation our dear community of Zgierz.

With blessings

Dr. Shmuel Sheps,
Geneva, Switzerland

[Page 186]

(From a letter to W. Fiszer)

Ramat Hasharon, 8 Sivan, 5735. May 18, 1975

To dear Wolfe, my friend and relative, greetings.

Through your great generosity, my library has been enriched with an important acquisition, the Book of Zgierz, which you saw fit to give me as a precious gift.

I hereby thank you for this from the depths of my heart, despite the fact that any form of thanks cannot express the value of this book; which, beyond any doubt, was a gigantic effort that was all yours, whether in its form, its content, or its importance.

I have not yet finished leafing through and reading it, and apparently more time will pass before I finish this holy duty, filled with experiences. This effort requires great focus and concentration, as well as quiet time.

However, while I was reading it, chapter by chapter, page by page, I am astounded and amazed anew how a person such as you could have had such knowledge, such good taste, such patience, such an iron will, such a talent to ascend beyond any sense of self – and especially that wisdom and talent, which all together contributed to the conclusion of this monumental creation.

My dear Zeev, you have done a great thing in perpetuating your hometown of Zgierz, a significant Jewish city. I read and read, and at times stop to think how wonderful it is that such a great deal of the values of culture and morality were concentrated in such a small community. Those are values that are so hard to find in the world we now live in. When I think about this, my heart again laments the terrible destruction and the unforgiveable crimes perpetrated upon us by the people of iniquity.

And certainly, I will not forget to express my appreciation that you knew how to perpetuate in such an honorable fashion the memories an merits of our ancestors, our fathers, mothers, and family members who were lost and are no more, as it says: "Wisdom that has the merit of ancestors is good. It is fortunate that the merit of the ancestors stands and illuminates it." (*Kohelet Rabba*, chapter 7).

With gratitude and appreciation,

Aryeh Ben–Menachem

[Page 187]

A Vanished World

by Y. Szmuelewicz

One needs to know that the Jewish community of Zgierz was barely 200 years old. Only about 5,000 Jews lived together in that town until the outbreak of the Second World War. As we read about the long history of Jewish Zgierz in the Yizkor Book, written mainly in Yiddish, but also with some Hebrew, a wonderful Jewish world unfolds before us.

Almost a half of the Yizkor Book presents the History of Zgierz in general as well as its Jewish community, with precise portrayals and appropriate numbers and facts. All the Jewish parties, organizations, and institutions are mentioned, along with their activities. One can see that everything was written and presented in an objective fashion, to the extent that such was possible. From this all, a clear picture emerges how the Jewish community began in Zgierz and grew there approximately 200 years ago.

*

A second important part of the book is the section "The Development of Jewish Zgierz." 45 articles are published there, which present in a detailed fashion everything that took place in Jewish life in Zgierz – in our modern time, this means until the outbreak of the Second World War, when Hitler's deluge came.

In that section, the exact statistics are supported with appropriately documented facts about all the Jewish political parties and their activities, about the local Jewish culture organizations, sports clubs, choirs, institutions of education, drama clubs, libraries, and the like. For the youth, the Jewish library in Zgierz served as a center of drawing knowledge and hope for a better and finer world.

*

In the third section of the Yizkor Book, entitled, "Personalities and Characters," there are 65 articles about various

[Page 188]

Jewish personalities and characters who emanated from the town of Zgierz during various periods of time. That interesting section begins with a description of the first rabi of Zgierz, and how he was received there.

*

Photographs and names of the murdered martyrs are printed on 126 pages of the book. Heartwarming Jewish eyes, covered over with fear and tears, peer out toward us. This is all accompanied by moving words, expressing the sorrow of the surviving relatives. "I will remember my near and dear relatives, victims of the Hitlerian murders, until the end of my life. We must never forgive the murderers of our people." (page 731).

Forward, July 4, 1975.[1]

Translator's Footnote:

1.   The Jewish Daily Forward: https://en.wikipedia.org/wiki/The_Forward

A Monument to the Jews of Zgierz

by A. Tosin

The Book of Zgierz (800 pages), published by the Zgierz Landsmanshaft in Israel, first of all deserves great praise for the scope and comprehensiveness with which the editors (David Shtokfish and Y. A. Malchieli) conducted their work.

Together with the material, which consists of memories told over by the former residents of the town, that book also contains a series of serious historical works regarding the life of the Jews in Zgierz and the history of the town in general – – –

Zgierz – a small town, which was constricted by its proximity to the large manufacturing city of Łódź, took in its own hues. Even though Zgierz lived in the shadow of Łódź, it appreciated its own uniqueness, the specific atmosphere that the Jewish community cherished through the entire time. This was expressed through the large number of different organizations: political, professional, religious, and cultural. Various social organizations were active there, beginning

[Page 189]

with the charitable fund and continuing with the professional groups. Many were involved with helping the poor and the sick.

– – The Jewish population of Zgierz excelled with its intensive societal activity. This plays out in this monumental book, in which the historians will find rich material to understand the vitality of the Jews in Zgierz in all areas of cultural and societal activity.

"Nowiny Kurier"

The City of Frischmann

by G. Kresel

The Book of Zgierz, an eternal memorial to a Jewish community of Poland. Editors: David Shtockfish and Y. A. Malchieli. Gathering and editing of the material: Zeev Fisher. Tel Aviv, 5735 / 1975. Hebrew and Yiddish. 800 pages.

Zgierz was famous in the Jewish world in general and in Hebrew literature in particular in the merit of David Frischmann. He was born there, and the city served as the background of no small number of his book (*Tikkun Leil Shavuot, Kiddush Levana, Hu Niftar*, the poem *Ophir*, and others). The city imbued Frischmann with great appreciation, and he was proud of the city. Even the poet Yaakov Cohen, who was not born there but rather was brought there when he was a one–year–old child, regarded Zgierz as his native city. In his own words: "It seems that I recall nothing of what, in truth, I always note as the city of my birth, that is the town of Zgierz near Łódź – that house and those damp walls in which I first found myself, and through which I first looked and saw the world, with its creativity and depth before me – – – ."

In the new era, Zgierz is considered a suburb of Łódź. However, there were times, and we have no small number of examples of such metamorphoses, when Łódź was listed as a neighborhood in the proximity of Zgierz. Those days are not that long ago – but in the previous century, there was a growth of manufacturing in Zgierz, and Łódź, "the Manchester of Poland" followed in its wake. When Łódź was still a village, Zgierz was in the midst of its development in the textile manufacturing sector. Jews began to arrive in Zgierz at the beginning of the previous century, and they slowly became the principals, as they later were in Łódź, in the establishment of modern manufacturing enterprises in Poland. At first, they were in a specific area, known as the Rewir.

[Page 190]

The history of the Jews of Zgierz is a story of the struggle to expand the bounds of the Rewir, until the Jews were permitted to break through their bounds of settlement in the 1860s. The reason for the permission was that they saw the Jews as a primary factor in the development of the city, and therefore, the anti–Semitism was tempered somewhat.

It is interesting and even amazing to see in our book how our Jewish brethren established manufacturing, despite all the restrictions and decrees imposed upon them. This manufacturing eventually spread to Łódź. Thus, the manufacturing in Łódź was built upon the gradual waning of the manufacturing center in Zgierz. The Jews introduced improvements and optimizations in manufacturing, as a result of which the name of Łódź as a manufacturing center spread throughout the world. It is interesting that the Jewish population grew there specifically during the time of the restriction of the areas in which Jews were allowed to live. The heads of Jewish manufacturing, who were seemingly also the heads of the community, are presented in the book. Thus, Jewish life was forged in Zgierz, as in all other Jewish communities of Eastern Europe, and it contributed to the totality of our treasures and culture, whether in the realm of literature or of art (i.e. the well–known Marek Szwarc).

Before us is a Jewish world, meaning: a way of life in all its colors, starting with the rabbinate and leading to modern enlightenment, and also factions in the new times; starting from the extreme Orthodox and leading to the Communists, "as was the customary situation" in all Jewish cities and towns in Eastern Europe. A unique phenomenon stood out here, and later in Łódź: the Germans who were active in the realm of manufacturing, i.e. the Volksdeutschen, who filled such a terrible role during the era of the Holocaust. This phenomenon is explained in the "German" background of Frischmann, who was the only one and unique among the writers in those days. Isucher Moshe Szwarc is presented as a scarlet thread passing almost through the entire book. He was a Hebrew writer and communal activist; whose name became famous even far from his native city. He would sign his name in Hebrew as Y. M. Shachor. There is barely a page in our book in which he is not mentioned. He was involved in Hebrew, Zionist, and general Jewish communal work. He was like a sort of "institution" in Poland. He also tells about Frischmann, his childhood friend, during his early days. Frischmann also expressed great love for him throughout all his days. He also merited having continuity: his son Shmuel Szwarc was a researcher who was involved in the era of the Marranos. His other son, Marek Szwarc, became known in the world of art and sculpting. Yaakov Binyamin Katznelson set up the first modern school in Zgierz. This school contributed a great deal to the forging of the Hebrew and Zionist culture here and in adjacent Łódź. The well–known phenomenon, that the people of Galicia disseminated Hebrew culture throughout all of Poland, was found here as well in the name of Avraham Yaakov Weisenfeld. He arrived in Łódź from his native Kraków at the time of his wedding, and his home immediately became a meeting place for writers and scholars.

The editors of the book did well in including chapters of memoirs of Yaakov Cohen, from which one can learn not only about the atmosphere in which he was raised and forged in Zgierz, but also about the Jewish way of life in an Eastern European town. There, we find details of his mother's family, Wandrowski and his uncle the Jewish writer Zalman Wendroff[1], who recently died in Soviet Russia at an old age.

[Page 191]

Here I will add in a closed, hidden and secret statement that Cohen tried to not become famous during his lifetime, and the writer of these lines only publicized him in public after his death (in my lexicon, section II, p. 118). Anyone who examines "The New Preacher" from the beginning of our century will find particularly sharp articles of criticism (including of the first anthology of the poems of Tshernikhovsky) signed "Akiva Wendroff." I wondered about this signature for days and years until I found out about the request for it not to be published in public (Cohen especially regretted his destructive criticism of Tshernikhovsky). From Yaakov Cohen, the book moves to Yitzchak Katznelson, who also includes the essence of Zgierz in his poems. It is appropriate to read and review the wonderful chapter by the splendid Jewish writer A. Litwin on the rabbi of Zgierz from his book Neshamot Yisrael).

Zgierz has a non–insignificant share of the *aliya* to the Land of Israel, and the article by Yehoshua Manoach about the Zgierz native Menachem Berliner, who made *aliya* during the period of the Second Aliya, is one of the most emotional and pleasant descriptions in the book. The book ends with chapters of the Holocaust, frightful testimonies to the destruction of a fundamental Jewish community, and the role that the German residents played in that murder, for they knew very well all the comings and goings of the Jewish homes.

It is necessary to note the significant role of Wolfe Fisher, who wrote many of the chapters of this memorial book, either with his own signature or with his many pseudonyms. He is an example of someone who is "crazy for a single matter," for if the book appears before us, it is primarily due to his diligence and efforts.

Al Hamishmar, January 2, 1976

Translator's Footnote:

1.   https://yivoencyclopedia.org/article.aspx/Vendrof_Zalmen

The Book of Zgierz

It is a comprehensive book in Hebrew and Yiddish, perpetuating the community of Zgierz, with a population of 5,000 individuals, destroyed by the Nazis and their assistants during the Holocaust years of the Second World War. The book was edited by David Shtokfish. It describes the origins of this small community in Poland, its phases of development, its struggles with the local authorities, and the conditions of the surrounding area. It is a mosaic of communal life, accompanied by many photographs of personalities and events, perpetuating the realities and people of the community who are no longer in existence. The book is divided into six sections: History of the City, the Development of Jewish Zgierz, Personalities and Characters, the Holocaust, Eternal Lights, and the Survivors. (Book of Zgierz, published by the Organization of Zgierz Natives in Israel. Tel Aviv, 5735 / 1975. 800 pages).

Maariv (?) June 6, 1975.

[Page 192]

Among Yizkor Books

by M. Czanin

The number of Yizkor books that have been created to this point to perpetuate the destroyed cities and towns already form a significantly large library. A library? No, the create a completely separate world, with their own climate. Every books that is published is another city, another town, which seems just yesterday to have lived, hoped, and dreamed, and today fits between the two covers of a book. So it is when I open the Book of Zgierz.

The Book of Zgierz

We come across a Jewish toiling city that, for 150 years, struggled for is existence, struggled with its own needs and with the often inimical surrounding environment. There in Zgierz, as in all cities of Poland, Jews had to fight not only for their economic existence, but also for their actual lives in the place, and for the rights to have a roof over their own heads. It was almost like a suburb of Łódź – Jews had a problem not only with the Polish majority, but also with the Germans, who were always given privileged rights by the authorities in contrast with the Jews – even though the Jews aspired to live in Poland and received legal recognition, and the Germans always had Political aims against Poland.

The two chapters of the book, "The History of Jews in Zgierz until 1862" written by the late A. Wolfe Yasni, and "View into Zgierz and the Life of its Jews from the Community Annals of the Years 1915–1930" by Y. A. Malchieli give a comprehensive view of the Jewish community that was bound together by toil, Torah, and idealism. Our own enemies considered the Jews in the destroyed communities as "thorny Jews," "loafers," and "parasites," "unwilling to live from work," and other disgusting lies.

As you read the Yizkor Book of Zgierz, you will see from the dry writings the type of wonderful toil, work ethic, an

[Page 193]

based their lives, even on uncertain terrain. Even the relatively small population in Zgierz of only 6–7 thousand people built Jewish institutions, struggled for ideals, and thought about the Land of Israel and about the entire world. The entire spectrum of ideologies of the Jews existed there. Through this, it fed the Jewish world, giving forth rabbis, leaders, activists, artists, and writers.

The Book of Zgierz was edited by David Shtokfish and vice–editor Y. A. Malchieli. One can feel very strongly in the book the untiring work of Wolfe Fisher, who collected, edited, and himself wrote worthwhile articles about his hometown of Zgierz, about the creation and destruction of that vital Jewish community.

Latzte Neies, October 15, 1776

The Book of Zgierz

by Sh. Worzoger

… Zeev Wolfe Fisher accurately states in the foreword – in the name of the "Committee for the Book of Zgierz": "We have attempted to present for the future generation the beginning and growth of the Zgierz community, and its development under the specific circumstances of the area."

The picture of Jewish life in Zgierz is truly comprehensive, and spreads a wide tapestry of the struggle for rights of residence, of a compact, organized life, communal activity, struggle for broadening the Jewish area of residence and area of building; and, incidentally, the stubborn opposition to the decree on clothing. We acquaint ourselves with reports on wide–branched cultural activity: a library named for David Frischmann who incidentally was a Zgierz native, as was the martyred artist Yitzchak Katznelson; the publishing of the Łódźer Tagblatt, as well as the literary evenings and artistic discussions, the activities of a drama club, a choir, the orphanage and children's home, elementary school, Agudat Hatzeirim [Young People's Organization], Young Zion, Hashomer Hatzir, and Beis Yaakov; sports groups and scouting organizations; a rich, impulsive Jewish life in all arenas. This was indeed characteristic for almost all Jewish towns in Poland – until the Second World War.

[Page 194]

… Read, and how many times will you be amazed by the heroism and dedication of the weak, tormented victims in the passive struggle against the totalitarian, dark forces. This was more than heroism during those inhuman, brutal events. This was faith, a belief that only the Jewish people was blessed and imbued with.

Points of light in the darkness were such testimonies such as "The Way of Martyrdom of a Jew from Zgierz," "Jumping from the Death Wagon" by Mordechai Grand, "The Miracle with a Child," and others.

Long, long, will you follow such personalities as Rabbi Tzvi HaKohen, Reb Yechiel Ichel Elberg, Reb Simcha Yehuda Leib HaKohen, Pinchas Zelig Gliksman, Reb Avraham Hersch Gliksman, and the lions of the group of maskilim – Reb Avraham Yaakov Weisenfeld, Reb Isucher Moshe Szwarc, the artist Yaakov Kohen, the writer Pinchas Bizberg, and the journalist A. Cincinatus. And how can one evaluate a city with Jews? No, it is not true that we can already understand what took place. First now, when we read the Yizkor Book of Zgierz, it will at first be incomprehensible, and the mystery of a human being and his deeds will grow greater.

Yisrael–Shtime: November 19, 1975

The Book of Zgierz

by Chaim Leib Fuchs

The Zgierz Yizkor Book, published by the Zgierz Jews in the State of Israel in 1975, is a book with its own spirit and content. On the one hand, it is full of longing and sorrow for the destroyed holy community; and on the other hand, it tells about the great creativity in all areas of Jewish life of that community. Through the course of its 200 years, it wrote heroic folios in the history book of Jewish life of Poland.

In the successful work of the historian A. W. Yasni of blessed memory about the history of the Zgierz Jewish community, he takes us into the first Jewish houses that arose in Zgierz through great sacrifice. We see the bitter struggle for the Jewish toilers, who , despite their difficult toil, also

[Page 195]

concerned themselves with the spiritual life of their community. The first residents pass before our eyes, who, even though they were struggling for simple livelihood, also had to dedicate great effort to repel the actions of their eternal enemies, the Poles; and furthermore – from the freshly arrived Volksdeutschen, who caused great trouble for the Jews of Zgierz.

The article by the engineer Shmuel Szwarc of blessed memory was very successful in giving a picture of the Szwarc family. Yaakov Pilowski's article about Pinchas Bizberg suffers from a dearth of detail about Bizberg's life in the State of Israel. There is also no information about his early death. It is a shame. There is important work about the following families: Hillel Zeidman about the Yehuda Leib Sczaransky; Rabbi Huberbrand about the destruction of Zgierz, and Malchieli's exploration (also the translation by Yehuda Elberg) about the rabbis Yechiel Ichel and Avraham Natan Elbeg, who disseminated Torah in Zgierz. In the work about the textile pioneers of Zgierz by Leon Rubenstein, important material is lacking, which can easily be found in Lazar Kahan's book "The Jewish Builders of the Textile Industry in Poland." It was strange to me that my uncle, Ozer Kohn, was first mentioned in the chapter about the first charitable fund in 1900. We know about his correspondence from Zgierz in *Hamagid, Hamelitz, Hatzefira*, and also about his activity among the maskilim, for example: about his friendship with Reb Wolfe Halterecht of blessed memory.

The section on the Holocaust presents a broad picture of the struggle and pain, causing the soul to tremble. I refer to the poem by Y. A. Malchieli, Wolf Fisher's writings, and F. Greenberg's memoirs. The entire chapter of Eternal Lights does not allow us to forget the martyrs.

In general, the Book of Zgierz is an important contribution to the Jewish struggle for existence and the eternal memory of Jewish Zgierz. A great thank you is owed to my friends Wolfe Fisher and Fabian Greenberg (I knew his cordial mother very well) who, through great efforts, ensured that Jewish Zgierz will never be forgotten – both the earthly Zgierz and the Zgierz of above.

Yiddisher Kemfer, December 5, 1975

[Page 196]

The Yizkor Book "Book of Zgierz"

by Fabian Greenberg

The Zgierz Jews who survived Hitler's murderous hand have not forgotten their city: they heard the voice of the 5,000 murdered Jews: "Do not forget us!"

The instrument through which the idea of erecting a monument to the Zgierz community was actualized is the Book of Zgierz, the Yizkor book that has now been published in Hebrew and Yiddish in the State of Israel, published by the Organization of Zgierz Natives with the help of the committee in New York, edited by David Shtokfish.

Zgierz is mentioned as a duchy already in the year 1231. The Yizkor Book presents many historical details that explain to us that it was not easy for the Jews to settle in Zgierz. About 250 years ago, there were only five or six Jewish families in the city, and this was too many for the Polish regime of the time. The Catholic church also had a hand in restricting the settlement of Jews in Zgierz. However, at the beginning of the 19th century, the situation of the very small community changed for the better. German weavers from Silesia arrived in Zgierz. They proposed to build textile factories in the city if they would be given free places to build and if they would be freed from paying taxes for a period of ten years. Their project was rejected by the Zgierz civic leaders of the time. However, the at the time small neighboring town of Łódź seized the moment and accepted the proposal. Seeing how the textile industry developed in Łódź with a great impact thanks to the Jews, the Zgierz municipal leaders permitted more Jews to settle in the city, especially those who knew how to help develop the textile industry.

Thus did the Jewish settlement slowly grow. The Jewish entrepreneurial spirit did wonders. Between the two world wars, 70% of the Zgierz textile factories were in Jewish hands, and they employed thousands of Christian workers, but few Jews. The rabbi of Zgierz convened

[Page 197]

a meeting of all the Jewish manufacturers, and decreed that every industrialist must employ at least 10% Jews. The manufacturers unanimously rejected the proposal of the Zgierz rabbi. This was a rare case where a rabbi took such strong interest in the economic situation of the workers in his community.

One can find articles in the Yizkor Book about a series of personalities who lived and worked in Zgierz, such as Isucher Szwarc, the father of the engineer Shmuel Szwarc the famous researcher on the Marranos of Portugal, and of Marek Szwarc, the well–known painter and sculptor in Paris. Isucher Szwarc himself wrote in various Hebrew periodicals under the pseudonym "Yam Shachor." Moshel Eiger is also mentioned, the partner in the well–known large textile firm "Sirkis and Eiger." His wealth did not stop him from writing poems in Hebrew and Yiddish, which were published in several books.

The *Maskilim* Isucher Szwarc and Tovia Lypszyc are also mentioned for their initiative in inviting the writer and pedagogue Yaakov Binyamin Katznelson to Zgierz to open a modern *cheder*, one of the most modern *cheders* in Poland. This made it possible for the enlightened fathers to give their children a modern education.

The great poet Yaakov Cohen, who spent his youth in Zgierz, grew up among those children. In the Yizkor Book, there are extracts of Yaakov Cohen's memoirs, in which he describes with great love and warmth the people with whom he came in contact in Zgierz. He described the city and even the surrounding forests. His younger friend was the son of the teacher Yaakov Binyamin Katznelson, Yitzchak Katznelson, the fine, sensitive, gifted poet, the lamenter over the destruction that cut him off at a young age[1]. Yitzchak Katznelson was influenced by his talented friend Yaakov Cohen. He wrote his first song in Zgierz, about children and a bird. Jewish children sung that song for many years in the German kindergartens.

Another renown personality was connected with Zgierz. That was the great writer, feuilletonist, and biting critic who strongly fought against every piece of trash that he found in Hebrew or Yiddish literature, David Frischmann. He was born in Zgierz in 1859. When

[Page 198]

the Jewish library of Zgierz was founded, the institution was named for the great native of the city.

In the chapter about personalities, we find interesting articles about the rabbis who led the Jewish community until the tragic end. There are also interesting details in the Yizkor Book about the rabbinical family of the renowned writer Yehuda Elberg, about his grandfather and father.

It is superfluous to state that all the Jewish parties in Poland, large and small, had their corner in Zgierz. The Yizkor Book describes all of them. Even those who brought no glory to the Jewish community of Zgierz, the two fine youngsters Yomele and Itshele, are written about in the Yizkor Book. They were simple thieves and blackmailers. Their victims were for the most part the Jewish maids. The poor girls had to pay protection money, and if not, the two wanton youths would beat them or threaten them with rape. Yomele and Itshele spent more time in prison than in freedom.

The other curious types in Zgierz are also described: Yoshke the "culture–carrier," the newspaper seller; Machla the Heaven Gazer and Chava–Ita, the two who concerned themselves with the poor people of Zgierz; and the porter Belas and his sister with their bizarre appearance; as well as many others.

The mood of the reader changes, however, when he comes to the chapter on the Holocaust. The memories of the Holocaust survivors about how the Poles and Germans of Zgierz assisted the Nazi murderers to confiscate Jewish belongings, torture and beat, and finally drive the Jews out of Zgierz, will shock the reader. The hearts of the survivors will be pained when they read about how their families were murdered – men, women and children. Hundreds of names and pictures are found in the book of the murdered people, the families of whom wished to memorialize them in the Zgierz Yizkor Book.

The 800–page book was splendidly produced. It is the product of more than two decades of hard work.

In the introduction it says: "We owe thanks to all those who lent a hand to the production of this book – the committee members in Tel Aviv and New York. The highest gratitude goes to the initiator and actualizer, Wolfe Fisher. Without him, the book of Zgierz would never have seen the light of day." It is difficult to

[Page 199]

note all of those who participated in Tel Aviv, for the committee changed over the years. In New York, the following people were very dedicated to the work: Leon Rubinstein, David Wechsler, P. Green, and the late Moshe Yaakov Grand.

The Yizkor Book "Book of Zgierz" is an important contribution to our Holocaust literature.

Freie Arbeiter Shtime, March 1976

Translator's Footnote:

1.   See https://en.wikipedia.org/wiki/Itzhak_Katzenelson

Belated Memory Books

by Nathan Ek

In recent times, new Yizkor Books have only rarely appeared. There are those that have been published late – mainly not due to a lack of interest or laziness, but certainly due to special difficulties. The Book of Zgierz (Zgierz near Łódź) was first published in 1975[1]. The editors relate that when the group of Zgierz Jews who survived gathered together in Łódź after the war, they quickly organized a landsmanshaft and made a decision (in 1947!) to "publish a book that will perpetuate the memory of the destroyed Jewish community" (see page 773). They then publicized an "appeal to all Zgierz natives" in which they clarified the character and content that the book (they called it a "Pinkas" at that time) should have. They also called on the Zgierz natives to help carry this out. What then was the reason for the delay? We read the following there: in the year 1948 "the evil winds of the Stalinist regime began to blow in Poland." All societal activities were controlled. Searches were conducted in the homes, and documents, letters and protocols

[Page 200]

that had a connection to societal activity were confiscated. In the interim, the Zgierz survivors began to prepare for *aliya* to the Israel. However, even though they were very busy, the Yizkor Book was not forgotten.

"Over 200 typewritten pages about the history of the Jewish settlement in Zgierz," so the editors relate, "were taken with us to Israel as ground material for the Yizkor Book." We hoped that it would not be too long before it was published. However, various obstacles and difficulties arose. The editor Shtokfish describes in the introduction that the main thing was "no organized financial help from overseas arrived." Here we must note that to this day, it was seldom possible to publish Yizkor Books without crucial financial support from the landsleit groups in the United States, Canada, or other overseas countries. Some Yizkor Books were even financed in their entirety, prepared, and published overseas. Apparently, the Committee for the Book of Zgierz in Israel also waited for help from a group of fellow natives in America. The introduction mentions that the Zgierz native in America, Fabian Greenberg, along with other American Zgierzers such as Leon Rubinstein and David Wechsler, "laid a hand" upon the committee members in America. The result of all the efforts was the impressive volume of about 800 pages with a wealth of literary and documentary material, as well as illustrations – in Hebrew and Yiddish.

*

Zgierz is one of the industrial towns that surround the large industrial center of Łódź. In 1939, prior to the outbreak of the Second World War, approximately 5,000 Jewish souls lived there. Despite the fact that an electric tramway lead to neighboring Łódź, and one could travel back and forth several times a day, the small community of Zgierz was not negligible in comparison to the large community of Łódź with its quarter of a million Jews. Rather, it had its own, strongly pulsating life in all areas. With love and longing, the Zgierz natives tell about the role of the local Jews in business and industry in their home city, about their social and cultural activities,

[Page 201]

their institutions, sports organizations, parties and youth organizations, from the right and the left – no lack of unity was felt there.

The largest portion of the book, almost 300 pages, is occupied by the section entitled "Personalities and Characters." There, we find descriptions, articles and portraits, starting with all kinds of well–pedigreed rabbis, writers, communal activists, wealthy people – and leading to the portrait of "Yaakov Aharon the water carrier." Some of the descriptions and articles were transcribed from earlier published books and periodicals (for example, fragments of the memoirs of the poet Yaakov Cohen regarding Zgierz, published in 1953). The largest portion, however, were written specifically for the Yizkor Book. Among the personalities that are mentioned there with a unique spirit are three renowned writer–poets who came from Zgierz: Yaakov Cohen, David Frischmann, and Yitzchak Katznelson, whose father (Y. B. Katznelson, a *maskil* and Hebrew writer) led a modern *cheder* there.

Zukunft, April 1976.

————————

Translator's Footnote:

1. 4. There is a footnote in the text here, as follows: "The Book of Zgierz, in Memory of a Jewish Community in Poland." Editors: David Shtokfish and Y. A. Malchieli; Material was collected and organized by Zeev Fisher. Published by the Organization of Zgierz Natives in Israel, 1975.

[Page 202]

Afterword

by Z. Fisher

In this book, we have a continuation of the large memorial book that was published ten years ago. Our aspiration to continue memorializing our town, which still lives within us, is still in our flesh and bones. We know that it is appropriate and worthwhile to erect a more complete and richer monument.

Jewish Zgierz was a city like all cities and towns of Poland. Nevertheless, there was something unique about it with respect to other holy communities. When I search my thoughts for the most characteristic trait of Zgierz Jewry, I am struck with the unique intensity that typified its residents. All colors of the rainbow were represented in Zgierz, from the extreme Hassidim to the Communists, from scholars who knew all of the Talmud by heart to the ignoramuses who could barely read the Siddur and the prayers; from renowned writers and poets to porters and wagon drivers – a Jewish settlement so deep with activity and individual deeds that stood out in all arenas of human endeavor, in economy and organization, in spiritual creativity and communal leadership, in science and art. They left their mark in all areas.

It was a young community in comparison with other communities, but it exemplified all the sides of Jewish fate in the latter generations: all the forms of existence and senses of spirit and ideology found expression in the community of Zgierz: the struggle of the old with the new, of tradition with revolution, the suffering of disbandment and birth pangs of world were painfully felt therein. The Holocaust destroyed it completely as it wiped hundreds of other Jewish communities of the map.

Much more will be told about our city, presenting a full world of Jewish life, cultural activity, religious realities and customs, the blend of practical life with great spiritual content. We hope in our hearts that people will yet come to draw close to the generations of the ancestors and add to the wide–branched Jewish life of our city, on the uniqueness and collectivity of the Jews of Zgierz.

At the end, I regard it as a pleasant duty to thank all members of the book committee who stood with me in bringing this book to print, each within their abilities.

With esteem and appreciation, I note the dedicated work of Mrs. Chaya Halperin, for her daily activities of preparing and publishing the book with deep connection to the sublime task. She spared no effort, and she helped with everything that was needed to memorialize the martyrs of Zgierz.

Here is the place to express gratitude to the editor of the book, Mr. Shimon Kanc, who dedicated his talent to the editing of the material, and also donated a great deal from the fruits of his own pen.

[Page 203]

{Same as 202, but in Yiddish rather than Hebrew}

[Page 204]

Members of the book committee: Yeshayahu Frogel, Shimon Kanc, Zeev Fisher, Mrs. Chaya Halperin, Rafael Katz, and Pinchas Sirkis.

[Page 205]

H: In Memory of the Departed

And these are the Names of the People of Zgierz
Who Have Gone to their Eternal World

During the years 5735–5745 (1975–1984)
And are memorialized in our annual gatherings.

May their memories be a blessing:

From among the tens who survived the Holocaust and came to Israel, and also from those who succeeded in coming to the Land even before the Holocaust – death has already taken no small number. Let us honor their memories and note their names, one by one, in order of their passing:

1975

Berger, Yehudit – wife of Aharon Yosef
Berger, Meir – son of Aharon Yosef
Gurner, Shlomo – son of Pesach
Harpazi-Celnik,Tzila – daughter of Berl Celnik
Mueskin–Sirkis, Sima – daughter of Daniel Sirkis
Srebnik, Moshe Yaakov – son of Shimon
Fogel, Chava – wife of Moshe
Reichert, Yisrael – son of Eliezer Chaim
Szapsowicz, Feivel–Shraga – son of Ziskind
Szpira, Avraham Yitzchak – son of Rafael Yaakov
Konski, Yehuda – son of Yeshayahu

[Page 206]

1976

Boas, Avraham – son of David
Greenberg, Regina–Rivka – daughter of Tzvi Cohen, wife of Fabiaı Greenberg
Hofstein, Chaya–Hela – daughter of Moshe Eliezer
Avishai, Yitzchak – husband of Ruth Czernikowska – Avishai
Weinstein, Yehuda Leibush – son of Shalom
Waldman–Gibralter, Henia – daughter of Mendel Gibralter
Shilek, Moshe–Morris – son of Yaakov Shilek
Schwartzbard, Yehuda – son of Natan

1977

Bornstein, Avraham Mordechai – son of Yerachmiel
Ber, Avraham – son of Emanuel
Baniel-Berliner, Yehoshua – son of David
Chanachowitz, Moshe–Max – son of Chaim
Tenenbaum, Aryeh–Leibel – son of Eliahu
Noiman, Leibel – son of Avraham
Frogel, Aryeh–Yehuda – son of Yisraelv Praszkier, Shalom – son of Feibish and Rache

Chernichovsky, Yitzchak–Sever – son of Mendel
Rotapel, Moshe – son of Yitzchak (in Denmark)
Sieradzki, Mendel – son of Tzvi (in Sweden)
Bialer, Yehuda Leib – son of Chanoch, husband of Yehudit Sirkis
Shuster, Moshe – husband of Bella, nee Szajngoltz

1978

Gotstat–Yakir, Chesia – daughter of…
Spiwak, Nota – son of Yoel
Haron, Mordechai – son of Yosef Meir and Rozia
Manoach, Yehoshua – son of … (a member of Degania)
Luksenburg, Menachem – son of Yaakov

[Page 207]

Meltzer, Yosef – husband of Yocheved, nee Weksler
Globichover, David – husband of Chana, nee Ickowitz
Landau, Yosef – son of Rabbi Dov Landau of Stryków
Domnakwitz, Yaakov – husband of Chaya, nee Cukier
Flam–Jozpowitz, Luba – daughter of Yeshayahu Jozpowitz

1979

Berger, David – son of Aharon Yosef
Gotthelf, Shmuel Leib – son of Nathan
Traub–Tzelgov, Esther – daughter of Yosef Celgow
Franbach, Yitzchak – husband of Chaya nee Abramowitz
Shiff–Kurshstein, Tova – daughter of Kirsztajn, Shimon David
Klonowski–Sherman Frania – daughter of Avraham Szerman
Stamler–Gotthelf, Miriam – daughter of Avraham
Szternfeld, Dov– son of Moshe
Reichert, Yehudit – daughter of Zeev and Machla

1980

Skosowski, Zeev – son of Moshe
Celnik, Nachum – son of Berl
Ber–Gotthelf, Esther – daughter of Nathan Gotthelf
Teichner–Nakritz, Mara – daughter of Barich Nakritz
Zylberberg, Hadassa – wife of Yehuda Zylberberg
Haber, Naftali – son of Yosef, husband of Rachel nee Tugendrajch
Pilboski–Shindler, Henia – daughter of Yona Shindler
Zadorf, Yisrael – son of Aharon Shimon
Eiger, Tzvi – son of Avraham
Szejwach, Mordechai – son of Mendel
Pichontka, Yisrael – son of Efraim, husband of Naomi, nee Jakier

[Page 208]

1981

Klurfeld, Meir – son of Avraham
Domnakowitz Nisan – son of Nachum
Rajchert, Zelig – son of Zeev
Slodiewicz, Shmuel – son of Wolf
Kapitolnik–Sirkis, Bronia – daughter of Daniel Sirkis
Franbach–Abramowitz, Chaya – daughter of Eliezer Abramowitz
Liberman, Leib – son of Nathan Dov
Gornicki, Yosef – son of Asher
Binder–Nowak, Regina – daughter of Yehuda (in France)
Sirkis–Yoskowitz, Bella – daughter of Shmuel, wife of Peretz Sirkis
Sirkis–Sczaranski Yael – daughter of Menachem wife of Pinchas Sirkis
Mankita–Shevach, Tzipora – daughter of Hirsch Shevach
Temerzon, Yissachar – son of Meir
Ravid, Yuval – son of Uri and Ira, grandson of Rafael Kac

1982

1981

Fisher–Shmukler, Esther – daughter of Avraham Leib, wife of
Wolfe Fiszer
Kirsztajn, Menachem – son of Shimon David
Nakritz, Nathan – son of Yitzchak
Celgow, Moshe – son of Yosef
Reler-Bornsztajn, Rachel – daughter of Mendel Siedlicer–
Bornstein
Fogel, Zelig – son of Meir
Fogel, Berl – son of Meir
Sirkis, Avraham – son of Eliezer
Pomeranc, Chaim – son of…
Kahan, Leon – son of Yehuda–Yudel (from France)
Szapszowicz, Baruch–Bulak – son of Avraham
Stupaj, Eliezer – husband of Mira, nee Akawie

[Page 209]

Shapan–Bori, Dvora – daughter of …
Friedman, Sonia – wife of Avraham
Konski, Shlomo – son of Yeshayahu

1983

Hershkowitz–Yakir, Chaya – wife of Avraham Yitzchak
Hershkowitz
Goldstein, Dorka – nee Szhiker, wife of Peretzv Reznik–Lewin,
Achva – daughter of Yehoshua Lewin
Yaffa–Katz, Dova – daughter of Nathan David Katz
Krol, Rafael – son of Shraga, husband of Esther, nee Jakubowicz

Ber, Yaakov – son of Emanuel
Lebowitz–Hershkowitz, Rachel – daughter of Moshe Yaakov
Hershkowitz
Fisherman-Yakir, Chana – wife of Chaim Fisherman
Eisenberg–Abramowitz, Sara – wife of Sender Eisenberg
Berliner, Yechezkel – son of …

1984

Zilberberg, Yehuda–Leibik – son of Yitzchak Meir
Finkelstein, Yisrael – husband of Hela, nee Goldberg
Blau, Chaya – daughter of …
Srebnik Leibush–Leon – son of Shimon Henich (in the United States)
Poznanski, Michael – son of …
Greenberg–Gryn, Fabian – son of Gedalia (in the United States)
Elberg–Harel, David–Tevel – son of Rabbi Nathan Elberg
Weisbrot–Finkielstein, Rachel – daughter of Avraham Petachia
Finkielstein (in Russia)
Pomerantz, Esther – daughter of Gerszon Gelkop
Szwartzbard, Mendel– son of Getzel (in Australia)
Wronska, Chaya (daughter of Shaul and Reila (in Australia)
Blusztajn, Yaakov – son of …

[Page 210]

Blank, Menachem – son of Moshe (in the United States)
Karpman, Simcha – son of Shmuel, husband of Esther Sher

1985

Baum, David – son of Shmuel Avraham Abba
Bornstein, Aharon – son of Mendel Siedlicer–Bornstein
Weinstein, Yosef – son of Shalom
Dubiner–Gurner, Genia – daughter of Pesach, from Kibbutz
Mizrav Glicksman, Miriam – daughter of Yechiel Margolis,
wife of Shlomo, died in the United States
Rotkowski–Rotkopf, Shmuel Asher – son of Avraham Ber
Goldberg–Trojanowski, Sara – daughter of Shaul and Golda
Moshkowitz, Nachum – from Kibbutz Givat Brenner
Piotrkowski, Gershon – son of Yaakov
Cytryn–Ber, Chana – died in the United States
Koza, Shimon
Wagman, Shmuel – son of Hershel and Esther nee Hollander,
died in the United States

[Page 211]

Zgierz Jews

by Shimon Kanc

(Excerpts from a lecture at the annual Zgierz memorial gathering, 17 Tevet 5745, December 19, 1985, Tel Aviv)

It is not easy to describe in a memorial book the distinctness and uniqueness of one city or town or another. We always turn to the general that characterizes all other Jewish communities. There were *cheders*, schools, *Beis Midrashes*, Hassidic *shtibels*, youth organizations and libraries everywhere; but every city has something that differentiates and separates it from others. However, there is a difficulty in defining that which is characteristic specifically of that community. On the other hand, in Zgierz, one's eyes immediately go to what is unique. In the Book of Zgierz, one immediately sees the uniqueness of the settlement, both in the whole, and also in separate people, simple Jews from the entire year, and personalities.

What must one have to be a personality? The question relates quite well to Zgierz, a city that gave forth many personalities, Orthodox and worldly, famous in the world. However, there were many more non–famous personalities, creative people in all realms. The element of creativity was especially characteristic of Zgierz Jews, and that is the test of the personality.

I am convinced that the future historian will unroll a wide canvass, a larger picture of Jewish life in Poland according to the example of one city from which one can learn a great deal. Whether it is a historian or a writer who wishes to create something from the world that has disappeared, I would hold up Zgierz as an appropriate example.

Zgierz embodied everything that characterizes Jewish life, from the Jewish reality of previous generations. In Zgierz, one could find the expression of all Jewish

[Page 212]

forms of life, manners, and spiritual streams. This come to expression in all realms: in work and business, in education and culture. Jews in Zgierz were involved in all types of work, and ran large–scale enterprises. They went with their merchandise to the farthest regions of Czarist Russia. They were overflowing with initiative and activity, from the small–scale handworkers to the large manufacturers. Thus, the Jews felt in their souls and spirit that Zgierz was their natural place of residence. The ways of life in the home and on the street, in the sacred and the secular, were through–and–through Jewish.

The first volume of the Book of Zgierz, a heavy book of 800 pages, already presents a broad picture of that succulent Jewish life. One feels the vibrant and simultaneously modest and clean life. The second volume broadens the picture, presents new passages, portrays and tells about new people, but did the second volume already cover everything? No – and this is to a large degree – it is specifically after the second volume that the feeling is to strengthen that no creation, even of a thousand pages, can capture the greatness and beauty of Jewish life. When one reads the writings of Mr. Wolfe Fisher, both in the Yeshiva and *Beis Midrash*, and with the Zionist youth, the community appears before one's eyes like a spring of enthusiasm for high ideals, national and general humanity, as for scholarship in Hassidism, morality, and fine traits.

Zgierz gave forth geniuses, rabbis, and Rebbes, but also great writers who created treasuries of Jewish culture. I know of no other city that gave forth such a large percentage of intellectuals, as Zgierz contributed to the rich Jewishness of Poland. This is all brought down in both volumes of the Book of Zgierz. The work of Wolfe Fisher is especially unique, written with great talent and great love. His descriptions of the originality and regionality of the advancement of Zgierz especially stands out. That uniqueness is the contributor to the organic whole of the Jewish monolith in Poland.

In the process of editing the manuscripts, I had the opportunity to get to know well several participants, especially Mrs. Chaya Halperin, who was the most active in preparing this book. She left Zgierz when she was very young, and I was left with the impression that she possesses all fine traits

[Page 213]

that are described in the book about the Jews of Zgierz: the chief qualities that characterized the Zgierz Jews are refinement and practicality, qualities which do not contradict each other. The Jews of Zgierz were practical with a longing for the additional soul[1]. The Jews of Zgierz were known in the Jewish world for these dignified qualities, and were finely exemplified in the local ideal woman with so much initiative in her work.

In truth, the memory of how terribly and cruelly such a superb Jewish community was cut off rests sadly and sorrowfully upon the heart. Zgierz is no more.

Those who remain, the survivors, recite Yizkor and write books. At times, perhaps the doubt tears through the heart: will those for whom the books are written, the future generation, read them? These are sad thoughts that come upon those who have given up many days and nights to write and collect the means to print and publish the books.

To them, the people who have given parts of their lives for this purpose, I wish to point out the phenomenon that in Israel, more and more schools are adopting destroyed Jewish communities. This is done with the help of the Yizkor Books. The students study the Yizkor Books, and we are witness to the fact that they are amazed by the new world that appear before them; world about which they knew very little. It is worthwhile to become familiar with the work that is written by the students, and with the great level of respect they show toward the world of truly great Jewishness that unfolds before them.

There is indeed a mystique in the awakening interest of the third and fourth generation. Previously, it had seemed that we had not succeeded in piquing their interest in our horrendous experiences or with the high moral and cultural level of our parents and grandparents. It is good, therefore, that the memory books have the mysterious power to awaken the interest of the future generations in the cut–off lives of our forebears.

Through the Yizkor Books, we also recite our collective Kaddish for those who were murdered, for our nearest and dearest. Thus, both holy volumes of the Zgierz book serve as a Kaddish for Jewish Zgierz, accompanied with the ancient Jewish adage: through your blood you shall live![2]

Translator's Footnotes:

    1.   This term generally refers to the additional soul said to be granted to Jews on the Sabbath. Here, it refers to general spiritual aspirations.
    2.   Ezekiel 16:6.

[Page 215]

I.   Eternal Light

ט

נר תמיד

[Page 216]

We will Remember

The natives of Zgierz – men, women and children, who were tortured and murdered in sanctification of the Divine Name by the German Enemies and their assistants, may their names be blotted out.

May G-d remember them for the good, and may their souls be bound in the bond of eternal life, and their rest be forever under the wings of the Divine Presence with all the martyrs of Israel.

With deep emotion, we recall the Jews of Zgierz who were so cruelly destroyed along with their families.

We also recall and perpetuate the memory of all those who left us during later years.

[Page 217]

In memory of our dear wife, mother and grandmother

Sarah Eisenberg

Daughter of Eliahu and Miriam Abramowicz
Died 4 Shevat 5733 – 1973 in Bat Yam

May her memory be blessed!

The perpetuators:
Husband Alexander Eisenberg
Daughters Rachel and Nathan Avi-Dan and family

Mira and Shalom Shapir and family

In memory of our dear husband, father and brother

Avraham Bornstein

The son of Yerachmiel and Freda
Born in Zgierz, 1911
Died on August 16, 1977 in Bat Yam

May his memory be blessed!

The perpetuators:
Wife Mina Bornstein (nee Przytyk)
Daughter Freida-Layaha Bornstein
Sister Miriam Bornstein and family in the United States
Cousin Alta-Ita Kurtz and family of the United States

[Page 218]

In eternal memory of our dear parents, grandfather and grandmother

Our father Reb David Baum the son of Reb Shmuel Avraham (Abba) of blessed memory of Zgierz. A fearer of Heaven and lover of his fellow, who performed acts of charity and benevolence, clean of hands and pure of heart. Died in Tel Aviv, first day of Passover, Sabbath 15 Nissan, 5745 (1985).

Our mother Rachel Baum the daughter of Reb Naftali Dov and Chava Nechama Rotenbach of blessed memory of Łódź. Noble of spirit, fearing Heaven, and all her ways were peaceful. Died in Tel Aviv, 29 Tevet 5718 (1958).

Our grandfather Reb Shmuel Avraham (Abba) Baum of Łódź, the son of Reb Yosef of blessed memory, an upright, pure, and pious man. Died in Tel Aviv, 19 Kislev 5702 – 1942.

Our grandmother Keila Hena Baum of Zgierz, daughter of Reb Elchanan of blessed memory. A woman of valor and many deeds, her hand was open to all in need. Died in Tel Aviv, 2 Kislev 5704 -1944.

May their memories be blessed! May their souls be bound in the bonds of eternal life.

Perpetuators:
Daughters, sons and families in Tel Aviv.

[Page 219]

In memory of my husband

Shmuel Leib Gotthelf

son of Nathan and Vicha
Died in Hadera, September 5, 1979

May his memory be blessed!

Perpetuator:
His wife Mania Jakubowicz-Gotthelf of Hadera.

In memory of my dear wife

Dorka Goldstein

Daughter of Ernestina and Bernard Sziker
Born in Poddębice near Łódź in 1897
Died in Tel Aviv, January 20, 1983

May her memory be blessed!

Perpetuator:
Husband Peretz Goldstein

[Page 220]

In memory of my dear wife

Mrs. Miriam Gliksman

Daughter of Yechiel Margolis
Died first day of Sukkot 5745 – 1984 in the United States

Perpetuator:
Husband Shlomo Gliksman, Miami Beach, United States

[Page 221]

A memorial candle to our dear aunt

Hela-Chaya Hofstein

Daugter of Reb Moshe Eliezer and Roiza
Died in Tel Aviv, 1976
May her memory be a blessing!

She was born in Zgierz, and left the city at a young age for Germany to assist her older sister Idit and her husband Gedalia Weisbaum with their two young daughters. When the Nazis came to power in 1933, the family escaped to Holland. Hela, the aunt as she was called by all of them, became the decisive personality. When the Germans invaded Holland, the entire family went underground. Hela, with her special talents to forge connections, knew how to find hiding places, to bring "food" to the house, and to lead the family. The sister and brother-in-law were captured in 1943 and deported to Auschwitz. The aunt Hela continued to take care of the children that remained.

The daughters made *aliya* to the Land after the war, and Hela began to search for the son with whom contact had been lost, until she found him. She concerned herself with his education. She endured difficulties to provide an honorable livelihood for herself and for the lad. She was also a support for the entire family. In consideration of her deeds in the Dutch underground, Queen Juliana granted her Dutch citizenship after the war as a token of sublime humaneness.

Perpetuators:
Children of his sisters; Chaya Hecht, nee Weisbaum, and family
Pesia Rosenthal, nee Weisbaum, and family
Dan Weisbaum and family

[Page 222]

A memorial candle to our dear parents

Our mother Tzila Harpazi daughter of Berl and Chaya Celnik.

Born in Zgierz,, June 30, 1914 – died in Negba September 20, 1975.

Our father Tzvi Harpazi, son of Kalman and Leah Goldberg.

Born in Włocławek, October 15, 1912 – died in Negba October 9, 1975.

To our grandfathers and grandmothers who perished in the Holocaust – a candle to their memory.

Our parents made *aliya* to the Land of Israel in 1934,
and were among the founders, builders, and defenders of Kibbutz Negba.

May their memories be a blessing!

Perpetuators:
Son Ehud and Adina Harpaz and family
Daughter Anat and Yaakov Maor and family
Daughter Leah Harpazi

[Page 223]

In memory of our dear parents, grandfather and grandmother

Celina Widislawski nee Messing

Perished in Auschwitz camp, August 1944.

Yaakov Widislawski son of Reb Chaim Leib
Perished in Łódź Ghetto, 1941.

May their memories be a blessing!

Perpetuators:
Their only daughter Marisha Cohen, who survived thanks to mother's sacrifice
Son-in-law Adam son of David Cohen, Melbourne, Australia
Granddaughter Celina Peleg nee Cohen, and children, Justin and Anton, Melbourne Australia
Granddaughter Jane Korman nee Cohen, her husband Yoram Korman, and their children Yasha, Sonia, and Jasmin, Moshav Ishi near Jerusalem.

[Page 224]

In memory of our dear husband and father

Yehuda Leib (Leibush) Weinstein

Son of Shalom and Leah of blessed memory.

A faithful, generous worker on behalf of the community.

Died in Tel Aviv, 10 Av 5636, August 6, 1976.

May his memory be a blessing!

Perpetuators:
His wife Yehudit Weinstein nee Librach
Son Meir Weinstein and family

[Page 225]

In memory of our dear

Rachel Weisbrot

Daughter of Reb Avraham Petachia and Freidel Finkelstein
Born in Zgierz
Died in Russia on September 7, 1984

May her memory be a blessing!

Perpetuators:
Her sisters Sarah Bernstein nee Finkelstein and husband Leibel, of the United States
Rivka Eichler nee Finkelstein and family of the United States
Her daughter Irina Kapol nee Weisbrot and family of Russia
Her son Izik Weisbrot and family of Russia

[Page 226]

In memory of our dear husband, father and brother

Shmuel the son of Hershel and Ester Wegman

Grandson of Reb Fishel Bunim of blessed memory Hollander,
the *shochet* [ritual slaughterer] of the city of Zgierz.

Born in the city of Łódź in 1909, active in the Hechalutz Hamerkazi movement
– made *aliya* in 1930,
did a great deal for the arriving *Chalutzim* [pioneers] as they arrived in the Land.

Died in the city of Brookline Massachusetts, United States, in the month of Av
5745 – August 1945.

May his memory be a blessing!

Perpetuators:
His wife Sonia Wegman, daughter of Reb Nachum Mordechai Pros of blessed
memory
Daughter Naomi Kirshstein, nee Wegman, and husband Harvey
Brother Shlomo Wegman and family, United States

[Page 227]

A memorial candle to the Zajdel Family

Our father Reb David Zajdel the son of Shlomo of Kaluisz, died in 1923 in Poland.

Our mother Rachel Leah Zajdel

daughter of Reb Leibel and Feiga Rivka Harun, died on 8 Tammuz 5696 (1936) in Tel Aviv.

Our sister Kresil-Naava Joskowicz, daughter of Reb David and Rachel Leah Zajdel.
Died on 26 Kislev 5731 – 1971 in Givatayim.

Our brother-in-law Moshe Shmuel Joskowicz,
died on August 1, 1969 in Givatayim.

Our brother Shlomo Zajdel the son of David and Rachel Leah.
Died on 12 Kislev 5734 – 1973 in Karkur.

Our sister-in-law Krula Zajdel nee Birnbaum.
Died 3 Shevat – 1979 in Karkur.

May their souls be bound in the bonds of eternal life

Perpetuators:
Lipshia Gelfman-Reuveni nee Zajdel and family
Avraham Zajdel
Moshe Zajdel and family

[Page 228]

In eternal memory of my dear family

My grandfather Reb Avraham Zisha Turcinski the son of Zeev
Yehuda of blessed memory,
died in Zgierz prior to the war.

My grandmother Yehudit Turczinski nee Radogowski,
perished in the Łódź Ghetto, 15 Sivan, may G-d avenge her blood.

My mother Hendel Turcinski, daughter of Reb Chaim Dowzinski of
blessed memory of Izbica.
Died on 9 Kislev in Zgierz, prior to the war.

My sister Tzipora (Potcza) and her husband Motel Blofarb, and their
children.
Perished in the Łódź Ghetto during the Holocaust.

My sister Hinda Chaya and her husband Yehuda (Leibish) Szwarc, and
their son.
Perished in the Łódź Ghetto during the Holocaust.

My brother Zeev Yehuda (Wolf Leib) Turcinski, son of Reb Yaakov
Meir.
Died in Zgierz in 1933.

May their souls be bound in the bonds of eternal life.

Perpetuator:
Yisrael Yitzchak and his wife Miriam Turcinski, Holon

[Page 229]

In memory of my family who perished in the Holocaust

My grandfather Reb Avraham Yaakov Jankelewic

My grandmother Sara Lea Jankelewic

They perished in Zgierz.

My father Reb Yisrael Yitzchak Zajdorf

son of Reb Aharon Shimon and Miriam Rachel.
Died 10 Iyar 1980 in Beni Brak.

My mother Rivka Zajdorf nee Jankelewic.
Perished in the Holocaust in 1942.

My brother Reb Chaim David Zajdorf, son of Yisrael-Yitzchak and Rivka.
Perished in the Holocaust in Poznan

My sister Sara-Liba Zajdorf, daughter of Yisrael-Yitzchak and Rivka.
Perished in the Łódź Ghetto in 1942.

[continued]

My sister Feiga Lea Zajdorf daughter of Yisrael-Yitzchak and Rivka.
Perished in Auschwitz during the Holocaust.

My aunt Mrs. Perl Brandes, nee Jankelewic, her husband and family.
Perished in the Łódź Ghetto.

My uncle Reb Pesach Jankelewic, the son of Avraham Yaakov, and family.
Died in the United States.

My uncle Reb Wolf Jankelewic, the son of Avraham Yaakov, and family.
Perished in the Łódź Ghetto.

My uncle Reb Shimon Jankelewic, son of Avraham Yaakov and family of Aleksander.
Perished in the Holocaust.

My uncle Reb Yitzchak Jankelewic, son of Avraham Yaakov and family.
Perished in the Holocaust.

May their souls be bound in the bonds of eternal life.

Perpetuators:
Yosef Leib Zajdorf and family
Guta-Tova Wirzbinski, daughter of Yisrael Yitzchak Zajdorf, and family

[Page 230]

In Memory of my dear grandfather and grandmother

The Torah scholar and Hassid, Reb Mordechai Yaakov Mondry.

And his wife Mrs. Reizel Mondry of Warsaw.

Died in Łódź prior to the war.

May their souls be bound in the bonds of eternal life.

Perpetuator:
Their granddaughter Mania Jakubowic-Gotthelf, nee Mondry

[Page 231]

In memory of our dear family

My father Reb Ber-Wolf Mondry, son of Reb Mordechai Yaakov of blessed memory.
Perished in the Łódź Ghetto.

My mother Mrs. Chaya Sara, daughter of Eliezer Cukier,
perished in the Holocaust.

My brother Shmuel Eliahu-Eliasz Mondry, his wife Feiga, nee Lichtensztajn of Łódź, and their
son Mordechai Yaakov.
Perished in Łódź.

My sister Sonia-Sheva Antygnus, nee Mondry, her husband Nathan, and daughters Lea and Esther
Antygnus.
Perished in Auschwitz.

My brother, the Torah scholar Reb Yisrael-Leib Mondry.
Perished in the Warsaw Ghetto.

His wife Perl, nee Najman, with their four children.
Perished in the Łódź Ghetto.

May their souls be bound in the bonds of eternal life.

In the photo: Eliahu-Eliasz Mondry. Sonia-Sheva Mondry-Antygnus

Perpetuators:
Manya Jakubowicz-Gotthelf, nee Mondry
Aharon the son of Eliahu Mondry

[Page 232]

In eternal memory

Reb Yisrael Hirsch Jakubowicz

Yenta Jakubowicz

Perished in the Warsaw Ghetto.

May their souls be bound in the bonds of eternal life.

Perpetuator:
Their daughter-in-law Manya Jakubowicz-Gotthelf

[Page 233]

In memory my dear husband, our father and grandfather

Reb Yaakov Yakir Michowicz

Son of Reb Shalom Dov of blessed memory, born in Zgierz
Died 29 Tevet 5735 – 1975 in Tel Aviv.

The late Reb Yaakov Yakir, son of Reb Shalom Dov Michowicz, was born in the city of Zgierz to a Hassidic family that basked in the presence and court of the Admor the Tzadik of Aleksander of holy blessed memory.

Reb Yaakov made *aliya* to the Land in 1930. He worked at the most difficult jobs out of love of the land, as a true pioneer. He accepted the difficulties of absorption with love. Despite all the hard suffering, he did everything he could to bring his parents and family to the Land.

Reb Yaakov was one of those who laid the foundations for the weaving industry in the Dan region. Along with his family, he set up a small enterprise. He made every effort to bring religious lads into the business, so that they could earn their livelihoods honorably. Through his hard work to sustain his family members, he established and founded a *minyan* [prayer quorum] for the Hassidim of Aleksander on HaKishon Street in Tel Aviv. He served as the chief *gabbai* [trustee] of this *Beis Midrash* until his last day. He did everything, with literal self-sacrifice, to strengthen and maintain this Hassidic house.

He educated his sons and daughters in that same spirit of Torah with worldly activity.

May his soul be bound in the bonds of eternal life.

Perpetuators:
His wife Sara Michowicz
Sons Dr. Moshe and Chana Michowicz and family, and Dr. Shalom Dov and Rachel Michowicz and family
Daughters Zahava and Aryeh Hoizler and family, Shoshana and Yehoshua Kula and family.

[Page 234]

An eternal light to my dear husband

Nathan Nakritz

The son of the Hassidic Torah scholar Reb Yitzchak of blessed memory
Born in Zgierz. Died on 25 Shvat 5742 – 1982 in Tel Aviv.

He was the scion of a Hassidic family, and studied in Yeshiva during his youth, where the personality of a lad thirsting for knowledge was forged. However, already at the outset of his path, he also had to bear the yoke of livelihood. He worked in a textile factory.

His *aliya* to the Land during the 1930s was a result both of straits and personal impetus. In the Land, he was tested with all the tribulations of absorption and acclimatization. He began to forge his path in life in accordance with the desires of his heart and the command of his conscience. From his parental home and it's environment in Zgierz, he brought a deep connection to the spiritual heritage of the nation. From the Zionist movement, he brought an aspiration for the redemption of the nation and mankind. He was chosen as a member of the committee when the activities for the publication of the memorial book for the martyrs of community commenced. He worked on the matter with interest.

Nathan Nakritz devoted special attention to a methodical collection of factual material and testimonies about Jewish life in its fullest until the Second World War, and about the Holocaust years. He was active, a man to whom it mattered, who knew no rest until his final day. He took interest in everything and was noted for his exemplary personal and social sense. Since he had a blessed pen, he excelled in writing journalistic articles on all sorts of communal problems. He did not avert his eye from any small injustice. A man of pure heart and straight path has left us, a man who comported himself with modesty, was dedicated and faithful.

It is sad for the individual and for everyone.

May his memory be blessed!

Perpetuator:
His wife Guta Nakritz, nee Katz

[Page 235]

In memory of my dear husband and daughter

Leon-Leibish Serebnik

the son of Reb Shimon Henech and Rivka
Born in Zgierz in 1913
Died January 26, 1984 in the United States.

Charna Serebnik, the daughter of Leon and Sara
Died in an automobile accident at the age of 22 in the United States.

May their souls be bound in the bonds of eternal life.

Perpetuator:
Sara Serebnik and family, United States.

In memory of our dedicated, dear father and grandfather

Moshe-Yaakov Serebnik

son of Shimon and Sheindel of blessed memory.

Born in Zgierz. Died on Friday 26 Cheshvan, October 30, 1975 in Tel Aviv.

May his memory be blessed!

Perpetuators:
Irka Serebnik
His daughter Aliza Dagan
His daughter and son-in-law Ora and Asaf Weigel
Grandchildren: Anat and Nimrod Weigel

[Page 236]

In memory of our dear wife, mother, mother-in-law, and grandmother

Esther Fisher (nee Schmukler)

daughter of Reb Avraham Leib Shafer of blessed memory,
A native of Vilna
Died 15 Nisan, first day of Passover, 5742 – 1982.

May her soul be bound in the bonds of eternal life.

Perpetuators:
Her husband Zeev Wolf Fisher
Her son and daughter-in-law Daniel and Tzafrira Shmukler
Her sister Rivka HaLevi
Her grandchildren Yitzchak, Shmuel, and Aryeh Shmulkler

In memory of our dear parents

Aryeh Frugel   Yafa Sheindel Frugel

son of Reb Yisrael, born on 15   nee Bulka-List, born in 1902
Shevat 1901   Died on 3 AdarI, 5733, February
Died on 23 Elul 5737 – 1977 in   5, 1973,
Tel Aviv.   in Tel Aviv.

May their souls be bound in the bonds of eternal life.

Perpetuators:
Sons Pinchas Pereg-Frugel and family
Moshe Frugel and family

[Page 237]

In memory of our dear wife and mother

Sonia Friedman nee Zylberman

Born in Warsaw in 1918.

Died on 10 Tevet 5743 – 1992 in Bat Yam.

Her parents Reb Shaul and Sara Zylberman, and her sisters Tova and
Manya Zylberman
Who perished in the Holocaust, may G-d avenge their blood.

May their souls be bound in the bonds of eternal life.

Perpetuators:
Her husband Avraham and Yaakof Friedman of Israel
Her sons Dr. Emanuel Friedman and family, United States
And Shaul Friedman and family, Israel

In memory of our dear husband and father

Nachum Celnik

son of Berel and Chaya Genendel
Born in Zgierz in 1911
Escaped to Russia during the war
Died on 18 Av 740, July 31, 1980 in Tel Aviv.

May his memory be blessed!

Perpetuators:
His wife Sara Celnik
His daughter Esther Yasur, nee Celnik and family
His son Dov Celnik and family

[Page 238]

In eternal memory of the Kuperman family

Our father Reb Chanoch Kuperman, the son of Reb Feivel and Tirtza, perished in the Holocaust in Russia.

Our mother Mrs. Reizel Kuperman

daughter of Machla and Reb Yaakov Moshe Wronski, perished in the Holocaust in Auschwitz.

Our brother Yitzchak Leib Kuperman, perished in the Holocaust in Russia.

Our brother Avraham Yisrael Kuperman, died before the war in Łódź.

[continued]

Our sister Yocheved Kuperman

Our sister Rivka Perl Kuperman

daughter of Chanoch and Reizel, perished in the Holocaust in Stutthof.

daughter of Chanoch and Reizel, perished in the Holocaust in Auschwitz.

[Continued]

[Page 239]

{continued from previous page}

Our brothers

Yaakov Moshe Kuperman

Eliahu Kuperman

son of Chanoch and Reizel

son of Chanoch and Reizel Perished in the Holocaust in Russia.

Our sister, my parents, brother and sister
Feiga Dembinski nee Kuperman {apparently lower left photo}

[Continued]

Her husband Meir and their children: Leibel, Sara, Yaakov, Moshe, Ezriel, and Tirtza

All perished in the Holocaust.

May their souls be bound in the bonds of eternal life.

Perpetuators:
Rachel Horn, nee Kuperman, and family
Bat-Sheva Danmark, nee Kuperman, and family
Yehoshua Dembinski the son of Meirand Feiga, and family

[Page 240]

In memory of my husband

Menachem Kirshstein

son of Sara and Shimon David
Born in Zgierz, Iyar 5665 (1905)
Died on 3 Shevat 5742 – 1982 in Givatayim.

He made *aliya* in 1924. The love of the land, its landscapes, and its people were natural to him. Menachem was known for his uncompromising uprightness, his clear language, his diligence, and his sense of humor. He always knew how to find an appropriate story for every event, and how to blend Hassidic stories with actual events. May his memory be blessed!
In memory of Shmuel (Stan) Kirshstein, son of Menachem and Shoshana, died at age 43 in 1975.

In memory of my brother-in-law Tova Schiff, nee Kirshstein, died on 18 Nisan 5739 – 1979.

And in memory of all Kirshstein family members who perished in the Holocaust.

Perpetuator:
Shoshana Kirshstein

In memory of my dear, beloved husband

Yisrael Rosenblum

son of Reb Reuven and Sara, nee Wigodni of blessed memory
A native of Łódź
Died on 27 Sivan 5743 – June 8, 1983, in Montreal, Canada.

May his memory be blessed!

Perpetuators:
His wife Tzesha Rosenblum, nee Fisher
Brothers-in-law Zeev Fisher, Israel
Yaakov and Franka Fisher, Israel
Marisha nee Fisher and her husband Moshe Fishman, Montreal

[Page 241]

Staff Sergeant Yuval Ravid

Killed in an accident in the line of duty on February 28, 1981, when he was only a youth of 20.

He had smiling eyes and the gaze of a fox – this was the image of Yuval from his childhood. Yuval was born on June 27, 1960 to his parents Era and Uri Ravid. He was a grandson of Polia nee Ickowicz and Rafael Katz. From his home, he absorbed the love of the Land of Israel, its landscape, the homeland, the love of his fellow, and social responsibility. He was greatly involved in the life of the group and the country. He studied computers at the Brenner and Ort Technikum in Givatayim. As a student, he excelled at his studies and in his contribution to the social life of the class and the school. He was drafted into the paratroopers in August 1978, and served in the operations division as a division sergeant. He participated in the Movil operation at the Lebanese border in August 1980. Upon his graduation, he delved into philosophy and preached a way of life according to intellect and logic.

May his memory be blessed!

In eternal memory

My father Reb Yosef Baruch Rubin the son of Yerachmiel of blessed memory.

My mother Frimet Rubin nee Reich.

My brothers and sisters Yaakov, Genia, Rivka, Perl, Shmuel, Sara, Esther, and Yenta.

All of whom perished in the Holocaust, may G-d avenge their blood.

May their souls be bound in the bonds of eternal life.

Perpetuator:
Their daughter and sister Chana Fridman, nee Rubin, and family

[Page 242]

In memory of our dear daughter and mother

Miriam Stamler

daughter of Esther and Avraham Gotthelf
Born in Zgierz in 1928,
died on 11 Nisan 5739 – April 8, 1979 in Akko, at the age of 51.

May her memory be blessed!

Perpetuators:
Her parents Esther and Avraham Gotthelf of Ramat Gan
Her son Pesach Stamler and family of Netanya

In memory of our dear husband, father, and grandfather

Shmuel Asher Rotkowski-Rotkopf

Son of Avraham Dov and Mindel, nee Celnik
Born in Zgierz on October 16, 1909
Died on 16 Kislev 5746, November 29, 1985 in Bat Yam.

May his memory be blessed!

Perpetuators:
His wife Rachel Rotkowski nee Friedman
His daughter Miriam Ronen nee Rotkowski and family
His daughter Ruth Apelbaum nee Rotkowski and family

[Page 243]

In memory of our family Szapshowicz-Abramowicz

My parents Risha nee Berka and Reb Shlomo Szapshowicz,
died before the Holocaust in Zgierz.

My brothers Ziskind, his wife Sara nee Fontowicz from Żyrardów,
their children Shlomo, Racha, and Chaya,
who perished in the Holocaust.
His son Feivel-Shraga who died in Petach Tikva, Israel, 2 Kislev – November 6,
1975.

Yaakov, his wife Ida-Yehudit, of the family of Rabbi Elberg,
and their children Chaya and Shlomek,
who perished in the Holocaust.

Shamsha, who perished in the Holocaust.

My sisters: Chaya Liba Cohen, nee Szapsowicz, her husband Yosef, and their
son Shlomo,
who perished in the Holocaust.

Esther-Etka Reler, nee Szapsowicz,
who died in Afula on March 1, 1974.

My cousin Zeev-Bulek the son of Avraham and Miriam Szapsowicz,
who died in Holon in 1982.

* * *

My parents Mindel nee Postabelski and Eliezer Abramowicz,
who died before the Holocaust.

My sisters Leah Roza Widowski, nee Abramowicz, and their daughter,
who perished in the Holocaust.

Her husband David Widowski,
who died before the Holocaust in Zgierz.

[Continued]

Naomi Gornicki nee Abramowicz, her husband Hirsch and their children,
who perished in the Holocaust.

Chaya Fernbach nee Abramowicz,
who died on June 4, 1981 in Tel Aviv.

Her husband Yitzchak Fernbach,
who died on January 29, 1979 in Tel Aviv.

My brothers Rafael Abramowicz, his wife, their daughters Adela, Manya, and Luba, and their son,
all of whom perished in the Holocaust.

Mordechai Abramowicz, his wife Arna nee Rosenthal in Germany,
who perished in the Holocaust.

Yisrael Hirsch-Herman Abramowicz, his wife Chana-Andza, and their son Izo,
who perished in the Holocaust.

Moshe, who fell in the Polish-Russian war during the period of 1919-1920.

May their souls be bound in the bonds of eternal life.

Perpetuators:
Franka nee Szapsowicz and Aharon Abramowicz
Yoram Aviram-Abramowicz and family

[Page 244]

In memory of my dear mother and our sisters

{ likely Miriam and Franka}

My mother Miriam-Regina Szerman, daughter of Mordechai and Chaya Kupfer,
perished in Majdanek in 1944.

My sister Franka-Freda Klinowski, daughter of Regina and Avraham Szerman,
a Holocaust survivor, who returned from Russia in 1946.
Died in Nazareth, Israel, on June 20, 1980.

[Continued]

My sister Hela-Chaya Szerman

daughter of Regina and Avraham.

Born in Zgierz. Died at the age of 22 in 1929.

My sister Fela-Feiga Szpic

daughter of Regina and Melech Sibirski, died in Rechovot in 1974.

Perpetuators:
Chana Librach nee Szerman
And her daughter Ilana Dobkin and family, Tel Aviv

NAME INDEX

www.ingramcontent.com/pod-product-compliance
Lightning Source LLC
Chambersburg PA
CBHW050412110426

42812CB00006BA/1867